LUTHERANS TODAY

American Lutheran Identity
in the Twenty-First Century

Edited by

Richard Cimino

William B. Eerdmans Publishing Company
Grand Rapids, Michigan / Cambridge, U.K.

Wm. B. Eerdmans Publishing Co.
255 Jefferson Ave. S.E., Grand Rapids, Michigan 49503 /
P.O. Box 163, Cambridge CB3 9PU U.K.

Printed in the United States of America

08 07 06 05 04 03   7 6 5 4 3 2 1

Library of Congress Cataloging-in-Publication Data

Lutherans today: American Lutheran identity in the twenty-first century /
   edited by Richard Cimino.
         p.   cm.
      Includes bibliographical references.
      ISBN 0-8028-1365-8 (pbk.: alk. paper)
      1. Lutheran Church — United States.   I. Cimino, Richard P.

   BX8041.L88   2003
   284.1'73 — dc22

                                                        200359948

www.eerdmans.com

Contents

Acknowledgments

I would like to thank Jon Pott at Eerdmans for his interest in my initial ideas about this book and his assistance throughout the project. I also appreciate the help of Gwen Penning and Jennifer Hoffman at Eerdmans in turning the manuscript into the finished book. Last but far from least is my thanks to the contributors of this book. Some took on the work of writing and researching their chapters when the future of the book was far from certain; others came on board later on short notice, yet finished their chapters on time. Their interest and enthusiasm about the project, recommending other potential contributors and suggesting new directions for the book, made the task of editing a pleasant experience.

Introduction

In 1958 American Lutherans were newsworthy enough to find themselves on the cover of *Time* magazine. They had not done anything sen-
sational, but they stood out in an era when American churches of different denominations were beginning to look and act alike as they
moved to suburbia and assimilated to mainstream America. Lutherans
were influenced by the same forces, but their strong confessional nature, with a stress on theology rather than practical Christian living, as
well as their liturgy and ethnicity, set this tradition apart from other
Protestants, suggesting a promising future. They were Protestants
with a difference at a time when differences were supposed to be dis-
solving in the American melting pot.[1]

Whether or not the 1950s was a golden age for American Lutheranism, there is the wide perception that the years that have followed
are posing serious questions to Lutheran identity. Disputes and concerns about the true nature of Lutheranism and the meaning of the
confessions in the United States have raged since the descendants of
the Reformation came ashore nearly four hundred years ago. But in
the current period of cultural and religious pluralism, the need for traditions and institutions to understand themselves and the routes they
should take in the future becomes more pressing. In fact, the pitched
battles over sexuality, the structure of ministry, ecumenism, and multiculturalism that have rocked Lutheranism in recent years all touch on
the central question of identity.

1. *Time* magazine, April 7, 1958; *Forum Letter,* April 25, 1987.

The matter of Lutheran identity has been debated and explored in conferences, books, theological journals, seminary classrooms, and congregations, but this book is nevertheless unique in that — in a rather un-Lutheran manner — it takes the accent off theology and doctrine and approaches the Lutheran tradition more through history and sociology. In other words, it examines Lutheran behavior as much as belief. Although Lutheranism, as Mark Noll points out in the first chapter, has produced a fair share of church historians, such scholars have tended to concentrate on American religious history in general and have not produced many works on American Lutheran history that might engage non-Lutheran scholars and laity. The same is true for sociology. Some of the leading sociologists of religion have come from Lutheran backgrounds, but the amount of research conducted on Lutheran churches, peoples, and other institutions is minuscule. Perhaps American Lutheranism, with its history of synods, splits, and mergers, doesn't have the ecclesial density and the mystique of Roman Catholicism or the Church of Jesus Christ of Latter Day Saints (Mormons) that would attract scholarly attention. Largely middle-class Lutheranism also lacks Episcopal social pedigree and the colorful and dramatic personality of Pentecostalism. Perhaps the shy Norwegian bachelor farmers populating Lake Wobegon Lutherandom symbolize Lutheran reticence about itself.

But whether it is researched and written about or not, the question of Lutheran identity, of how Lutherans fit into the American Christian mosaic, will not go away. Identity itself has become a more complex matter than was the case forty or fifty years ago. The myriad ethnic identities and corresponding synods have now faded into the Lutheran past. Even those groups with remaining ethnic ties don't pay much attention to their particular heritages and attempt to be multicultural in outreach. The ethnic divisions of the past have given way to greater ideological and theological pluralism within even conservative denominations. This "restructuring of American religion," to use sociologist Robert Wuthnow's phrase, means that divisions do not arise only between denominations but also within these bodies.[2] A liturgical "evangelical catholic" Lutheran congregation may have more in com-

2. Robert Wuthnow, *The Restructuring of American Religion* (Princeton, N.J.: Princeton University Press, 1988).

mon with the High Church Episcopal parish down the block than with its more liberal sister church of the same denomination downtown. Since the late 1960s, there has also been a tendency, particularly among the baby boomer generation and subsequent generations, to divorce one's spirituality from involvement in a religious tradition and denomination. This split can be expressed in bypassing religious institutions altogether and searching for spiritual sustenance through the self-help seminars, books, and meditation centers that comprise what Wade Clark Roof calls the "seeker culture."[3] Or, more commonly, it could mean remaining loyal to one's congregation while selectively adopting spiritual practices from other traditions.

The dissonance surrounding modern denominations implies that church members may find their Christian identity in many places aside from their church body and its official structures, views, teachings, and practices. The charismatic Lutheran may well accept basic denominational and confessional teachings, but she locates her primary faith identity in her prayer group and pays more attention to the teachings found in an interdenominational evangelical magazine than to those in official church statements. There has been a dramatic growth of parachurch groups, renewal movements, and caucuses within and on the edges of denominational life during the past forty years, and Lutherans have not been exempt from this trend. This is one of the reasons that part of this book examines the different movements that have formed among Lutherans.

Some may argue that the average Lutheran is not strongly involved in the movements discussed in this book but, rather, far more involved in his or her local congregation. Many congregations, however, have been directly and indirectly influenced by these movements. This is especially the case with the clergy who preach and teach to the laity every week. They are shaped by seminaries with distinct histories and teachings, and they have been far more exposed to theologies and ideologies outside of congregational channels than the laity. In the case of Lutheranism, many of these movements and groups have existed longer than the denominations, particularly in the case of the Evangelical Lutheran Church in America (ELCA), which was only

---

3. Wade Clark Roof, *Spiritual Marketplace: Baby Boomers and the Remaking of American Religion* (Princeton, N.J.: Princeton University Press, 1999).

formed in 1988. It is not improbable that these older movements often can elicit greater allegiance among both laity and clergy than the official denomination itself.

Change and Movements within American Lutheranism

This book gathers together contributors from a wide range of fields to address issues of Lutheran identity. They include historians, sociologists, political scientists, church officials, journalists, and other laypeople with experience and expertise in their particular corner of American Lutheranism. The contributors were asked to fulfill two requirements: to present research on their particular subject and then to apply such findings to the question of what it means to be a Lutheran in the twenty-first-century United States.

In order to explore the divisions and even multiple identities of American Lutherans, the first part of the book attempts to map the Lutheran landscape. The standard descriptions of denominations and their beliefs and practices no longer do justice to a complex situation where conflicting movements, organizations, and caucuses now exist within the same church body. Concerns about internal pluralism in American Catholicism were enough to spur a scholarly project that explored specific wings of the church — liberal, moderate, and conservative — and that produced a book on each category. I hope that the first part of this book, although on a smaller scale, will serve a similar mapping function in contemporary Lutheranism.

Although complete objectivity is difficult to attain, each contributor was asked to approach his or her particular field with a measure of disinterest. One may well discern some sympathy on the part of a contributor toward the movement he or she is examining, but readers will find that these chapters provide an invaluable guide to movements and groups that have received far too little attention in the past.

The book begins with an overview of historical and contemporary American Lutheranism by Mark Noll, who elucidates the "Lutheran difference" cited above. In the next chapter, Mary Todd narrows the focus somewhat to examine American Lutheranism's most historic institution — the Lutheran Church–Missouri Synod (LCMS). Maria Erling's chapter on Lutherans on the left recounts how a defined left wing in Lutheranism was incorporated into the denominational structure of the ELCA. In Mark Granquist's chapter, we hear the complex story of the passage of the Called to Common Mission (CCM) agreement between the Episcopal Church and the ELCA. The protest movement stirred among Lutherans as a result of the acceptance of the historic episcopate reflects a larger challenge denominational structures are facing over issues of centralization. My chapter on the evangelical catholics also involves a group largely in conflict with the denominational leadership, in both the ELCA and the LCMS. The chapter tells the story of how this movement has changed as it seeks to flesh out a vision of Lutheranism in the United States that is confessional, ecumenical, and shaped by Western catholic liturgy. Scott Thumma and Jim Petersen present recent research showing the rapid growth of megachurches in the ELCA, and ask whether denominational ties and Lutheran heritage are or will continue to be important to these congregational "Goliaths." Finally, in comparing the Lutheran charismatic renewal to expressions of the movement in other mainline and Catholic bodies, Robert Longman chronicles how charismatics in the ELCA and LCMS have had particular difficulty in sustaining their unique practices and beliefs.

Trends and Issues among American Lutherans

In Part II we turn from mapping the Lutheran landscape to look at various trends and issues involving Lutheran identity. The chapters in this part of the volume range from the strictly social scientific to the more polemical. Yet these contributions are all based on original and recent research as well as a concern to relate these findings to the question of Lutheran identity.

In the first chapter, Jeff Walz, Steve Montreal, and Dan Hofrenning present their survey research on the political views and involvement of Lutheran clergy. As in matters of doctrine, the authors find a widening chasm in the political views and activism of LCMS and ELCA clergy. In Mark Granquist's second contribution to the volume, he traces the waves of immigration and migration that have shaped Lutheran life — including the recent influx of newcomers from Asia, Africa, Latin America, and the Caribbean — and questions whether such immigrants are really best ministered to by centralized church structures. In the following chapter, Alvin Schmidt expands his previous research and writing on multiculturalism in American society to examine how this ideology has influenced all the major Lutheran bodies. Robert Benne provides an overview of the sweeping secularization that has taken hold of many Lutheran colleges and universities in the United States and investigates why some schools manage to retain and build on their Lutheran identity.

How else to end a book on Lutheran identity in twenty-first-century America than with a chapter on the upcoming generation of youth in the churches? Eugene Roehlkepartain draws on surveys and studies of young people in the ELCA and LCMS and finds conflicting patterns of commitment and loose ties to the faith community.

Readers will no doubt think of other subjects, movements, and issues deserving inclusion in a book on Lutheran identity. There is not much attention given to the smaller Lutheran bodies, for example, although an effort was made to include them in the discussions and analyses of several chapters. The dynamics of Lutheran congregations, the beliefs and practices of new Lutheran ethnic groups, the leaderships and bureaucracies in Lutheran denominations, the issue of Lutheran schooling, and the state of Lutheran pietism are, among others, subjects begging for further exploration. If this book kindles an interest in these "Protestants with a difference," convincing readers that this is a subject worthy of more discussion and research, then this work will have been well worth the effort.

I Change and Movements in American Lutheranism

American Lutherans Yesterday and Today

MARK NOLL

In the United States, according to the 2002 *Yearbook of American and Canadian Churches*, there are now more than 19,000 Lutheran churches, ministered to by almost 29,000 clergy, and numbering an "inclusive membership" of about 8.5 million people.[1] The number of Americans who describe themselves to pollsters as "Lutherans" is roughly twice as large as those whom the churches count in some kind of formal membership.[2] This is a lot of Lutherans. But for the history of religion in America, not to speak of the more important history of Christianity in the world, it is not immediately clear what this sizable contingent of present-day American Lutherans signifies. One reason for ambiguity is the obvious fact that the total of American Lutherans is divided into at least three fairly distinctive sub-clusters. There are, first, a number of smaller Lutheran bodies marked by pietistic, confessional, or ethnic distinctives, like the Church of the Lutheran Brethren, the Evangelical Lutheran Synod, and the Latvian Evangelical Lutheran Church in America (in sum, about 4 percent of the churches, 1.5 percent of the constituency, and 3.5 percent of the ministers). Then there are two major confessional bodies, the Lutheran Church–Missouri Synod (LCMS)

1. Ellen Lindner, ed., *Yearbook of American and Canadian Churches 2002* (Nashville: Abingdon, 2002).

2. Barry A. Kosmin and Seymour P. Lachman, *One Nation Under God: Religion in Contemporary American Society* (New York: Crown, 1993), p. 109; George Gallup, *Religion in America 1992-1993: 1994 Supplement* (Princeton, N.J.: Princeton Religious Research Center, 1994), p. 3.

and the Wisconsin Evangelical Lutheran Synod (WELS), which, though they are nervous about each other, can be classified together because of a common insistence on strict adherence to the Augsburg Confession and a considerable degree of separation from other Christian groups, often especially other Lutheran groups. (Together, these two bodies contain about 39 percent of the churches, 38 percent of the constituents, and 35 percent of the ministers, with the LCMS four to five times as numerous in each category.) The largest sub-grouping is the Evangelical Lutheran Church in America (ELCA), the latest and grandest result of the amalgamating process that over the course of American history has witnessed increasingly more comprehensive denominations built out of the multitudes of ethnic, regional, and personality-driven individual Lutheran bodies that once inhabited the American landscape. The ELCA is a broad church where hereditary Lutheran practices and principles have been (depending on perspective) blessed or cursed by extensive engagement with modern American culture. Within American Lutheranism as a whole, its churches account for 57 percent of the total, its constituents for 60 percent, and its clergy for 61 percent.

An even larger reason for ambiguity about what Lutheranism means in America concerns the bearing of the Lutheran past on the Lutheran present. The history of Lutheranism in America is complex primarily because Lutherans seem to have both easily accommodated to American ways of life, including religious ways of life, and never accommodated to American ways. Analysis of how accommodation and non-accommodation mark contemporary Lutheran life is the burden of the chapters making up this book, although their authors have better ways of framing that discussion than simply accommodation or non-accommodation. The task of this chapter, by contrast, is to provide some sense of history for the Lutheran presence in America; in addition, the chapter provides a brief opportunity for a non-Lutheran to say something, from an outsider's perspective, about the potential for Lutheranism in America.

American Lutherans between the Old World and the New

The historic source of Lutheran differences from the rest of American Protestantism is the Reformation itself. While most American denominations descend from the Reformed or Calvinist side of the Reformation — albeit in nearly infinite variety — Lutherans bear the stamp of their human founder. Following Martin Luther, Lutherans traditionally have stressed the biblical themes of Law and gospel. Lutherans typically ask how particular Scripture passages illuminate the standing of the reader before God in sin or grace, instead of seeking immediately (as most other American Protestants do) to discover their imperatives for action. On the Continent, Lutherans also developed a strong two-kingdoms theology in which a sharp divide was drawn between the proper business of the church in announcing sin and grace, and the proper business of the state in maintaining public order.[3] Early polemics with Calvinists over the meaning of the Lord's Supper, and later skirmishing with Anabaptists and Baptists on the question of who should be baptized and at what stage of life, gave the Lutherans — who, of course, could also cite literal chapter and verse when it suited their needs — a habit of defending their distinctive views on the real presence of Christ in the Lord's Supper and baptismal regeneration for infants as much from the general meaning of the whole Bible as from the dictate of any one text.

In the century before the ratification of the United States Constitution in 1789, about 120,000 German-speaking immigrants arrived in the thirteen colonies.[4] By the 1790s there were nearly 250 Lutheran congregations in Pennsylvania and a scattering of other Lutherans in New York, Maryland, Virginia, and the Carolinas. From the beginning of immigration, Lutheran ministers, no less than their people, were relating old-world expectations to circumstances in the New. In particular, they were forced to adjust habits of political deference, aristocratic authority, religious uniformity, and liturgical worship to American tendencies toward democracy, republicanism, religious pluralism, and revivalism.

3. Quentin Skinner, *The Foundations of Modern Political Thought*, vol. 2: *The Age of Reformation* (New York: Cambridge University Press, 1978), pp. 65-73.

4. A. G. Roeber, *Palatines, Liberty, and Property: German Lutherans in Colonial British America* (Baltimore: Johns Hopkins University Press, 1993), pp. 274, 291, 342n.; Christa Klein, "Lutheranism," in *Encyclopedia of the American Religious Experience*, ed. Charles H. Lippy and Peter W. Williams, 3 vols. (New York: Scribners, 1988), 1:431-35; Theodore G. Tappert, "The Church's Infancy, 1650-1790," in *The Lutherans in North America*, ed. E. Clifford Nelson (Philadelphia: Fortress, 1975), p. 37.

By the time of the Revolution, Lutherans were being drawn closer to the web of political and social conceptions sustained by English-language colonists. The forces at work in this process of acculturation can be illustrated by the family of Henry Melchior Muhlenberg (1711-1787), patriarch of American Lutheranism who, after arriving from Halle, Germany, in 1742, oversaw the organization of a viable Lutheran presence in North America. Muhlenberg himself remained neutral in the struggle for American independence, though two of his sons enlisted for active service with the Patriots.

During and after the Revolutionary War, Muhlenberg made a self-conscious accommodation to the assumptions of American public life. In 1763, he reported on how some parties in the Lutheran churches were insisting upon an "American liberty" to select their own pastors. Soon he passed from acknowledgment to acceptance, as in counsel to a fellow pastor in New York: "the English Constitution, the American climate, and many other considerations, demanded . . . that each member in each community must have the right to vote or at least have a hand in voting."[5] By the 1770s, in other words, German-speaking Lutherans, while not completely abandoning the social and political inheritance of their homelands, had begun to accommodate to American political realities.

What he did not accommodate, however, was theology. Muhlenberg, in fact, continued to insist on theological fidelity to the Augsburg Confession and the liturgical practice of sacramental realism (belief in the saving power of baptism and communion that other Americans have always had difficulty distinguishing from Roman Catholic sacramental realism). In his dealings with German immigrants, many of whom were drifting away from their hereditary church, Muhlenberg consistently upheld his own seamless brand of pious orthodoxy. On the Lord's Supper, he warned against the extremes of Roman Catholic transubstantiation and against Reformed or Baptist memorialism. Especially in America, those who in celebrating the Lord's Supper wanted to "exchange the real for the shadow" became a major problem. Baptism, Muhlenberg insisted with similar loyalty to Lutheran tradition, was genuinely "a rebirth." Although baptism was not conversion, it did mean "being cut off from the guilty and corrupt family

---

5. Quoted in Roeber, *Palatines, Liberty, and Property*, pp. 274, 291, 342n.

of Adam and being translated, ingrafted, or incorporated into Christ's kingdom of grace."[6] Muhlenberg eventually became a skillful speaker of English, but the conceptual languages of the colonies did not exert a noticeable effect on the traditional language of his faith.

Muhlenberg's successor as the leading American Lutheran, J. H. C. Helmuth, spoke out even more sharply than his predecessor about the need to retain Lutheran hermeneutics as well as Lutheran doctrine in the American sea of democratic individualism. In 1793 he registered a Lutheran protest to what, even at that time, was becoming the characteristic American approach to the Bible. Helmuth thought that it was "altogether harmful when someone reads his whims and fantasies into this holy book." This was, according to Helmuth, "to make a weathervane out of Scripture and so turn it in every direction of the imagination. . . . This is to play with the Bible as children play with a puppet. This is to explain Scripture as if the Holy Spirit must obey the bidding of the imagination of any old person, regardless of how confused. This is to make the Bible into a dark chaos." Treating the Bible like this meant for Helmuth that "the pure religion of Jesus is made an object of scorn and derision."[7]

After Helmuth, however, and before the massive German migrations of mid-century restored a stronger confessional emphasis, American Lutheran theology moved gradually in a more "American" direction.[8] Frederick Henry Quitman of New York City was among the leading American Lutherans in the generation after Helmuth, but he breathed a quite different spirit. Quitman's catechism and hymnal, both published in 1814, revealed much less confessionalism, much more Americanization. Instead of traditional Lutheran insistence on

6. Henry M. Muhlenberg, *The Journals of Henry Melchior Mühlenberg,* vol. 2, trans. Theodore G. Tappert and John W. Doberstein (Philadelphia: Fortress, 1945), pp. 118, 162; Leonard Riforgiato, *Missionary of Moderation: Henry Melchior Mühlenberg and the Lutheran Church in English America* (Lewisburg, Pa.: Bucknell University Press, 1980), pp. 137-57.

7. J. H. C. Helmuth, *Betrachtung der Evangelischen Lehre von der Heiligen Schrift und Taufe; samt einigen Gedanken von den gegenwärtigen Zeiten* (Germantown, Pa.: Michael Billmeyer, 1793), p. 67. I thank A. G. Roeber for pointing me to this important work by Helmuth.

8. Paul P. Kuenning, *Rise and Fall of American Lutheran Pietism* (Macon, Ga.: Mercer University Press, 1988); David A. Gustafson, *Lutherans in Crisis: The Question of Identity in the American Republic* (Minneapolis: Fortress, 1993).

the self-authenticating power of the living Word (Christ) as discovered in the written word (Scripture), Quitman's catechism set out "the grounds that ought to constitute the basis of rational belief" as "either natural perception and experience; or the authority of competent witnesses; or finally, unquestioned arguments of reason." Only later did Quitman bring in the Scriptures, but then insisted that everything having to do with the Bible and its testimony to Jesus as the Son of God needed to "coincide with the dictates of reason."[9]

Likewise, Quitman's hymnal featured Anglo-American tributes to the great designer of the moral universe more than the ardently Trinitarian hymns that had been customary in hymnals prepared by Muhlenberg. Thus, the first selection in Muhlenberg's hymnal had been a hymn of gracious salvation:

> Ach Herr Gott! gib uns deine Geist von oben,
> der uns beystand leist, im ohren und im lehren:
> vergib die Sund', andacht verlieh,
> das herz bereite, daß es sey munter zu deinen ehren.

> Oh Lord God! Give us your Spirit from above,
> who brings us aid for hearing and learning;
> forgive our sin, bring us to worship,
> prepare our heart to be joyful in your glory.[10]

With Quitman, by contrast, things began with a more Reformed (and also American) evocation of divine power:

> Before Jehovah's awful throne,
> Ye nations bow with sacred joy:
> Know that the Lord is God alone;
> He can create, and he destroy.[11]

---

9. Frederick Henry Quitman, *Evangelical Catechism: Or a Short Exposition of the Principal Doctrines and Precepts of the Christian Religion; for the Use of the Churches Belonging to the Evangelical Lutheran Synod of New York* (Hudson, N.Y.: W. E. Norman, 1814), p. 6.

10. Henry M. Mühlenberg, *Erbauliche Lieder-Sammlung zum Gottesdienstlichem Gebrauch in den Vereinigten Evangelisch-Lutherischen Gemeinen in Pennsylvanien*, second ed. (Germantown, Pa.: Liebert & Billmeyer, 1785).

11. Frederick Henry Quitman, *A Collection of Hymns and Liturgy, for the Use of Evangelical Lutheran Churches* (Philadelphia: G. & D. Billmeyer, 1814).

In local situations during the first decades of the nineteenth century, Lutherans experienced the same tensions as Roman Catholic immigrants over how far to follow American norms of democratic republicanism. On the ground in Pennsylvania, some of the Lutherans, with also some German Reformed, eagerly embraced a Whig kind of American republicanism, while others held out for a more community-based traditionalism. Many of the latter were politically Democrats, often because of solicitude for old-world patterns of communal authority.[12] Battles among Lutherans over church government frequently had a thoroughly American sound, as when in 1831 the Western Pennsylvania Synod urged support for denominational higher education since that kind of effort testified "to a church whose organization agrees entirely with the republican principles of your government."[13]

By the time of the Civil War, Lutheranism was burgeoning. Rising tides of German immigration and the firstfruits of an impending Scandinavian harvest joined the increasingly vigorous churches of the colonial period to constitute a substantial Lutheran presence in several American regions. The number of Lutheran churches grew from something less than 300 in 1790 to 1,217 in 1850 and then 2,128 in 1860.[14] The formation of the Lutheran General Synod in 1820, and then the establishment of Gettysburg Theological Seminary, under the dynamic leadership of Samuel Schmucker, in 1826, testified to the Lutherans' growing institutional maturity.

Schmucker (1799-1873), the most prominent American Lutheran voice from the founding of Gettysburg Seminary until the confessional surge of the mid 1850s, posed a problem by how moderately, yet also how resolutely, he pushed the process of Americanization. By the mid 1830s, Schmucker too was expressing high opinions of republican government and also championing the authority of common-sense rea-

12. Steven M. Nolt, "Becoming Ethnic Americans in the Early Republic: Pennsylvania German Reaction to Evangelical Protestant Reformism," *Journal of the Early Republic* 20 (Fall 2000): 423-46.

13. Paul A. Baglyos, "In This Land of Liberty: American Lutherans and the Young Republic, 1787-1837" (Ph.D. diss., University of Chicago, 1997), pp. 78-79.

14. Edmund S. Gaustad, *Historical Atlas of Religion in America*, rev. ed. (New York: Harper and Row, 1976), pp. 15, 28, 72, 102; Edmund S. Gaustad and Philip L. Barlow, *New Historical Atlas of Religion in America* (New York: Oxford University Press, 2001), p. 390.

soning. The work in which such opinions appeared was a popular apology written for those who might be suspicious of the Lutherans. It proceeded in what was then the common American pattern by first considering "the intellectual structures of man, the extent of the religion of reason, and the evidences of revelation," before beginning "the discussion of the Christian doctrines" proper. The same work also stressed that "the Lutheran divines are strenuous advocates for liberty of thought, and free, untrammeled investigation of God's word," and that principles of "moral government" provided the best possible way of understanding the doctrine of election. It also declared that the Augsburg Confession contained principles to justify the American Revolution, which was a reversal from the more quietistic interpretation of Augsburg that had become standard in Europe.[15]

In later public appeals on behalf of the Lutheran faith, Schmucker made the same sort of adaptation to the standard American hermeneutic: theology, he held, was "to be governed entirely by the word of God, interpreted according to the correct principles of common sense, which is the only true system of Historical Exegesis." And literal exegesis could only be set aside "when the passage literally interpreted *contradicts natural reason, common sense,* or the testimony of our senses."[16] Schmucker is well known in American religious history for eventually proposing alterations to the Augsburg Confession that would have eliminated, or much reduced, the traditional Lutheran insistence on baptismal regeneration and the real presence of Christ in the Lord's Supper.[17] In making these proposals he was following an "American" path that had been successful in broadening the appeal of Lutheranism beyond its traditional ethnic constituencies.

Schmucker's point of view came close to prevailing until about the mid nineteenth century. Then, however, the growing numbers of immigrants from Germany and Scandinavia and a revival of interest in the roots of the Reformation combined to lessen his influence.

15. S. S. Schmucker, *Elements of Popular Theology, with Special Reference to the Doctrines of the Reformation, as Avowed Before the Diet of Augsburg, MDXXX,* second ed. (New York: Leavitt, Lord, 1834), pp. 2, 42, 98, 275.

16. Schmucker, *The American Lutheran Church, Historically, Doctrinally, and Practically Delineated* (Springfield, Ohio: D. Harbaugh, 1851), pp. 121, 123.

17. L. DeAne Lagerquist, *The Lutherans* (Westport, Conn.: Greenwood, 1999), pp. 74-77.

Schmucker's books, such as *A Fraternal Appeal to the American Churches* (1838), pleased his friends but worried immigrants, especially with their American detractions from traditional Lutheran beliefs. The anonymous *Definite Synodical Platform* of 1855, which proposed a revision of the Augsburg Confession along lines favored by Schmucker, precipitated a clash of interests that eventually led to the mobilization of "European" Lutheranism against the trends favored by Schmucker.

In the struggle between "American" and "European" Lutherans, defenders of old ways also enjoyed capable leaders. One of these was the American-born Charles Porterfield Krauth (1823-1883), whose book, *The Conservative Reformation and Its Theology*, provided a forthright rationale for maintaining strict old-world standards for Lutheran teaching, even in the confines of the New World. For Krauth, a belief in the general correctness of the Augsburg Confession was not enough. This document, rather, needed to be affirmed in its details, for it was "the greatest work, regarded in its historical relations, in which pure religion has been sustained by human hands. . . . It is our shield and our sword, our ensign and our arming, the constitution of our state, the life of our body, the germ of our being."[18]

An even more energetic conservative was Carl Ferdinand Wilhelm Walther (1811-1887), a native of Saxony who migrated to the United States in 1838. Walther was every bit as active as an American revivalist, but it would have been an insult to tell him so. He pastored a church in St. Louis, helped start a training institute for ministerial candidates, founded a publishing house, a newspaper, and a theological journal, and worked to unite several different Lutheran synods. He became president of the German Evangelical Lutheran Synod of Missouri, Ohio, and Other States (forerunner of the modern LCMS), and was a leading figure in the Evangelical Lutheran Synodical Conference of North America that came into existence in 1872. Although Walther leaned toward congregationalism and proclaimed such high views of God's grace that he was called a "crypto-Calvinist," he shared with Krauth the conviction that the Lutherans' main task in the New World was to maintain old-world distinctiveness rather than to adjust to

18. Charles Porterfield Krauth, "The Conservative Reformation and Its Confessions," in *Lutheran Confessional Theology in America, 1840-1880,* ed. Theodore G. Tappert (New York: Oxford University Press, 1972), pp. 50-51.

American ways. Walther, therefore, insisted that ministers, as a condition of their service, affirm

> that without any exception the doctrinal contents of the confessions of our church are in complete agreement with the Holy Scriptures and are not in conflict with the same in any point, whether a major or a secondary point. Accordingly, [the minister] declares that he heartily believes the contents of the confessions to be divine truth and that he intends to preach it without adulteration.[19]

Following Krauth, Walther, and like-minded confessionalists, American Lutheranism turned back toward Europe. With other ethnic Protestants such as the Dutch Reformed, some of the Lutherans also established their own system of private schools at a time when most other American Protestants were becoming stronger supporters of public education. Thus, the first coming of American Lutheranism came to an end. American Lutherans turned their backs on what Schmucker had thought was a pious form of Americanized Lutheranism, but what his detractors concluded was only a mildly Lutheranized form of American pietism. Connections to the wider worlds of American religion would not be reestablished to any significant degree until after World War II. Whatever brought about this situation — the upsurge of immigration, a more strictly theological solicitude for Lutheran traditions, or a morally suspect retreat from public activism to social quietism — the course of Lutheranism was unalterably changed.

Immigration and Consolidating the Churches

Reference to immigration also helps clarify a great deal about more recent Lutheran history. If anyone doubted the securely German and Scandinavian heritage of American Lutherans, it is necessary only to construct a basic bibliography. Before too long the ethnic roots of Lutherans — of Ahlstrom, Anderson, Bachman, Fevold, Gritsch, Hildebrandt, Jenson, Jordahl, Kuenning, Mattson, Nelson, Nodtvedt, Rol-

---

19. C. F. W. Walther, "The Kind of Confessional Subscription Required," in ibid., p. 56.

vaag, Schneider, Tappert, Wolf — would be obvious. Once this fact is established, much is revealed about the course of recent Lutheran history in the Census Department's *Historical Statistics of the United States.* Its pages are jammed with figures, but the conclusions of the immigration tables could not be plainer. German migration was extraordinarily strong from 1840 to the First World War, with over five million new Americans. Scandinavia contributed almost as many immigrants as Germany during the thirty-five years before World War I, with almost two million new residents from Denmark, Sweden, Norway, and Finland. After 1914, the numbers shrank dramatically.[20] American legislation that in the mid 1920s choked off the immigrant tide was also an important fact for Lutheran history.

With this understanding about the end of massive immigration, the course of twentieth-century Lutheran history follows a general pattern for religious migration to America.[21] The proliferation of ethnically defined Lutheran denominations in the period from 1870 to 1915, as well as a siphoning off of countless hereditary Lutherans into American sects or into nonobservance, is completely predictable. Just as unremarkable is a gradual process of consolidation in the next generation as the use of English and adjustment to American ways replaced particular European practices. A minority's tenacious grasp on old-world languages and forms is also quite typical.

By the third generation following the end of large-scale immigration, most immigrant communities experience even greater consolidation, but also greater controversy over the pace of assimilation. By this stage in the immigrant experience, there has been enough time to move out of rural or urban enclaves into the suburbs, to make a lot more money, to see increasing numbers of the rising generation marry outsiders, and to provide more and more young people with higher education beyond that provided by the immigrant community itself. For Lutherans, this third generation arrived at different times, but, for most, large-scale immigration had receded far into the background by the 1970s and 1980s. It would only be expected, therefore, that consoli-

20. *Historical Statistics of the United States: Colonial Times to 1957* (Washington, D.C.: Bureau of Census, 1960), pp. 58-59.

21. Mark Noll, "The Fate of European Traditions — Lutherans and Roman Catholics," chap. 11 in *The Old Religion in a New World: The History of North American Christianity* (Grand Rapids: Eerdmans, 2002).

dation transcending ethnic traditions would occur, as has been the case with the Evangelical Lutheran Church in America (ELCA), and that acrimonious debate would also take place over how much of the old-world inheritance to modify in the light of conditions in the New World, as has been the case in almost all Lutheran denominations. Both of these conditions — the consolidation and the quarreling — are common to immigrant communities as they move out of strictly separated ethnic enclaves into the main paths of American life.

After Lutherans began to engage the larger American culture in the second half of the twentieth century, it was not entirely clear that traditional Lutheran distinctives were going to be preserved. The largest Lutheran denomination, the ELCA, was the result of countless mergers between separate ethnic denominations over the course of the twentieth century. Its very existence, therefore, is a signpost to the weakening of ethnic identity, since the mergers that contributed to this denomination took place only after ties with Europe faded and English replaced the German, Swedish, Norwegian, Danish, and Finnish languages. The critical question for the history of anything distinctly Lutheran is whether the ELCA's movement beyond ethnic, linguistically separated identities necessarily entails also an evisceration of Lutheran tradition itself. At least one study — on the social pronouncements in the 1960s and 1970s of one of the denominations that merged to form the ELCA — suggests that these Lutherans were responding to American society pretty much along the lines of the mainline Protestant denominations.[22] That is, they were reacting to American events in the mildly liberal fashion that had come to characterize denominations associated with the National Council of Churches. Lutheran distinctives, like Luther's two-kingdoms theology or his effort to proclaim a theology of the cross, were largely absent. In recent years, moreover, the issues most hotly debated in the ELCA have concerned proposals for the ordination of practicing homosexuals and other progressive sexual matters — in other words, the very issues that have engaged a great deal of attention from other mainline Protestant denominations. The Austrian-born sociologist Peter Berger takes a dim view

22. Christa R. Klein, with Christian K. von Dehsen, *Politics and Policy: The Genesis and Theology of Social Statements in the Lutheran Church in America* (Minneapolis: Fortress, 1989).

of the modern ELCA; in fact, so watered-down does he feel the ELCA's theological position has become that Berger, a lifelong Lutheran, describes himself now as "ecclesiastically homeless."[23] In such an interpretation of the Lutheran tradition in America, the conclusion might be that nineteenth-century traditional Lutherans preserved something distinctive from their European theological inheritance only to sacrifice it, in the late twentieth century, on the altar of mainline Protestant convention.

A mirrored account is possible for the conservative Lutheran Church–Missouri Synod (LCMS) and the Wisconsin Evangelical Lutheran Synod (WELS). In the 1970s, the LCMS was torn by internal dissension sparked by the desire of seminary teachers and other church leaders to employ some of the methods of biblical scholarship and some of the assumptions about modern learning that had become standard in the universities and many of the mainline Protestant denominations.[24] In this dispute, however, the Missouri Synod moved opposite the ELCA. It reaffirmed conservative positions on the inerrancy of the Bible, the reservation of the ordained ministry to men only, and firm rejection of modern sexual ethics. Missouri has also numbered many leaders who look kindly on creation science, conservative politics, seeker-sensitive worship, and other traits of recent American fundamentalism or evangelicalism. To some observers, these moves by the Missouri Synod seemed to have been influenced more by their American circumstances than by historic Lutheranism.

It might be possible, therefore, to conclude that American Lutherans turned aside from Samuel Schmucker's American modifications of Lutheranism in the nineteenth century only to yield to Americanizing pressures in the twentieth century — for the ELCA, becoming less and less distinguishable from older mainline Protestant denominations, and for the LCMS, taking on the colors of American fundamentalism.

23. Peter L. Berger, "Reflections of an Ecclesiastical Expatriate," *Christian Century* (October 24, 1990): 969.

24. John H. Tietjen, *Memoirs in Exile: Confessional Hope and Institutional Conflict* (Minneapolis: Fortress, 1990); Bryan V. Hillis, *Can Two Walk Together Unless They Be Agreed? American Religious Schisms in the 1970s* (Brooklyn, N.Y.: Carlson, 1991); Mary Todd, *Authority Vested: A Story of Identity and Change in the Lutheran Church–Missouri Synod* (Grand Rapids: Eerdmans, 2000).

Such a judgment could be premature. Considerable interest in distinctly Lutheran theological traditions remains alive in the ELCA, as found in periodicals such as *Lutheran Forum* and *Pro Ecclesia*. There is also a long tradition in the Missouri Synod of sharing tactical positions with American fundamentalists while preserving a distinctive Lutheran identity.[25] Clearly, however, the decisions that faced the generation of Schmucker, Krauth, and Walther are decisions still confronting American Lutherans at the start of the twenty-first century. Pressures to Americanize can take several forms, but they seem to be ever-present. In the nineteenth century, Lutherans took steps to resist that pressure; whether they are willing to do so again — especially since historical study shows so clearly the isolation that resulted from that earlier choice — remains an open question.

Waning Lutheran Identity and the Missed Opportunity

For those who are concerned about the special character of Lutheran history, modern public polling does not offer an altogether hopeful prospect. The Lutheran conception of Law and gospel, steady reliance on a Christ-centered understanding of Scripture, commitment to catechizing the young with materials originating from Martin Luther, belief in a redeeming work of God in, with, and under the sacraments, and vigorous advocacy of a two-kingdoms theology — these Lutheran distinctives are hard to find in the results gathered by social scientists through mass polling.

To be sure, when Lutherans are plotted on large-scale maps of contemporary American religion, there is a distinctive, but it is geographical rather than theological. A fairly recent county-by-county survey of American religious allegiance documents this distinctive. It shows that Lutherans were the largest religious body in 259 counties throughout the United States. Of those counties, over 80 percent were located in seven midwestern states: Wisconsin, Minnesota, Iowa, North Dakota, South Dakota, Nebraska, and Montana. Of the 109 counties where Lutherans made up at least 50 percent of the church

25. Milton L. Rudnick, *Fundamentalism and the Missouri Synod: A Historical Study of Their Interaction and Mutual Influence* (St. Louis: Concordia, 1966).

members, 98 percent were in these same seven states, with 61 percent found in Minnesota and North Dakota alone.[26]

When, however, it comes to religious attitudes and practices charted for the rest of American Christians, Lutherans as a whole fade into the pack. An extensive Gallup poll in the late 1970s found Lutherans as a group showing nothing very distinctive, when compared with other Christian families, on a whole range of beliefs and practices. For example, about the same proportion of Lutherans as other Christians found religion consoling, believed that Christ was the Son of God, felt that humanity had originated with Adam and Eve, knew at least five of the Ten Commandments, believed in the Bible as a religious authority, and thought the Ten Commandments were still valid. (Lutherans were like other Americans in that about twice as many considered the Ten Commandments still valid as could name even half of them.) Similarly, about the same proportion of Lutherans had spoken in tongues, were active members of a church, did volunteer work in the local congregation, and attended services. Where Lutherans as a communion were distinctive was both an encouragement and discouragement to their leaders. Lutherans turned out to be quite a bit less likely than members of other communions to have had a life-changing religious experience or to believe in the devil as a personal being. They were also quite a bit less likely than Baptists to visit the sick, give ten percent or more of their income to religious causes, or to know that Jesus said "you must be born again" to Nicodemus. On the other hand, more Lutherans believed the Bible did not make mistakes than Methodists. Lutherans were more likely than Methodists to read the Bible at least two or three times a week, and they spent more time in youth work than even the Baptists.[27]

In searching for aggregate information on the beliefs and practices of Americans, survey researchers find Lutherans as a category neither esoteric nor marginalized. Wade Clark Roof and William McKinney in their major study of American mainline religion had little difficulty

26. "Ranking Christian Denominations by Counties of the United States: 1971," color-coded map provided by National Council of Churches of Christ in the U.S.A., 1974.

27. "Evangelical Christianity in the United States: National Parallel Surveys of General Public and Clergy," conducted for *Christianity Today* by the Gallup organization (1979); Mark Noll, "Are Protestants and Catholics Really that Different?" *Christianity Today* (April 18, 1980): 28-31.

classifying the Lutherans as "moderate Protestants" along with Methodists, Disciples of Christ, Northern Baptists, and the Reformed. On questions concerning civil liberties, racial justice, women's rights, and the new morality, Lutheran attitudes were all but indistinguishable from those of these other Protestant groups, who in general were a touch more conservative than Roman Catholics, a great deal more conservative than Episcopalians and Congregationalists, but quite a bit more liberal than Southern Baptists, fundamentalists, Pentecostals, and (except on questions related to race) black Protestants.[28]

The same kind of results appeared when researchers explored the money-religion relationship. A recent comparative study that took in Southern Baptists and Assemblies of God along with congregations' of the ELCA, Presbyterian Church in the United States of America, and Roman Catholics found Lutherans to be about as financially supportive of their churches as the Presbyterians, a tad more generous than the Catholics, but much less so than the Baptists or Assemblies of God.[29] The many charts and graphs generated by the large Kosmin-Lachman survey of the early 1990s regularly found Lutherans as a block reporting results that appeared similar to Methodists as a block.[30] In politics, although a recent study finds strong "liberal" and Democratic adherence among ELCA ministers, poll after poll of the populace at large shows Lutherans with the same heavy tilt toward "conservative" and Republican candidates as other largely Caucasian, mainline Protestant bodies.[31]

When analysis moves beyond polling to more general historical considerations, Lutherans seem to fade even more into the American background. Students of American history with an eye for religion, for

28. Wade Clark Roof and William McKinney, *American Mainline Religion: Its Changing Shape and Future* (New Brunswick, N.J.: Rutgers University Press, 1987), pp. 195, 200, 209, 214.

29. Dean R. Hoge et al., *Money Matters: Personal Giving in American Churches* (Louisville: Westminster/John Knox, 1996), pp. 11-27.

30. Barry A. Kosmin and Seymour P. Lachman, *One Nation Under God: Religion in Contemporary American Society* (New York: Crown, 1993), p. 109.

31. Jeff Walz, Steve Montreal, and Dan Hofrenning, "Pastors in the Two Kingdoms: The Social Theology of Lutheran Pastors," unpublished paper; Lyman A. Kellstedt and Mark A. Noll, "Religion, Voting for President, and Party Identification, 1948-1984," in *Religion and American Politics from the Colonial Period to the 1980s*, ed. Mark Noll (New York: Oxford University Press, 1990), p. 360.

instance, cannot help but notice the comparative absence of Lutherans from national political life. However many Lutherans may have served as governor of Minnesota, as mayor of Fargo, or in the South Dakota state legislature, Lutherans have still been seriously under-represented at the national level. There are now in the United States more than four times as many Lutherans as Episcopalians, nearly three times as many as either Presbyterians or Jews, and almost as many as Methodists; yet in the 107th Congress (1999-2001), there were about twice as many Jews as Lutherans, more than twice as many Presby-terians and Episcopalians, and more than three times as many Meth-odists. The highest national office ever filled by a Lutheran is Chief Justice of the United States Supreme Court, and only recently with the appointment of William Rehnquist. Many United States presidents have been Episcopalians, several Presbyterians and Congregational-ists, one a Disciple of Christ, and two Quakers, but none has ever been Lutheran, even though Lutherans for several decades have been more numerous than the Episcopalians, Presbyterians, Congregationalists, Disciples, and Quakers combined.

There is a similar pattern in a very different sphere. Lutherans have long been distinguished for producing outstanding general his-torians of American religion and of more general church history, as the names Sydney Ahlstrom, Jaroslav Pelikan, and Martin Marty so richly attest. Yet it is also a mark of something peculiar that, though there ex-ist rank after rank of competent studies on various aspects of Ameri-can Lutheran history, there is no truly great monograph to compare, for example, with George Marsden's history of fundamentalism, Philip Gleason's work on Roman Catholicism, Donald Mathews's in-terpretation of antebellum Southern evangelicalism, Grant Wacker on the early Pentecostals, Dee Andrews and other historians recently on the Methodists, or the excellent books by Joseph Haroutunian, Nor-man Fiering, Harry Stout, and others on the American Puritans.

It is, thus, surprising for those who know the penetrating vision of Luther, the scholarly aplomb of Melanchthon, the irenic efficiency of the Concord formulators, the surging brilliance of Bach, the passionate wisdom of Kierkegaard, or the heroic integrity of Bonhoeffer to wit-ness the relatively inconspicuous presence of Lutherans in America. Granted, Lutherans have been leaders in health care, as at the Lu-theran General complex of hospitals and related agencies just north of

Chicago; and many noteworthy philanthropies, such as Bread for the World, have a visible Lutheran foundation. But beyond a few noteworthy exceptions, it is difficult to locate identifiably Lutheran contributions to the larger history of Christianity in America.

If I have been even reasonably accurate in what I have described, it means that American Lutherans are missing an opportunity for assisting their fellow American Christians, and especially their fellow Protestants. Most American Protestants are descended from the Reformation, but because they have become so much at home in the historic American culture, their links to the Reformation are obscured. Protestantism has been one of the truly formative influences in American history, but in the process much of the original Protestant vision has been modified, distorted, or lost. Lutherans are the major denominational family in the best position to redeem the deficiency.

Among the most important elements of historic Lutheranism is the Augustinian conception of human nature. Given the great liberal American confidence in the human ability to shape the political future, the great confidence springing from the American Enlightenment in mastering human motivation, and the great confidence of American revivalists in discerning spiritual ends and means, Augustinianism had little chance. In America, it was simply too much to believe that *sinfulness*, an ineluctable bent of character, was a greater problem than *sins*, the freely chosen acts of the will. The result was that American Protestants lost something important from the Reformation's understanding of the labyrinthine depths of human evil and the majestic power of God's grace in Christ, themes that were foundational to Martin Luther's witness.

A related casualty was the Reformation conviction about the objectivity of salvation. Particularly with the American confidence in human willpower, it has been difficult to retain historic emphases on the objective work of God in salvation. The American tendency has been to preserve the importance of preaching, Bible reading, the ordinances, and Christian fellowship, but to interpret these activities as occasions for human action. That *God* saves in baptism, that *God* gives himself in the Lord's Supper, that *God* announces his word in the sermon, that *God* is the best interpreter of his written Word — these early convictions, which no one stated better than Martin Luther, have been consistently obscured by the American stress on human capacity.

It is the same with the church. If a great strength of American religion has been the creative power of voluntary agencies, so also has it
been an American weakness simply to think of the church as another
voluntary society. Protestants might acknowledge a spiritual truth in
Luther's claim that "outside the Christian church there is no truth, no
Christ, and no salvation."[32] But the prevailing tendency is to treat all
ecclesiastical organization as either a product of human creativity or as
merely a Christian parallel to the world's other modes of religious organization. The American confidence in the ability to fashion political
and social institutions has spilled over into thinking about the church.
Creativity, flexibility, marketability, and adaptability are the result, but
not necessarily the voice of God.

Perhaps most importantly, characteristically American Christianity has gone its way without any check from what might be called the
Lutheran gift for ambiguity. Americans have much more easily followed the Calvinist tendency to seek cultural transformation according to the then-prevailing religious vision. Or some Protestants have
turned in the opposite direction and pretended to abandon the world.
Rarely have American Christians considered Luther's tension with
culture, which saw him committed to Christian activity, but always
with the sharpest reservations. The paradoxes of Lutheranism — *simul
justus et peccator*, Law and gospel as two sides of the same thing, the
theology of the cross — have not flourished in America or especially
among American Protestants, for whom relations with the world are
more simply yea or nay.[33]

Whether Lutherans are in a position to offer such gifts from their
own tradition to Americans more generally would seem to depend on
two matters: on how much genuine Lutheranism is left in American
Lutheranism, and on whether Lutherans can bring this Lutheranism to
bear. The chapters that follow mark an important start in answering
such questions.

32. Paul Althaus, *The Theology of Martin Luther* (Philadelphia: Fortress, 1966),
p. 291.

33. Robert Benne, *The Paradoxical Vision: A Public Theology for the Twenty-First Cen-
tury* (Minneapolis: Fortress, 1995); Mark R. Schwehn, "Lutheran Higher Education in the
Twenty-First Century," in *The Future of Religious Colleges,* ed. Paul Dovre (Grand Rapids:
Eerdmans, 2002), pp. 208-23.

BIBLIOGRAPHY

Althaus, Paul. *The Theology of Martin Luther.* Philadelphia: Fortress, 1966.

Benne, Robert. *The Paradoxical Vision: A Public Theology for the Twenty-First Century.* Minneapolis: Fortress, 1995.

Berger, Peter L. "Reflections of an Ecclesiastical Expatriate." *Christian Century* (October 24, 1990): 969.

Das Evangelische Magazin der Evangelisch-Lutherischen Kirche 2 (February 1831): 146, as quoted in the helpful dissertation of Paul A. Baglyos, "In This Land of Liberty: American Lutherans and the Young Republic, 1787-1837," Ph.D. diss., University of Chicago, 1997, pp. 78-79.

"Evangelical Christianity in the United States: National Parallel Surveys of General Public and Clergy," conducted for *Christianity Today* by the Gallup organization (1979).

Gallup, George. *Religion in America 1992-1993: 1994 Supplement.* Princeton, N.J.: Princeton Religious Research Center, 1994.

Gaustad, Edmund S. *Historical Atlas of Religion in America,* rev. ed. New York: Harper and Row, 1976.

Gaustad, Edmund S., and Philip L. Barlow. *New Historical Atlas of Religion in America.* New York: Oxford University Press, 2001.

Gustafson, David A. *Lutherans in Crisis: The Question of Identity in the American Republic.* Minneapolis: Fortress, 1993.

Helmuth, J. H. C. *Betrachtung der Evangelischen Lehre von der Heiligen Schrift und Taufe; samt einigen Gedanken von den gegenwärtigen Zeiten.* Germantown, Pa.: Michael Billmeyer, 1793. (I thank A. G. Roeber for pointing me to this important work by Helmuth.)

Hillis, Bryan V. *Can Two Walk Together Unless They Be Agreed? American Religious Schisms in the 1970s.* Brooklyn, N.Y.: Carlson, 1991.

Historical Statistics of the United States: Colonial Times to 1957. Washington, D.C.: Bureau of Census, 1960.

Hoge, Dean R., et al. *Money Matters: Personal Giving in American Churches.* Louisville: Westminster/John Knox, 1996.

http://www.adherents.com/adh_congress.html (August 2, 2002). Religious statistics for members of the United States Congress are available at this site.

Kellstedt, Lyman A., and Mark A. Noll. "Religion, Voting for President, and Party Identification, 1948-1984." In *Religion and American Politics from the Colonial Period to the 1980s,* ed. Mark Noll. New York: Oxford University Press, 1990.

Klein, Christa. "Lutheranism." In *Encyclopedia of the American Religious Experience,* ed. Charles H. Lippy and Peter W. Williams, 3 vols., 1:431-35. New York: Scribners, 1988.

Klein, Christa R., with Christian K. von Dehsen. *Politics and Policy: The Genesis and Theology of Social Statements in the Lutheran Church in America.* Minneapolis: Fortress, 1989.

Kosmin, Barry A., and Seymour P. Lachman. *One Nation Under God: Religion in Contemporary American Society.* New York: Crown, 1993.

Krauth, Charles Porterfield. "The Conservative Reformation and Its Confessions." In *Lutheran Confessional Theology in America, 1840-1880,* ed. Theodore G. Tappert. New York: Oxford University Press, 1972.

Kuenning, Paul P. *Rise and Fall of American Lutheran Pietism.* Macon, Ga.: Mercer University Press, 1988.

Lagerquist, L. DeAne. *The Lutherans.* Westport, Conn.: Greenwood, 1999.

Lindner, Ellen, ed. *Yearbook of American and Canadian Churches 2002.* Nashville: Abingdon, 2002.

Mühlenberg, Henry M. *Erbauliche Lieder-Sammlung zum Gottesdienstlichem Gebrauch in den Vereinigten Evangelisch-Lutherischen Gemeinen in Pennsylvanien.* Second ed. Germantown, Pa.: Liebert & Billmeyer, 1785.

―――. *The Journals of Henry Melchior Mühlenberg,* vol. 2. Trans. Theodore G. Tappert and John W. Doberstein. Philadelphia: Fortress, 1945.

Noll, Mark. *America's God, from Jonathan Edwards to Abraham Lincoln.* New York: Oxford University Press, 2002. See chap. 7, "Colonial Theologies in the Age of Revolution," and chap. 20, "Failed Alternatives."

―――. "Are Protestants and Catholics Really that Different?" *Christianity Today* (April 18, 1980): 28-31.

―――. "Children of the Reformation in a Brave New World: Why 'American Evangelicals' Differ from 'Lutheran Evangelicals.'" *Dialog: A Journal of Theology* 24 (Summer 1985): 176-80.

―――. "Ethnic, American, or Lutheran? Dilemmas for a Historic Confession in the New World." *The Lutheran Theological Seminary Review* (Winter 1991): 17-38.

―――. "The Lutheran Difference." *First Things* (April 1992): 31-40.

―――. *The Old Religion in a New World: The History of North American*

Christianity. Grand Rapids: Eerdmans, 2002. See chap. 11, "The Fate of European Traditions — Lutherans and Roman Catholics."

————. "Whither Lutheranism? . . . An Evangelical Protestant Perspective." *Word and World* 11 (Summer 1991): 312-15.

Nolt, Steven M. "Becoming Ethnic Americans in the Early Republic: Pennsylvania German Reaction to Evangelical Protestant Reformism." *Journal of the Early Republic* 20 (Fall 2000): 423-46.

Quitman, Frederick Henry. *A Collection of Hymns and Liturgy, for the Use of Evangelical Lutheran Churches.* Philadelphia: G. & D. Billmeyer, 1814.

————. *Evangelical Catechism: Or a Short Exposition of the Principal Doctrines and Precepts of the Christian Religion; for the Use of the Churches Belonging to the Evangelical Lutheran Synod of New York.* Hudson, N.Y.: W. E. Norman, 1814.

"Ranking Christian Denominations by Counties of the United States: 1971." Color-coded map provided by the National Council of Churches of Christ in the U.S.A., 1974.

Riforgiato, Leonard. *Missionary of Moderation: Henry Melchior Mühlenberg and the Lutheran Church in English America.* Lewisburg, Pa.: Bucknell University Press, 1980.

Roeber, A. G. *Palatines, Liberty, and Property: German Lutherans in Colonial British America.* Baltimore: Johns Hopkins University Press, 1993.

Roof, Wade Clark, and William McKinney. *American Mainline Religion: Its Changing Shape and Future.* New Brunswick, N.J.: Rutgers University Press, 1987.

Rudnick, Milton L. *Fundamentalism and the Missouri Synod: A Historical Study of Their Interaction and Mutual Influence.* St. Louis: Concordia, 1966.

Schmucker, Samuel. *The American Lutheran Church, Historically, Doctrinally, and Practically Delineated.* Springfield, Ohio: D. Harbaugh, 1851.

————. *Elements of Popular Theology, with Special Reference to the Doctrines of the Reformation, as Avowed Before the Diet of Augsburg, MDXXX.* Second ed. New York: Leavitt, Lord, 1834.

Schwehn, Mark R. "Lutheran Higher Education in the Twenty-First Century." In *The Future of Religious Colleges,* ed. Paul Dovre, pp. 208-23. Grand Rapids: Eerdmans, 2002.

Skinner, Quentin. *The Foundations of Modern Political Thought,* vol. 2: *The Age of Reformation.* New York: Cambridge University Press, 1978.

Tappert, Theodore G. "The Church's Infancy, 1650-1790." In *The Lutherans in North America,* ed. E. Clifford Nelson. Philadelphia: Fortress, 1975.

Tietjen, John H. *Memoirs in Exile: Confessional Hope and Institutional Conflict.* Minneapolis: Fortress, 1990.

Todd, Mary. *Authority Vested: A Story of Identity and Change in the Lutheran Church–Missouri Synod.* Grand Rapids: Eerdmans, 2000.

Walther, C. F. W. "The Kind of Confessional Subscription Required." In *Lutheran Confessional Theology in America, 1840-1880.* Edited by Theodore G. Tappert. New York: Oxford University Press, 1972.

Walz, Jeff, Steve Montreal, and Dan Hofrenning. "Pastors in the Two Kingdoms: The Social Theology of Lutheran Pastors." Unpublished paper.

The Curious Case of the Missouri Synod

MARY TODD

My brother used to call it the Misery Synod. We'd grown up in a parsonage where dinner table conversation frequently included talk of developments local or larger that had to do with the church, in our case the Lutheran Church–Missouri Synod. Our father was a pastor, as was an older brother. We held the unenviable position of PK — preacher's kids. But in post–World War II America, the synod felt like family; thus everyone around the table understood my brother's reference as much more a term of endearment than a pejorative.

A wordsmith would have a delicate task deconstructing the use of language in this church, especially in the wake of September 11, 2001. Within months of that national tragedy, the Missouri Synod — the tenth largest church body in the United States and the only American Lutheran synod never to have merged with others in a strikingly long institutional history — found itself on the brink of schism for the second time in thirty years. Words had everything to do with how it got there.

The hallmark of American religion since World War II, according to sociologist Robert Wuthnow and others, has been the restructuring of denominations along conservative and moderate-to-liberal positions. Such division is particularly true of the 2.5 million–member Missouri Synod, whose history since 1945 has been marked by an ideological struggle for the soul of the church, played out in the politics of elections and appointments.

The cynic would say, politics is politics, at whatever level and in whatever context. The realities of raw politics tend to bring even the cynic up short, however, when found in the church. What we know about American politics in general since the 1960s — that conservatives are better organized and far better funded — tends to be true of church politics as well, and has been the case in the Missouri Synod. The corollary to that truth is the usual description of moderates, that they respond late to the conservative challenge, tend to be less overtly political, and usually have to scramble for funds. That, too, has been the case in the Missouri Synod.

Though by nature religion itself is conservative, the label "conservative" is still useful within a religious denomination both to reflect political reality and to locate various camps. (The same can be said of the term "liberal.") The last quarter of the twentieth century saw not only conservative takeovers but attendant response by moderate elements in several Protestant church bodies, notably the Southern Baptist Convention and the Lutheran Church–Missouri Synod. The two stories in fact present an interesting parallel.

Missouri's expression of a more open attitude in the 1960s was met by conservative backlash in the 1970s that led to a schism and the departure of the most moderate-to-liberal clergy and congregations. The post-purge honeymoon did not last, however, as a growing unhappiness over what the most conservative perceived to be relaxation on doctrinal matters generated their renewed political activism over the course of the 1990s. Moderate voices, fearful of what looked to them like a rising fundamentalism in the synod, belatedly and loosely organized into an uneasy coalition that succeeded at the 2001 convention in electing a moderate candidate as president of the synod. But the signal action of that same convention — a resolution declaring, "We cannot consider [the Evangelical Lutheran Church in America] an orthodox Lutheran church body" — reflected the agenda of conservatives to keep the synod doctrinally distinct from the main body of American and world Lutheranism.

Early Divisions

In order to unravel or at all understand the current state of the church, it is essential to look to its history. Since its founding in 1847, the synod has been wary of other Lutherans in America and has jealously guarded its doctrinal position by refusing any sort of union without first establishing full doctrinal agreement. "No union without unity" was the motto that was to keep the synod from engaging in the dreaded "unionism." And for the first half of its history, the fact that the synod spoke, wrote, and worshiped only in its native German language kept the pool of potential partners small.

But the twentieth century challenged the very identity of the synod when America went to war with people who spoke German, not only in Europe but in the 100 percent Americanism crusade on the home front. The synod responded by changing its name (originally the German Evangelical Lutheran Synod of Missouri, Ohio and Other States) and its native tongue in short order. And, while World War I brought many of the ethnic Lutheran synods together into a collaborative effort that Missouri did not join — the National Lutheran Council — the synod did agree to participate in fellowship talks in the 1920s with four other ethnic synods. In 1928 the five Lutheran bodies issued a statement on a number of doctrines about which they found themselves in agreement. It seemed the Missouri Lutherans were ready to leave their historic insularity at last.

The synod in convention the following year, however, rejected the fellowship document and called instead for a brief statement of its own doctrinal position, and in 1932 adopted what *really* is called the "Brief Statement." Intended to serve only as clarification of the synod's stance on the controverted issues of the day, the document later became the basis for future fellowship talks, and over time took on an importance far beyond its original purpose. As talks with a newly merged ethnic synod, the American Lutheran Church (ALC), continued, concern grew in some quarters of the synod about the question of fellowship. In 1940 an unofficial partisan publication appeared, the *Confessional Lutheran*, edited by the Reverend Paul Burgdorf. From this time forward, the more conservative position in the Missouri Synod would declare itself the confessional position. Those who disagreed were not only perceived to be but called liberal. In truth, the division was between the very conservative and the more moderately conservative.

The spirit of the church darkened as increasingly strident voices spoke out against the fellowship discussions with the ALC. By 1944 the situation had grown critical. The church had reached a new low, according to worried pastors, with the synod caught in a theological climate of insinuation and fault-finding. Forty-four leading clergy met in Chicago in September 1945 to discuss their concerns over the direction their church body seemed to be taking. The result of their meeting was a document simply called "A Statement," a series of twelve theses that identified tendencies and trends those in attendance considered abuses of the synod's evangelical heritage. The Forty-Four stood at odds with those in Missouri who took what they believed to be the "wrong approach" to Scripture, leading to "a tragic misconception of the very essence of the Gospel and the nature, functions and mission of the Church."[1] They were concerned not only about the spirit within the synod — one they described in terms of legalism, negative attitudes, narrowness, and a "disregard for the fundamental law of Christian love" — but with what those attitudes might mean for the church in a rapidly changing world: a retreat into separatist isolationism.

The Forty-Four sent their Statement to all pastors in the synod with a cover letter that set the document in context. Within weeks several hundred more clergy signed on. But to the conservatives whose actions and attitudes had prompted the Statement, the document was very nearly heresy. They demanded its retraction and called for synodical discipline of those responsible for writing and disseminating it, especially those who were members of the faculty of Concordia Seminary St. Louis.

There would be no resolution to the controversy over the Statement of the Forty-Four. Attempts made at finding common ground between the opposing opinions found none beyond both sides' acceptance of the Lutheran principle of *Sola Scriptura*, or Scripture alone. In early 1947 the synodical president, John Behnken, asked the Forty-Four to withdraw but not recant their Statement. And so they did, "for the sake of peace." The compromise meant that the centennial convention of the synod that summer would not be wracked by conflict. But it also meant that the deep divisions evidenced by this episode would go underground, certain to be revived.

One of the signers of "A Statement," *Lutheran Witness* editor and seminary professor Theodore Graebner, wrote several cautionary es-

1. Cited in Mary Todd, *Authority Vested: A Story of Identity and Change in The Lutheran Church–Missouri Synod* (Grand Rapids: Eerdmans, 2000), p. 131 n. 129.

says in the late 1940s about what he considered dangerous trends in his church body that had not diminished despite the efforts of the Forty-Four. Graebner called his church to repentance and blamed its seminaries for not properly training its clergy, observing that in a conservative church body, legalism is the obvious outgrowth of inadequate scholarship. In a vein similar to Garry Wills' recent analysis of the Roman Catholic Church in *Papal Sin,* and strongly critical of what he called the synod's "burden of infallibility," the editor argued that Missouri suffered from a bad habit of quoting itself while eschewing any possibility that it might ever have been wrong in the past. Additionally, Graebner complained, "Heresy hunting has developed into a profession," and he cited the particular case of seminary professor Dr. Richard Caemmerer, who, with the endorsement and approval of his local clergy conference, participated in a public event to commemorate V-E Day in 1945, only to have another group of clergy demand that he be removed from office.[2] The treatment accorded his faculty colleague was but one example in the outraged Graebner's lengthy list of evidence of division in his beloved synod.

Struggle and Schism

When Theodore Graebner died in 1950, the churches of America were embarking on a decade of remarkable growth. The Missouri Synod reaped the benefits of the Baby Boom and suburban sprawl as much as other church bodies. Between 1945 and 1965 its number of baptized members nearly doubled and the synod added half again as many congregations. Growth required Missouri to add both offices and agencies to meet the demands for researching and financing new mission starts. The seminary in St. Louis added several new faculty to prepare pastors for new congregations and old. The dissension of the previous decade appeared to have faded from memory. By the early 1960s Missouri was the only one of three leading Lutheran church bodies in the United States — mergers in 1960 and 1962 had led to the creation of the American Lutheran Church (ALC) and the Lutheran Church in

2. Theodore Graebner, "For a Penitent Jubilee" (1946), *Concordia Historical Institute Quarterly* 45 (1972): 3-28.

America (LCA) — not to be the product of a merger. Its long institutional history and the reputation of its seminary in St. Louis had earned the synod recognition as theologically rigorous but not uncompromising, the doctrinal conscience of American Lutheranism.

The contagious spirit of Vatican II even led the synod to open a few of its windows to the outside world to let fresh air in. The 1962 convention established a permanent advisory body, the Commission on Theology and Church Relations, to deal with theological questions that had formerly been sent to seminary faculties for an opinion. And in 1965 Missouri joined with the two other primary Lutheran bodies, the ALC and the LCA, to form the Lutheran Council in the United States (LCUSA), a pan-Lutheran agency for cooperative activities and study. Both actions — a commission whose name deliberately included church relations, and partnership in a national agency for the first time — gave the appearance that the synod was open to other Lutherans in ways it had not previously been. The 1965 convention also received and adopted a visionary report called the Mission Affirmations, the result of a self-study on the theological mission of the church by former missionary to India Martin Kretzmann. But in typical fashion of synodical conventions, Missouri sent mixed messages by both adopting progressive proposals and reaffirming (a favorite word) prior positions.

The mixed mood of the 1960s was in part due to the renewed energy of Missouri conservatives, who saw reasons to worry in the progressive leadership of new synodical president Oliver Harms, the convention decisions regarding inter-Lutheran cooperation, and the moderate majority on the faculty of the St. Louis seminary. Additionally, already in 1964 Missouri renewed its longstanding conversation on altar and pulpit fellowship with the American Lutheran Church.

A key player in this story is an unofficial weekly publication, *Christian News,* successor to the *Confessional Lutheran,* and its editor-publisher, Herman Otten. Since 1962, Otten, who was refused certification for ordination by Concordia Seminary, St. Louis, for criticism of the faculty who taught him, but who serves a congregation of the synod in New Haven, Missouri, has wielded disproportionate influence in advancing candidates, issues, and positions. Even a schism in Missouri in the 1970s did not satisfy Otten's desire for pure doctrine and leadership, as he has repeatedly grown impatient with leaders he earlier supported. Depending on one's perspective, Otten certainly belongs in the twentieth-century Lutheran Hall of Fame or Shame.

Otten began publishing his newspaper under the masthead *Lutheran News,* convinced that "liberalism was infiltrating Lutheranism" in America, but changed its name in 1968 to *Christian News.*[3] The paper beat the familiar drum of right-wing America in the 1960s — anti-Communist, anti–social activism, anti-intellectual, anti-modern — and resonated with conservatives who feared social change and its impact on the church. Alan Graebner, historian of Missouri's laity, locates Otten and his publication in the synodical landscape of the time:

> Otten did not cause the conservative resurgence of the 1960s, nor was he its chief tactician. He was not even the first to raise the alarm. But he was the main publicist of the movement. His paper, intended for laity as well as clergy, was an essential instrument for arousing the disgruntled to action, for putting them in touch with one another, and for maintaining morale. The *News* is therefore an important window on the outlook and susceptibility of an influential group of clergy and laity.[4]

In 1967 Otten sent copies of his publication to all delegates to the synodical convention, in support of the conservative goal of replacing Oliver Harms with a leader who would turn back the dangerous tendencies toward Lutheran unity that Harms had been championing. The political machine was driven by a group called Balance, Inc., under the leadership of Pastor E. J. Otto and layman Harold Olsen. Together with Otten, Balance advanced the candidacy of Jacob A. O. Preus to challenge Harms in 1969. At the Denver convention in July of that year, the conservatives were successful in capturing the presidency of synod, but in long-standing Missouri tradition, the convention delivered a mixed message, as delegates voted to enter into pulpit and altar fellowship with the American Lutheran Church and, for the first time, extended the right to vote to women in congregational meetings.

Jacob Preus, son of a former governor of Minnesota, had come to the Missouri Synod with his brother Robert in the late 1950s from the

---

3. Christian News website (http://luther_news.tripod.com/).
4. Alan Graebner, *Uncertain Saints: The Laity in the Lutheran Church–Missouri Synod, 1900-1970* (Westport, Conn.: Greenwood, 1975), p. 190.

"little Norwegian" synod, the Evangelical Lutheran Synod (ELS), when the brothers joined the faculties of Missouri's seminaries. Upon his election, he announced that the primary issue facing the synod was the proper understanding of Scripture, particularly as it was being taught at the St. Louis seminary. He launched an investigation that eventually resulted in the suspension of the seminary president, Dr. John Tietjen. As developments in the church unfolded, Balance in 1971 began publishing a monthly newsletter called *Affirm*, calling for action against the faculty of Concordia Seminary, St. Louis, and speaking against fellowship with the ALC. *Affirm* came to be recognized as the journal of the Preus camp. The moderates had no comparable publication until they organized as Evangelical Lutherans in Mission (ELIM) in 1973 and began publishing *Missouri in Perspective.*

Newsweek in 1971 declared the Missouri Synod "easily the most polarized Protestant denomination in the United States."[5] By the summer of 1973, when the synod met in convention in New Orleans, a showdown seemed inevitable. Preus declared the church to be at a doctrinal crossroads, and the "spiritual carnage" that followed earned the convention the label "battle of New Orleans."[6] No matter what side one was on, few disputed the combat reference. Lay people struggled to understand what was tearing their church apart in what appeared to be a "monk's battle"; conservative pastors told their congregants that this was a battle for the Bible itself, because the liberals were "taking your Bible away."

In February 1974, with their president suspended and their faculty under accusation, 85 percent of the students walked off the campus of Concordia Seminary, St. Louis, followed by 90 percent of their teachers. They formed a seminary in exile (Seminex) with the assistance of Eden Theological Seminary and St. Louis University.

The "urge to purge" extended through the synod as college faculties came under the close scrutiny of the Preus camp. Concordia Teachers College in River Forest, Illinois, held the reputation as not only the oldest of the Concordias but also the so-called flagship of the synod's institutions of higher education. In 1974 Preus sent Paul

---

5. "Lutherans to the Right," *Newsweek*, July 12, 1971, p. 64.

6. E. Clifford Nelson, ed., *The Lutherans in North America*, revised ed. (Philadelphia: Fortress, 1980), p. 531.

Zimmerman, formerly president of the Ann Arbor campus and chair of the Fact Finding Committee that had examined the St. Louis faculty, to serve as president at River Forest, in a direct response to the River Forest faculty's support of the St. Louis exiles. At Concordia, Seward, Nebraska, President W. T. Janzow was replaced for allegedly tolerating liberals on his campus.

The walkout was not the end of the controversy, however, as no one had yet left the church, only positions of authority within it. The final chapter would come with the question of whether graduates of Seminex could be ordained and called to congregations of the Missouri Synod. Eight district presidents thought so, and authorized such ordinations. In April 1976, Jacob Preus fired four of the eight district presidents, and that summer the exodus out of Missouri began. The moderates formed the Association of Evangelical Lutheran Churches (AELC), and 150 congregations followed. An early goal of the AELC was unity with other Lutherans, a goal achieved twelve years later in the formation of the Evangelical Lutheran Church in America (ELCA).

LCMS Presses on for Doctrinal Purity

Had the purge been complete, the story of political division in Missouri would be history, but we know that is not the case. The demand for doctrinal purity abated in the aftermath of the schism. Jacob Preus retired in 1981 and was succeeded by St. Louis seminary president Ralph Bohlmann, whose eleven years in office introduced a spirit of moderation. Conservatives began to lose patience with Bohlmann, especially as he became embroiled in a power struggle with Robert Preus over the presidency of the seminary in Fort Wayne, Indiana. Additionally, his establishment and support of a Commission on Women led some on the right to believe he was a shadow supporter of the ordination of women. Because the Missouri Synod remains one of the few Protestant church bodies to prohibit women in the pastoral office, a renewed fear of change gave conservatives in the synod a new issue. At the 1992 convention, Ralph Bohlmann was stunned to lose his bid for reelection by twelve votes to a relatively unknown district president from Iowa, Alvin Barry.

The Barry years returned Missouri to politics full force, but not immediately. Watchful moderates grew concerned as the 1998 convention neared, where the report of a Blue Ribbon panel proposed a significant restructuring of the synod that looked like a centralization of power in the president's office. Given that the historic self-understanding of the synod is advisory to its congregations, the panel's proposal appeared ominous. A group calling itself Lutherans Alive! published a newsletter called *Forward*, designed to "inform, educate, and uplift" the synod and move it forward in mission and ministry. The underlying fear obvious in the title of their publication was that the synod was again moving backward toward insularity. While the feared restructuring did not come to pass, the tone of the 1998 convention was grim. Parliamentary finesses, floor maneuvering, discouraged delegates who went home early, and election of virtually the entire conservative United List of candidates to church boards and offices left moderates depressed and uneasy about the future of their church.

Renewed Moderate Resistance

Three moderate clergy met together one evening in a hotel bar during that convention and agreed that some sort of support network for moderate voices in the synod needed to be established, a means by which people could communicate more regularly and effectively in order to try to change the direction of the synod. Within six months of that informal gathering, the Daystar Network debuted as an electronic discussion group. As the group expanded, its leadership proposed a meeting so that those who knew each other only through the Internet might gather in person.

The first Daystar free conference was held in January 2000 in Portland, Oregon, at Zion Lutheran Church, where Stephen C. Krueger, founding president of Daystar, was pastor. The free conference idea renewed a tradition begun by C. F. W. Walther, first president of the Missouri Synod. In 1856 Walther had issued an open invitation to "truly believing Lutherans" to "venture openly to inquire." The only requirements were that participants pledge subscription to the Augsburg Confession and that no one was to serve or represent the church in any official capacity.

Over two hundred people attended the two-day conference on the theme of Freedom for Ministry. A second conference was held in October of that same year in Mundelein, Illinois, its smaller attendance reflecting perhaps the spirit in the Midwest, which was more fearful than that along the geographic edges of the synod, in what are known as the saltwater districts. The theme of "One Body, One Spirit" addressed critical differences in the synod over issues of church and ministry.

More than six hundred clergy and laypersons subscribe to an active but restricted e-mail list called Daystar. Serving as something of a moderate think tank for the synod, Daystar hosts a public website that features documents, articles, free conference essays, and commentary on synodical concerns, as well as an e-zine called *Daystar Arising*.[7]

Daystars find themselves labeled liberals by the right wing of the synod, and are even considered too extreme by their fellow moderates in Jesus First. The more political of the two moderate groups formed more or less concurrently, the organization known as Jesus First Leadership began in August 1998 when a small group of clergymen and laywomen shared their concerns about the leadership of the church following the just-concluded synodical convention. The idea was initially conceived in a back-porch conversation between two pastors struggling with the increasing polarity in their synod. The answer, according to Pastors Richard Lessman and David Luecke, was a different vision of leadership. The model would be Jesus himself. The name was coined by one of the laity at the organizational meeting, who said, "I want a church that sees Jesus first."

Lessman and Luecke assembled a team of supporters and drafted a statement, "A Call to Affirm Jesus-First Leadership." Their goal was simply to get the endorsement of as many in the synod as they could, and to that end they called on the "thousands of people of the Lutheran Church–Missouri Synod [who] are concluding that church and ministry values important to them are no longer being expressed by major segments of church leadership," as evidenced in "disturbing displays of diminished mission urgency, increased legalism, disrespect for the priesthood of all believers, exaggerated pastoral authority, misplaced uniformity, resistance to cultural diversity, avoidance of other Christians, overstepping the advisory nature of Synod, and a growing spirit of fear and intimidation." The call included eight

---

7. Daystar website (http://day-star.net/).

relatively nonspecific pairings, each containing a statement of affirmation of the gospel supported by a Bible passage and a rejection of tendencies toward legalism, coercion, or injustice in church practice.[8]

Within weeks more than six hundred names had been attached to the Jesus First document, and JFL leaders had been labeled liberals who wanted to take over the church. Jesus First describes itself as having begun as "an effort to bring a change in the leadership" of the synod.[9] It does so by formulating strategic plans to influence delegate selection; nominate moderate candidates for synodical offices, boards, and commissions; and publicize issues through its newsletter, which it sends to each of the six thousand congregations in the synod.

Just as the two moderate groups were organizing themselves, a political hot potato fell into their laps. On Reformation Day 1999 the Lutheran World Federation and the Roman Catholic Church signed the Joint Declaration on the Doctrine of Justification in Augsburg, Germany, ending more than four centuries of condemnations about Martin Luther's fundamental doctrine of salvation by grace through faith. Both parties recognized that "in their respective histories our churches have come to new insights. Developments have taken place which not only make possible, but also require the churches to examine the divisive questions and condemnations and see them in a new light."[10] Despite the agreement between the majority of Lutherans and the Roman Catholics, the condemnations were not ended; the Missouri Synod was quick to condemn the action. Five weeks later, Alvin Barry took the unprecedented step of placing an ad in *USA Today* and fifteen other national newspapers expressing his profound disapproval over the agreement and misrepresenting Roman Catholic theology in the process. Missouri moderates, outraged and embarrassed by the Barry ad, despite the fact that synodical funds had not been used to pay for it, found renewed energy to work for change in synodical leadership as a result of their president's actions.

8. Jesus First Leadership website (http://www.jesusfirst.net/).

9. Jesus First Leadership website (http://www.jesusfirst.net/).

10. Joint Declaration on the Doctrine of Justification, which can be found at http://www.justification.org/.

The Growth of Fundamentalism

And what of the conservatives? Since the schism, but especially since 1992, the synod has shown evidence of both fundamentalism and sectarianism. The right wing of the synod has been splintered since the 1960s, when different groups began to organize for different purposes. In the tradition of Paul Burgdorf's *Confessional Lutheran,* all like to call themselves "confessional" Lutherans, but their use of the term is rarely defined aside from their subscription to the Book of Concord, the collection of documents from Luther and other reformers published in 1580. In that regard *all* Lutherans are confessional, since the confessions offer the lens through which Lutherans understand Scripture. But there is a difference in *how* Lutherans use the confessions. Dean Lueking's distinction between two kinds of confessionalism identifies trends that can be traced from the synod's founding and that exist in "implicit tension" throughout its history. Evangelical confessionalism focuses on the ecumenical character of the Lutheran confessions, seeing them "as a bridge to the rest of Christendom rather than a wall barring it." Scholastic confessionalism, on the other hand, deeply influenced by pietism and seventeenth-century Lutheran orthodoxy, focuses on the correctness of belief and uses the confessions to "cut off all dissidents in any given doctrine from participation in the visible congregation of those who possessed the truth of God in its full purity."[11] In the conservative appropriation of the term "confessional" as a boundary, and in their fairly black/white thinking, everyone who does not subscribe to their self-understanding is considered a liberal or, worse, not a true Lutheran.

The Internet has caused their number to proliferate, as different groups organize regionally or around a particular issue, especially the pastoral office. Those who subscribe to a "high view" of the ministry renounce the so-called functionalist view of the office as described by the founding father of the synod, C. F. W. Walther. They believe the pastor is the ambassador of Christ and that the Great Commission in Matthew 28 refers to clergy only. This perspective is most often represented by men associated with the Fort Wayne seminary, some of

---

11. F. Dean Lueking, *Mission in the Making: The Missionary Enterprise among Missouri Synod Lutherans, 1846-1963* (St. Louis: Concordia Publishing House, 1964), pp. 15-16.

whom even appear to treat ordination as a sacrament. Websites such as Jack Cascione's Reclaiming Walther and Lutherquest sites[12] argue instead for historic congregational authority and against the high view of the ministry and a "hyper-Euro Lutheran" hierarchical church.

Some organizations are more lay-led than clergy-dominated, while others — such as the Lutheran Concerns Association of attorney Robert Doggett, former Congressman William Dannemeyer, and former corporate executive Edwin Hinnefeld — are more concerned with the management of synod than with its theology. Others claim they wish only to confess the historic creeds and confessions of the church (Confess and Teach For Unity or CAT 41[13] and Consensus[14]) or to espouse the "correct" Lutheran doctrines (Concord-Texas[15]) or seek an end to partisan politics through an approach based on Scripture (Reformation Today[16]). Certain of the discussion boards or e-lists attempt to maintain civility in the conversations carried on there, but others do not, and it is not uncommon to find references to "true Lutherans" as opposed to "false Lutherans," and even to the "Evil Lutheran Church in America," a particularly scurrilous reference to the ELCA. The pejorative rhetoric that has long been a characteristic of Missouri politics seems custom-made for the Internet.

While Herman Otten continues to distribute his weekly paper by conventional means, supporters have started an "unofficial" website for *Christian News*. After forty years of publication, Otten's paper still sounds the tocsin for conservatives in Missouri to remain vigilant in their stand against the dangers of church growth, ecumenism/unionism, feminism, modernism, postmodernism, and psychology, and for doctrinal purity as defined by Otten. A curious and not infrequent topic is Holocaust denial. Unwavering in his now forty-five-year-long campaign to be certified for ordination in a synod that has repeatedly denied him that status, Herman Otten remains the chief publicist of its right wing.

A number of major players on the right have a common heritage as alumni of Bethany Lutheran College in Mankato, Minnesota, or

12. http://www.reclaimingwalther.org and www.lutherquest.org.
13. http://www.cat41.org.
14. http://www.consusenslutheran.org.
15. http://www.concordtx.org.
16. http://www.reformationtoday.tripod.com.

roots in the Evangelical Lutheran Synod. Like Jacob Preus, Alvin Barry was not a native Missourian. He attended a Wisconsin Synod seminary and served a Wisconsin Synod parish before coming into the Missouri Synod. In like manner, a number of the major players on the left — though most would prefer to call themselves moderates rather than liberals — have common heritage deep in Missouri history, many coming from families with long synodical pedigrees. Some share a perspective learned as undergraduates at Valparaiso University, a school long tied to the synod but independent of any official affiliation. Most would likely share Alan Graebner's description of "left wing . . . within a Lutheran context" as being

> Characterized by an unwillingness to accept the fundamentalist view of Scriptural inerrancy, by strong sacramental and liturgical emphases, high commitment to ecumenicity, insistence upon institutional involvement in social concerns, [and] impressive intellectual qualifications.[17]

The LCMS in a Pluralist Society

The issues that divide Missouri are those at the core of its Lutheran faith — Law and gospel, the Eucharist, worship, the authority of Scripture and the ministry. The church is kept at odds by the things that matter to it most. And one of those things is fellowship with other Lutherans and other Christians in an increasingly pluralist society and world, the issue at the center of recent controversy. But the fellowship question is merely one aspect of the larger question challenging the synod: how should the church respond to the culture that surrounds it? Should it embrace or reject ideas that have influenced American society in the past generation? One issue that perpetually seems to lie just below the surface is the question of the service of women in the church. Conservatives insist that the changes introduced by feminism must be resisted; moderates worry that women will leave a church that does not recognize either their gifts or their desire to serve. Rather than discuss the issue, the synod continues to

17. Graebner, *Uncertain Saints*, pp. 194-95.

reaffirm its position against change, frustrating those like the moderate group Voices/Vision, women who want their church to grapple with the question.

The death of its president just months before the triennial convention in 2001 left Missouri with a leadership vacuum. The conservatives had no heir apparent to Alvin Barry, and the moderates were not agreed on who would be best to fill the position. The subsequent election of a moderate president left Jesus First and Daystar encouraged, but conservative gains on the synod's Board of Directors and other key boards left the post-convention direction of the church body not only uncertain but highly politicized.

Gerald Kieschnick was installed as president of the Missouri Synod on Saturday, September 8, 2001. Before he could outline the goals of his administration, the events of September 11 replaced the agenda of America and its churches. Eight days later, Kieschnick and the presiding bishop of the ELCA, H. George Anderson, each with his church body's director of disaster relief, visited Ground Zero and afterward met at a nearby church to pray, sing hymns, and share Scripture with exhausted relief workers from the World Trade Center site.

The following week, Kieschnick received a call from the president (bishop) of the Atlantic District of the synod, the Reverend David Benke, who had been invited by New York City Mayor Rudolph Giuliani to the Prayer for America event to be hosted by Oprah Winfrey at Yankee Stadium on Sunday, September 23. Given the Missouri Synod's persistent fears of unionism, Benke asked for his president's opinion on his participation, and Kieschnick agreed that Benke should take part. Benke also consulted with his district board of directors and with the Brooklyn congregation that he serves as pastor.

There are many Missouri Synod Lutherans — many Lutherans, really — who were proud to see a representative of their tradition participate in the Yankee Stadium event. A much smaller number of Missouri Synod Lutherans were not. In mid November charges were brought against President Kieschnick by two pastors and against David Benke by six pastors, a list that eventually grew to twenty-one. Among Benke's accusers was Walter Otten, brother of the editor of *Christian News* and a leader of the Northern Illinois Confessional Lutheran group (NICL).

To some of these men, the presence and prayer of a pastor from their church body at Yankee Stadium became more significant than September 11 itself, because of the blurring of lines between Christianity and other religions which the Missouri Synod constitution calls syncretism. To that end, Benke was accused not only of prayer fellowship with other Christians — the dreaded unionism — but of praying with non-Christians. His accusers demanded his repentance or his removal from the clergy roster.

The distance between the two camps widened as the Benke case became a flashpoint for the already seriously divided synod. The Northern Illinois Confessional Lutherans issued a statement on church fellowship in light of the Yankee Stadium event, "That They May Be One," and began to gather signatures.[18] The Daystar webpage had earlier collected names of those supporting Kieschnick and Benke.[19]

Raw politics exposed the deep chasm in Missouri. The charges against Kieschnick were dismissed, yet the president was enjoined from ruling on Benke's case and the first vice president, Daniel Preus, was as well, for publicly taking issue with his president. The matter fell to the second vice president, Wallace Schulz, to decide. In late June 2002, Schulz, longtime associate speaker on the synod's Lutheran Hour radio broadcasts, was appointed primary speaker. Several days later he issued his decision in the Benke case, suspending Benke and relieving him of his duties as Atlantic District president and chair of the Board of Regents of Concordia University, Bronxville, New York. The suspension allowed Benke to continue serving St. Peter's, his congregation in Brooklyn. Benke immediately appealed the ruling and the case proceeded to a dispute resolution panel. Schulz, in the meantime, was relieved of his duties as Lutheran Hour speaker, and in September was terminated by the Board of Governors of the Lutheran Laymen's League/Lutheran Hour Ministries. The League's Executive Committee had earlier asked Schulz to recuse himself from adjudicating the Benke matter in order to avoid a conflict of interest. In Jauary 2003 Schulz and Benke appeared before a dispute resolution panel. Following the hearing, during the panel's deliberations, the synod's Commission on Constitutional Matters issued several opinions favorable to

18. Northern Illinois Confessional Lutherans website (http://www.cat41.org/NICL/).

19. Daystar website (http://day-star.net/).

Benke's case. In May President Kieschnick released the report of the panel that lifted Benke's suspension and returned him to office. The unanimous decision determined that Benke's participation in A Prayer for America had been "a discretionary response to a quite extraordinary set of circumstances in a quite unordinary event — a terrorist attack on the United States," and thus an allowable action according to a resolution on the Lutheran understanding of fellowship adopted by the synod at its 2001 convention. Wallace Schulz did not appeal. A month later the Atlantic District reelected David Benke as its president/bishop. Had the panel ruled otherwise, he would have been removed from the synod's clergy roster.

In an effort to address the growing conflict in his church body, Kieschnick had previously called for theological convocations to discuss the question at the heart of the Benke matter — fellowship. A model event was held in August 2002 in Phoenix, Arizona, and was replicated in each of the synod's thirty-five districts in the months following. Despite the deliberate attempt at dialogue, the battle lines remained drawn. In May 2003 Kieschnick encouraged the Council of (district) Presidents to apply "evangelical admonition and ecclesiastical discipline" to the signers of the NICL statement, given that they had not followed appropriate procedure in introducing what appeared to be a doctrinal statement.

In reporting the resolution of the Benke case to his church body, Gerald Kieschnick wrote that, in the year and a half since September 11, "The identity and reputation of The Lutheran Church–Missouri Synod . . . [has] been misinterpreted and misunderstood by many. Conflict and consternation have been witnessed and experienced by pastors and laity throughout the Synod." He urged his pastors and people to "improve the way we walk together," the very meaning of the word "synod."

As developments in this curious case unfold, Missouri once again finds itself, as *Newsweek* had described it in 1971, "easily the most polarized Protestant denomination in the United States," and caught up in what a friend calls the eschatology of the next convention. Delegates to the July 2004 convention will not only vote on the reelection of Gerald Kieschnick as synodical president, but will surely be faced with questions from congregations and districts on the Benke matter. The final resolution will depend on whether David Benke's prayer was an offense against or an extension of the gospel of Jesus Christ. And how that question gets answered will determine not only how the Missouri Synod understands itself in the future but whether the misery will continue.

BIBLIOGRAPHY

Christian News website (http://luther_news.tripod.com/).

Daystar website (http://day-star.net/).

Graebner, Alan. *Uncertain Saints: The Laity in the Lutheran Church–Missouri Synod, 1900-1970.* Westport, Conn.: Greenwood, 1975.

Graebner, Theodore. "The Burden of Infallibility: A Study in the History of Dogma" (1948). *Concordia Historical Institute Quarterly* 38 (1965): 88-94.

————. "For a Penitent Jubilee" (1946). *Concordia Historical Institute Quarterly* 45 (1972): 3-28.

Jesus First Leadership website (http://www.jesusfirst.net/).

Joint Declaration on the Doctrine of Justification. This document can be found at http://www.justification.org/.

Lueking, F. Dean. *Mission in the Making: The Missionary Enterprise among Missouri Synod Lutherans, 1846-1963.* St. Louis: Concordia Publishing House, 1964.

Lutheran Church–Missouri Synod website (http://www.cms.org/).

"Lutherans to the Right." *Newsweek* (July 12, 1971): 64.

Nelson, E. Clifford, ed. *The Lutherans in North America,* revised ed. Philadelphia: Fortress, 1980.

Northern Illinois Confessional Lutherans website (http://www.cat41.org/NICL/).

Todd, Mary. *Authority Vested: A Story of Identity and Change in The Lutheran Church–Missouri Synod.* Grand Rapids: Eerdmans, 2000.

The Lutheran Left: From Movement to Church Commitment

MARIA ERLING

The Lutheran "left" is hard to locate today. I set out to ask church leaders, veteran pastors, young people, and longtime Lutherans to refer me to people and places I should contact to learn more about the left in Lutheranism. Pastors and laypeople alike referred me to retirees and veteran advocates who organized and protested a couple of decades ago. These individuals are now just as deeply committed to issues of social justice and to organizing and advocating for causes as they were during the heyday of Lutheran protesting in the '70s and '80s, but they are not recruiting new leaders. In the historic locations for more activist political engagement among Lutherans, such as campus and urban ministry, the present-day successors to these social justice warriors do not command the wider audience that their predecessors once held within the church. A visible, organized movement of left-thinking and left-acting Lutherans seems not to be actively defining, at least from these familiar locations, a presence that must be noticed when decisions are being made by the church. It would seem that the Lutheran left, if it did once have a role in the development of modern American Lutheranism, did not generate a cadre of followers or an institutional presence that would sustain a continuing identifiable voice.

Concluding that the Lutheran left has already had its moment and is now invisible or in disarray would, however, be premature. This assessment would too narrowly depend on the assumption that Lutheran "leftness" would take shape as a movement. For a variety of historical reasons, the story is more complex. A key, defining complication in explaining the role of the left within contemporary Lutheranism is the enormous institutional and personal energy exerted by Lutherans on the several stages of merger among Lutherans during the second half of the twentieth century.

I contend in this chapter that the left functioned as one of the players defining how Lutheranism, both theologically and socially, would define itself as a church in the world. Because this voice was a recognized presence during these constructive phases of church "building," the story of the left within contemporary Lutheranism is more complex than the simple account of a movement functioning in a defined way over and against a given establishment. A better account of the role of the Lutheran left within contemporary Lutheranism would be able to account for the way the left functioned in the merger, and would describe the way that many of its commitments now are discussed and enunciated, though less pointedly, in the discourse of the denomination itself.

Less noticeable than other facets of contemporary Lutheranism, and not prominent as a definable movement with coherent goals, recognizable leaders, a mechanism for promoting a vision, and an active recruitment strategy, the Lutheran left should be described as a more inchoate sensibility among a large segment of active Lutherans. This sensibility provides good reasons to lay claim to an ongoing tradition of progressive, socially minded activism within American Lutheranism. If the left wing within Lutheranism should not be named a movement, the elements of a progressive theological and activist perspective can still be recognized as operative within the church. Well-articulated assumptions about justice and the church's public role that are informed by the stances once taken by activists in the years of protest against the Vietnam War, against racism, and against sexism still guide many Lutherans who, rather than organizing a movement to push the church from without, choose to play the role of insider in promoting their vision within the church structure.

A Golden Age

There were and are many who express frustration at the perceived absence of a visible, identifiable left wing within contemporary Lutheranism. And the lament that arises from former activists, and the children of activists, recalls a golden age and cherished places and offices where the left existed, even flourished — a coffee shop and bookstore near Augsburg College in Minnesota, the community at Holden Village in Washington State, and colorful chaplains and lively ministries at college campuses throughout the country. These persons and locations have not been joined by new faces and places on the map. Lutherans remember the once-active role of protesters at church conventions, when the Lutheran Peace Fellowship, and Clergy and Laity Concerned, challenged delegates to go beyond the drafting of statements to take direct action. Organized national protests in which Lutherans gained some visibility outside the church walls also figure in the memories of some. Those who remember getting arrested during a protest against the threat of nuclear war at the Soviet Embassy in New York in April of 1982 consider the current church to exhibit a relative failure of courage, a lack of nerve, compared with the public voice once wielded by activist leaders.

If there was any kind of organized "movement" of left-wing Lutherans, the Lutheran Peace Fellowship (LPF) provides the most readily available example of how this dynamic emerged within Lutheranism. Founded in the late 1930s, the Fellowship focused its attention during the 1960s on supporting conscientious objectors and providing information and means for church people to express, as church people, their opposition to the Vietnam War.[1] As the war ended, the Lutheran Peace Fellowship broadened its work to educate members of the church on the continuing need for a peace fellowship, since the causes of war, poverty, and injustice still existed. A particularly dangerous threat remained in the buildup of nuclear weapons.

When the Lutheran Peace Fellowship began in the late 1930s and the early 1940s — the actual founding date is unclear — the work emerged in the context of America's widespread reluctance to be involved in yet another war in Europe. Lutherans particularly were sympathetic to the grievances that Germany sustained at the end of WWI. At the same time, significant leaders within American Protestantism also advocated a pacifist stance as the true Christian foundation for involvement in the world, and so Lutherans seeking partnership on this

---

1. Stephen Schroeder, *A Community and a Perspective: Lutheran Peace Fellowship and the Edge of the Church, 1941-1991* (Lanham, Md.: University Press of America, 1993).

issue found it readily. Building on the efforts within the several Lutheran denominations during the late 1930s to develop a Lutheran pacifist response to the war, the Fellowship consciously emulated the work and structures modeled by historic pacifist churches, and approached its own Lutheran constituency on an explicitly ecumenical basis; it provided means by which Lutherans could learn about other pacifist efforts and incorporate these perspectives and models within their own church setting. The LPF did not belong to any one of the Lutheran denominations — Missouri Synod, Augustana Church, United Lutheran Church, American Lutheran Church, or Evangelical Lutheran Church, to name only the largest American Lutheran groups at the time. Instead, the Fellowship gathered together leaders from disparate strands and emphases of Lutheranism and provided an important mechanism for intra-Lutheran thinking and activism.

The key Lutheran denominations involved in the start of the Lutheran Peace Fellowship were the Augustana Lutheran Church and the United Lutheran Church. (The Augustana Synod, founded in 1860, was one of the church bodies that would merge to create the Lutheran Church in America in 1962. The United Lutheran Church was founded in 1918 out of the General Synod, General Council, and General Synod South, three German Lutheran churches. It too would merge into the Lutheran Church in America in 1962.) The Evangelical Lutheran Church, founded in 1918 as a merger of Norwegian American Lutheranism, provided leadership for the Fellowship in the 1950s. (This church body merged into the American Lutheran Church in 1960.) The Lutheran Church–Missouri Synod contributed energy and leadership to several "leftist" organizations in the 1960s, particularly to the Lutheran Human Relations organization (which dealt with racism concerns) and to Clergy and Laity Concerned (an anti-war group). Other Lutheran denominations at mid century included the more confessionally and biblically conservative American Lutheran Church, founded in 1930 by Ohio, Buffalo, and Iowa Synod Lutherans, and smaller ethnic Lutheran synods of Danes, Finns, Slovaks, Icelanders, and Norwegians that would later variously merge into the American Lutheran Church, the Lutheran Church in America, and the Lutheran Church–Missouri Synod. Individual pastors and members within these smaller groups often did not know of the existence of the Lutheran Peace Fellowship, as their own church-body leaders did not themselves promote the cause. It was more often the case that individuals would have to discover Lutheran activists in the other churches on their own.

The Lutheran Peace Fellowship, with its pacifist concerns, was by no means the only cause that appealed to Lutherans who had commitments to social justice causes, or for that matter to a progressive theological agenda. It did, however, provide a rallying point and organizational center for the articulation of an alternative vision for the church's role in the world. A commitment to pacifism itself preceded any kind of organizational commitment to the Fellowship for its own sake, but the newly evolving organization did provide an important arena for the staging of a wider, intra-Lutheran conversation about the church's role within society. Within the several Lutheran churches, means for bringing the issue to a wider membership depended in part on how each church was structured. Though the Lutheran Peace Fellowship was never officially sponsored by any Lutheran denomination, within the United Lutheran Church a group of leaders in central Pennsylvania organized a special committee to assist pastors in providing information to members on conscientious objection. In the Augustana Church, a wider exposure to the issue was provided for members when the editor of *The Lutheran Companion*, the church's weekly newspaper, brought the issue to the attention of his readers.

A centrally driven organizational impulse characterized the efforts of those churches that would later form the Lutheran Church in America, headquartered in New York City. In their approach to bringing social issues before church members — creating committees and identifying causes with key leaders within the structure of the church — the resulting institutional commitment to the consideration of selected social issues tended to forestall the development of grassroots agitation over against the church establishment. The church itself would move along in addressing social issues, perhaps not at breakneck speed, but in relation to selected issues with some consequence. Particularly in relation to issues that could be defined as left-wing, but also in relation to theological and liturgical concerns, the issues dominating the agenda at church conventions may not have reflected the concerns of people in the congregations as much as they did the perspectives of the leaders in the church. Bringing the theological and ethical concerns of pacifism, for instance, to members of congregations, including the wider perspective that peace-seeking and peace-making efforts would ultimately depend on a sustained commitment among Christians to the elimination of poverty and the assurance of social justice for all people, was seen as the natural exercise of the teaching role of pastors and church leaders.

A contrasting development, involving a more detached and sometimes wary relationship between the grassroots and the central church, evolved within the American Lutheran Church, headquartered in Minneapolis, Minnesota. With its population center farther west rather than in the Eastern states, the left is remembered as having a separate geographical location from the "mother church" in Minneapolis. The west has always been under-represented within Lutheranism, and perhaps because of its minority status or perhaps because of the more fragile economic basis for churches and institutions there, a regional consciousness over against establishment Lutheranism developed there. Though there were certainly those living in Iowa, Minnesota, and the Dakotas who also agitated for alternative perspectives, voices from California, and perhaps even more fervently from the Pacific Northwest, enunciated a grassroots left that was decidedly anti-establishment in its Lutheranism.

Holden Village, an institution that was formed during the late 1950s and early 1960s, incorporated much of the countercultural ethos of its founding years. Located on the property of an abandoned lumber camp in Washington State, it now provides a retreat setting for a Lutheran community, but also an organizational hub for the articulation of a vital grassroots, commercial-free Lutheranism. Its "word of mouth" reputation — no Internet hookups at Holden Village, or roads for that matter — is countercultural in the sense that a consistent, critical perspective is maintained over against the many ways that established economies, theologies, hierarchies, and societies threaten to subsume Christian, Lutheran values and replace them with a consumer mentality. One observer, who remembers hiking to Holden Village with his activist father during the early '60s, states that the village could be seen today as a place that harbors a "revivalist left."

When it was founded at the end of the 1950s, leadership for the retreat community was sought from those who had already been involved in youth ministry. During the '60s as well, Holden continued to be of service to youth, who through the Luther League were a well-organized dimension of the church in the region. Leadership for the Luther League in the Northwest was itself committed to anti-war and social justice movements, and in their yearly conventions resolutions were routinely passed on from the Luther League to the conventions of the church.[2] The activist, set-apart dynamic of Lutheranism in the Northwest was fed both by the inheritance of Hans Nielsen Hauge's lay-oriented churchmanship that influenced Norwegian American Lutherans who settled the region, and by the independence of Lutheranism in the Pacific Northwest. Hauge's churchly legacy was drawn on to cultivate a perspective that located the authority of the church within the congregation, particularly within the agitated, or revived, conscience of the individual Christian. As this spiritual independence was nurtured, it gave Lutherans in the region resources to resist efforts of leaders at "church headquarters" to determine the course of the church. Luther Leaguers and students involved in campus student associations, like the Lutheran Student Movement, participated in a wide network of advocacy that was oriented to change, social justice, and to developing independent theological and spiritual grounding to use as leverage against a church leadership that was perceived as geographically, culturally, and economically distant from the concerns of the region.

The spirit of revolt and the resistance to authority characteristic of student movements affected the institutional health of the Lutheran left, particularly when the international links to other student movements in Europe, Asia, Africa, and Latin America were broken down. Risto Lehtonen's *Story of a Storm: The Ecumenical Student Movement in the Turmoil of Revolution* (1998) recounts how the student revolt of the 1970s weakened ecumenical and political ties between churches as one after another of the Christian student movements dismantled their programs in the interest of noninstitutional and nonhierarchical forms of involvement.

The Promise of a New Lutheran Church

Each of the several streams of Lutheranism that joined to form the Commission for a New Lutheran Church (CNLC) in 1982, and later

2. Charles Lutz, *Surprising Gifts: The Story of Holden Village, Church Renewal Center* (Holden Village Press, 1987).

merged as the Evangelical Lutheran Church in America in 1988, had its own well-formed notion of the nature and purpose of the church. The different traditions relied on the same confessional tradition to support their own ecclesial understanding, but each church, because of its separate history and experience in America, developed significant differences. The American context for the development of these distinctive understandings of the balance of authority and autonomy in the various dimensions, or expressions (as they came to be called), of the church — the congregation, the district or synod, and the national church — meant that each church participating in the merger brought long traditions of effective church governance to the merger negotiations. The varied conceptions of the location of power, or authority, within the church necessarily affected the way in which each church's "left" functioned in its own church body.

The LCA, as described above, though it did experience agitation from special interest caucuses, tended to identify and corral these emphases into a national structure that had considerable autonomy vis-à-vis congregations. Its official social statements, adopted after extensive internal discussion and consultation, expressed the commitments of the church in the social arena and had directive force within the structure of the denomination. The ALC, as described above, located the genesis and fount of authority more specifically within congregations and with believers. One mark of this difference was the number of social statements passed by each body as of the time of the merger. There were nineteen social statements passed by the LCA, and over five times as many, ninety-five, passed by the ALC, along with an additional sixty resolutions. The two churches had obvious differences in the way that they generated, discussed, and produced statements. The development of social statements within the ALC, by contrast with the LCA, occurred through a more rapid, task-force-oriented process. Congregations were consulted, but the issues and statements occurred with such frequency that the more systemic, methodical, and institutional attention that may have been possible with fewer statements could not occur.

When the work of designing and planning a new Lutheran church began in 1982, Lutherans in the separate denominations — ALC, LCA, and the Association of Evangelical Lutheran Churches (AELC, whose members were former Missouri Lutheran congregations) — were to come together as one, and old assumptions and insti tutional cultures were to pass away, while a new Lutheran church would be fashioned according to new principles. Of course, the separate church bodies had much in common — the same hymnal, common processes for theological education, and easy transfer of membership among the churches. Networks of the left had functioned in part as bridges between and among Lutheran churches; now these networks could and did provide the foundation for collaborative work within the merger negotiations. People from various church bodies knew each other through organizations like the Lutheran Peace Fellowship and were ready to work together to build a foundation that would advance specific goals.

Already in the predecessor church bodies, a particular goal of becoming more inclusive of Native American, Black, Asian, and Hispanic persons in membership as well as in the decision-making processes of the church was quite well established. In the LCA, the 1984 convention in Toronto committed that church to working toward increasing membership of these groups by 12 percent annually, and to designate that 25 percent of all new congregations would be located in communities of diversity. The ALC in 1984 agreed by an almost unanimous vote (758-4 with 5 abstentions) to the dissemination of a report from the task force on racial inclusiveness. *Visions of an Inclusive Church* was not binding on the church, but instead was transmitted to congregations for the "stimulation and reflection of their members." The choice to propose a "vision" of inclusiveness was banked on the premise that a vision could itself prompt "profound change," and that just as Jesus used such teaching devices to inspire his followers, the task force could also propose to the congregations a new way to imagine the American Lutheran Church.

Much of the spirit and commitment to inclusiveness demonstrated by the separate statements adopted by the LCA and the ALC in 1984 stemmed from the ongoing discussion of the topic at the meetings of the Commission for a New Lutheran Church (CNLC). The members of the CNLC were themselves selected by their churches, who were guided by the principle of quotas — the group of seventy included forty-eight laypersons and thirty-two clergy, forty-two men and twenty-eight women, with sixteen people who represented minorities, or what later became known as "people of color, or whose language is other than English." In fashioning or imagining the new church, Lutherans built their hopes for a more culturally diverse church into the very structure of the new denomination.

The work of constructing a new Lutheran church was necessarily focused on constitutions, structural relationships, political arrangements, and the distribution of resources rather than on articulating a vision for the way the church would function or work in the world. The work of the commission focused on nuts and bolts rather than on movements or hopes. The Lutheran left could well be identified with the very pragmatic, structural goals that had been incorporated in the merger commission's commitment to what they called inclusivity. The concerns of women for broader representation in the leadership of the church, the push to develop more intentional strategies for expanding minority membership, and the broader concern that the church address issues presented to it by the world rather than by its largely white and male clerical leadership all became linked in the actual working of the CNLC. Edgar Trexler, in describing the way that participants functioned in the meetings, pointed to the power of a coalition formed by women, minority members, and the representatives from the AELC to ensure that decisions would be made on the basis of a broader representation, rather than on the theological or ecclesiological expertise of the clergy.[3]

Issues and concerns of the Lutheran left were still very much present in the churches during the process of the merger, and these sometimes even made their way to the floor of the commission. Agitating the church from the outside, pastors in the Pittsburgh area had formed an organization known as the Denominational Mission Strategy (DMS), which, after the pastors leading the group became subject to discipline and removal from the clergy roster of the LCA, staged dramatic, convention-disturbing events to protest the corporate nature of church merger and the preoccupation in the church with business as usual. Daniel Solberg and Douglas Roth — pastors whose social advocacy on behalf of unemployed steel workers in the Pittsburgh area had become so divisive in their synod that they were disciplined for violating the constitution — took their frustration to a meeting of the com-

---

3. Edgar R. Trexler, *Anatomy of a Merger: People, Dynamics and Decisions That Shaped the ELCA* (Minneapolis: Augsburg, 1991).

mission in Minneapolis in February, and later to the LCA's 1986 convention in Milwaukee, where they linked their own fight with Mellon Bank in Pittsburgh to a broader protest against the corporate nature of the church's merger. During the live telephone hook-up with the three participating churches to announce the positive votes for the merger, the connection was disrupted, and instead of the positive announcement of the vote by Presiding Bishop James Crumley, Solberg's voice announced, "I hate your adulterous merger." Crumley had the podium microphone disconnected.

Daniel Solberg's damning of the merger was a dramatic gesture intended to wrest the attention of the church away from its preoccupation with structure and constitutional issues. Advocates for divestment of the pension funds from companies doing business in South Africa were also agitated by the corporate style of the merger, including the polished, burnished reports to the consistory, and they joined sympathetically, if not physically, with Solberg's insistence that there were more important concerns of social justice that were being set aside for the moment. During his protest at the Milwaukee convention, delegates clapped their hands to drown out his voice. At the next joint meeting to effect the merger in Columbus, Ohio, leaders anticipated a similar attempt to interrupt the proceedings. Protesters took a four-foot replica of a South African Krugerrand with them as they attempted to take over the podium, but delegates were prompted by an organist and began singing "A Mighty Fortress," the battle hymn of Lutheranism. This time establishment singing drowned out the shouts of protesters.

The frustrated and at times frantic actions of Solberg and others who had been defrocked for their involvement in DMS in Pittsburgh signaled that some voices on the Lutheran left did not rest easy with the promise of representation and structural reform that advocates for diversity had written into the constitution of the new church. Dissatisfaction with vague promises that new voices would advance justice in the church and thereby provide a more authentic voice when the church spoke to society foreshadowed the problems with visibility and momentum that attend the left in contemporary Lutheranism. The left had brought its coalition-building expertise and networking ability to the merger process, and now they belonged in a different, more integrated way in the church they had fashioned.

Realism for More Conservative Times

The enthusiasm for newness waned rather quickly during the first years of the ELCA as a sequence of budget shortfalls first led to a reconfiguring of the envisioned structure of the church. Congregations and pastors also weathered a sometimes choppy transition to new styles of leadership. Quotas designed to ensure a minimum level of diversity in decision-making were an immediate reality that all levels of the new church had to abide by in setting up new synod leadership. In all levels of work, quotas ensured that 60 percent of the participants would be lay, divided equally between men and women, while 40 percent would be clergy. In addition, 10 percent of the participants needed to be people of color or speakers of a language other than English. To these fixed allotments informal quotas were also honored, to ensure that leadership came from all geographical areas of the church and that the separate predecessor church bodies would have proportional representation on boards and committees. All of these provisions made many experienced, white, male pastors feel very much out of the loop in the new arrangements, while others were tapped for leadership who had before been invisible participants.

Even while most members of the new denomination were still getting to know each other, there was an impatience with the time it would take to accomplish this necessary preliminary task of organization. Many had been waiting for the church to express itself in relationship to controversial social issues like homosexuality, and to resolve the conflict over divestment of church pension funds from companies doing business in South Africa. Others concerned about the lack of progress on theological matters in the merger commission wanted the church to address the new church's understanding of ministry, particularly the diaconate — a topic that had been too difficult for the merger commission to resolve — and to respond to the agreements and recommendations of ecumenical dialogues. Many church people had been waiting for their issues and concerns to receive appropriate attention. Many were disappointed to find that the resources were less than expected, and the process for decision-making unclear.

Although statements on abortion, church and society, and the death penalty were drafted, circulated, and approved at the second ELCA assembly in 1991, the pace of study and production of social statements has slowed since then. Ten years later there were only seven social statements. One reason for the more deliberate pace was the derailing of a study on human sexuality that had been slated to come before the 1997 church-wide assembly (along with three ecumenical proposals on relationships with Roman Catholics, Reformed Churches, and the Episcopal Church, USA, which also would command considerable institutional attention). After a draft version of the social statement was circulated in 1993, the negative reaction to the statement was so strong, particularly in relationship to its position on homosexuality, that it was pulled back from consideration and rewritten by a new team of "consultants." Even so, the new attempt was deemed "too liberal by the majority, and too conservative by the rest," according to the official press release issued by the ELCA just before the 1995 church-wide assembly, where the members were informed that no statement would come before the next assembly, and that "no social statement on human sexuality will be brought to a vote in the foreseeable future." The foreseeable future is now upon the ELCA Lutherans, however, as the 2001 assembly of the church, responding to memorials and requests from five synods, agreed by a large margin of 899 to 115 to create a study document on homosexuality, and by a narrower 561 to 386 margin to begin the process of creating a social statement. The task force charged with creating the study document was named in the spring of 2002 and met during the summer of that year.

The issue of homosexuality represents the most visible topic that now commands the attention of the ELCA, and it is one in which conservatives and liberals, the right and the left within Lutheranism, will no doubt take sides. It is not a foregone conclusion that the lines will be drawn in the familiar places, however, or that the chosen way for either side to advance their cause is to agitate or form a movement pressing the church from without. There are likely to be many identified leaders within the denomination who will work hard to guard the process of study so that sides do not become polarized. Thus it is that the church has already produced workbooks and guidelines for congregations to assist them in facing this issue, the most recent being *Talking Together About Tough Social Issues,* a resource provided by the Division for Church and Society. These procedural safeguards will, one hopes, forestall fighting and schism.

At the church's 2001 assembly, speakers took the floor arguing that the time for changing the church's rules about ordination of homosexual persons is now. Protesters from the national network of nonviolent protest on behalf of gay, lesbian, bisexual, and transgendered persons, called Soulforce, gathered outside the convention hall after the assembly delegates failed to amend their ordination requirements. Former Presiding Bishop Herbert Chilstrom was at the helm of the denomination when the first irregular ordinations were performed in San Francisco in 1989. He was directly involved in the establishment of the current policy, but has come some way in reexamining his position since then. He was asked by another delegate to address the assembly during the floor discussion and was granted the privilege of voice. He described himself as "an evangelical conservative with a radical social conscience" who has been "haunted by letters and parents' stories." Now he "longs for the day when this church has the opportunity to bless same gender relationships and for the day when it allows some congregations to call noncelibate homosexuals as pastors."

Chilstrom's invocation of his evangelical conservatism with a radical social conscience hearkened to the Lutheran tradition of deeply engaging the biblical text, as well as the Lutheran theological and devotional tradition, as a way to find guidance in dealing with the issues and concerns emerging in the contemporary social context. Lutherans on the left and on the right argue about how to interpret their theological and biblical heritage, and, particularly with regard to the social issue of homosexuality, the Lutheran debate will largely focus on issues of biblical interpretation.

Dealing with Christianity's long tradition of silence about and/ or condemnation of homosexuality will not be an easy task for any task force or study group to assume. Though there are repeated requests to change church policy, there are also signs that even in those regions where some support for a change in church policy had emerged, reactionary forces have mustered the numbers to defeat and even rescind the previous commitments of assemblies. The June 2002 meeting of the Delaware/Maryland Synod passed a resolution, submitted by former Bishop George Mocko, that overturned the previous year's action of the synod to be a "Reconciling in Christ" Synod, one which adopted a formal policy of welcome to all gay and lesbian persons. The synod did, however, keep the option open for congregations to declare themselves to be "Reconciling in Christ" congregations.

Theological and Historical Excavations

As the sides line up on the contentious issue of homosexuality, the Lutheran left will find a main source of support within the ecumenical and broader social movement seeking wider acceptance for gay and lesbian people. It is in the ecumenical and (to an even greater degree) in the wider interfaith domain that the Lutheran left is providing a way to reconsider and examine again the heritage of Lutheran theology and social involvement. One such effort at self-examination by Lutherans occurred at the same 1993 assembly that received the initial report that the church had developed cold feet on producing a statement on sexuality. It was at this assembly that a group from the Northwestern Minnesota Synod asked that Lutheran-Jewish relations be given top priority by the ecumenical department, and a request was also made by the New England Synod that a statement or declaration be made by the ELCA to the Jewish community, repudiating Luther's anti-Jewish rhetoric.

The Reverend Richard Koenig, a veteran pastor in New England, drafted the original request that came from the New England Synod, where it passed handily. It stalled when it reached church headquarters, however, where the staff recommended that rather than bringing it to the floor of the assembly in Kansas City, it should instead be considered in an en bloc group of resolutions to be passed on to the Department of Ecumenical Affairs. Koenig's long experience with maneuvering through conventions came in handy in this case. He worked with one of the synod's pastors who would be attending the national assembly, the Reverend John Stendahl, who lined up a couple of speakers, including the New England Synod Bishop Robert Isaksen, to bring the request out of the set of resolutions and directly to the floor. Stendahl remembers the sequence of speaking, first his introduction of the motion to bring the issue to the floor and his rationale, and then Bishop Isaksen's reading of a sampling of Luther's writings. The assembly was very quiet after hearing a sampling from the list of Luther's 1543 recommendations to secular authorities on how to handle the Jews at that time: burning Jewish synagogues, schools, homes, and books, revoking safe conduct on highways, confiscating their money and property, forcing labor, and expelling them from the territory.

The motion, as passed on August 31, 1993, by a margin of 905 to

38, with 3 abstentions, requested that the Department of Ecumenical Affairs

> prepare a declaration addressed to the Jewish community (1) repudiating the anti-Judaic rhetoric and violent recommendations of Martin Luther and grieving the tragic effects of such words on subsequent generations, and (2) affirming our desire to live out our faith in Jesus Christ in love and respect for the Jewish people by pledging to oppose the deadly working of anti-Semitism in church and society.

Koenig was inspired to bring the issue before his church because he was disheartened and ashamed that Luther's 1543 recommendations to secular authorities on how to deal with Jews were still being quoted in contemporary publications. He felt that modern-day Lutherans needed to "abjure Luther's writings against the Jews in order to make it clear that they are unacceptable to Lutherans today." His way of addressing that concern was to have his church make such a statement, and his efforts to move the church to such a declaration have been noticed appreciatively by the Jewish community, by concerned Lutherans, and even by young people. Today the ELCA declaration is cited at the Washington, D.C., Holocaust Museum after the film on the history of anti-Semitism, which includes Luther's violent rhetoric, is aired. On my recent visit to the museum I was accompanied by my sixteen-year-old daughter who, after viewing the film and the ELCA statement, declared, "Can you believe it took the church that long to say this?"

The difficulty of standing in judgment on the past is a real one, and those who seek to reform the church and turn it in a new direction, either socially or theologically, can be tempted to resort to simplistic and anachronistic standards by which to judge historical figures. Lutherans, however, have always had a robust sense of the reality of sin in persons, and in the world, and such scrutiny as they might give to bygone statements or positions of their own church rightly can and should be turned on themselves as well. In order to stand in a tradition, certainly a flawed one, one must go deeper than the actual statements and declarations of a given place and time so as to begin to understand them, and respect the fact that sometimes, tragically, even our heroes did not see as clearly as we'd like. The Lutheran left also stands in a tradition, a flawed one, but one that holds out the hope of being found faithful to its heritage. The Lutheran left belongs to a church, which makes it unsurprising that movement politics do not provide the best mechanism for advancing its goals. So to move Lutherans as Lutherans, and not only as advocates of one or another single issue, the Lutheran left seems now to have committed itself to a more halting, perhaps realistic, pace.

BIBLIOGRAPHY

Lehtonen, Risto. *Story of a Storm: The Ecumenical Student Movement in the Turmoil of Revolution, 1968 to 1973*. Grand Rapids: Eerdmans, 1998.

Lutz, Charles. *Surprising Gifts: The Story of Holden Village, Church Renewal Center*. Holden Village Press, 1987.

Schroeder, Stephen. *A Community and a Perspective: Lutheran Peace Fellowship and the Edge of the Church, 1941-1991*. Lanham, Md.: University Press of America, 1993.

Trexler, Edgar R. *Anatomy of a Merger: People, Dynamics and Decisions That Shaped the ELCA*. Minneapolis: Augsburg, 1991.

Word Alone and the Future
of Lutheran Denominationalism

MARK GRANQUIST

Much of the history of American Lutheranism is told in the tale of synodical mergers and the march to ever larger and more complex denominational structures. Indeed, this is a reasonable, descriptive approach to at least part of American Lutheran history; while there were over one hundred synods in twelve major groupings in the mid nineteenth century, today 95 percent of the 8.5 million American Lutherans are members of the two largest denominations, the Evangelical Lutheran Church in America (5.1 million members) and the Lutheran Church–Missouri Synod (2.6 million members). The next largest group is the Wisconsin Evangelical Lutheran Synod (400,000 members), and after that there are perhaps a dozen or so of very small Lutheran groups, many of which were the dissenters from previous mergers. The consolidation of American Lutheranism into two major denominations is perhaps one of the most important developments of its twentieth-century history.[1]

There is, however, a potential danger in telling this history in terms of merger, because the historiographical tendency is to view this process of consolidation as inevitable and uniformly beneficial. Mergers are celebrated as the natural outcome of the guidance of the Holy Spirit, and as a fulfillment of the will of God; in other words, bigger is better, and merger is what God wants for his Lutheran children in North America. But this romantic view of denominational history is

---

1. John H. Tietjen, *Which Way to Lutheran Unity?* (St. Louis: Clayton, 1966).

greatly flawed, in that it pays no attention to the very real costs and problems associated with the process of consolidation and institutional realignment. Mergers are difficult to arrange, take enormous amounts of time and energy, lead inevitably to hard feelings and disenchantment in some quarters, and generally expose the theological and ecclesiastical cracks that are endemic to American Lutheranism. Mergers upset the normal ties of loyalty and trust within denominations, as new leaders are installed, new headquarters are established, and new procedures and structures are implemented. The process of merger is, as well, ultimately inwardly directed, and inevitably draws resources away from evangelism and outreach, which is perhaps part of the reason that American Lutherans have seen their share of the American religious "market" drop steadily throughout the twentieth century. Even ignoring the theological question as to whether institutional rearrangement can be attributed to the will of God, the actual process of merger and consolidation must be seen to be at best a mixed blessing, and perhaps a great diversion of effort from necessary tasks.

Dilemmas of the ELCA Merger

The formation of the Evangelical Lutheran Church in America (ELCA) in 1988 can be traced back to four waves of merger, dating back to the First World War. The establishment of the Norwegian Lutheran Church in America in 1917, and the United Lutheran Church in America in 1918, and the merger that produced the old American Lutheran Church (1930-1960), were preludes to the formation of the newer American Lutheran Church (1960-1988) and the Lutheran Church in America (1962-1988), which led in turn to the formation of the ELCA itself. Forgotten in these historical events was the turmoil and negative consequences of the mergers themselves. Out of many of these mergers there were splinter groups that left the main bodies in protest: the Lutheran Free Church, the Evangelical Lutheran Synod, the Association of Free Lutheran Congregations, and the American Association of Lutheran Churches, among others. Yet simply measuring the size of small splinter groups does not nearly begin to tell the cost of mergers; indeed, the more important issue is the numbers of disaffected congregations and pastors who did not break away from the denominations themselves, but for one reason or another remained within them. As the mergers progressed throughout the twentieth century, the mechanics of leaving a particular Lutheran denomination have become harder and more complex, so some pastors and congregations have found themselves trapped in a denomination that they believe has strayed from the course of true Lutheranism as they understand it. This, of course, has led to tensions within the denomination and to political and ecclesiastical struggles for power and control, struggles that are well documented within the history of American Lutheranism.[2]

The formation of the ELCA demonstrated all of these tensions and problems. American Lutherans generally lag about twenty to thirty years behind the rest of their mainline Protestant cousins, so the great wave of Protestant mergers that formed the United Church of Christ, the United Methodist Church, the Presbyterian Church (USA), and others in the 1950s and 1960s was much past its peak when the ELCA was formed. Indeed, the very real problems evidenced by these other mainline Protestant consolidations were beginning to be seen by the time of the ELCA merger, although it is not clear that such lessons were taken seriously. The Commission for a New Lutheran Church (CNLC) had as its vision a new kind of Lutheran church in North America — new not only as a new Lutheran denomination, but also as a new kind of structure for American Lutheranism. It mandated a power-sharing arrangement where women, laypeople, and minority Lutherans would have a constitutionally set power base through the use of quotas and other restrictions. The CNLC also set ambitious goals for raising the levels of minority and non-English-speaking membership, and even if this goal has not come close to reality, it still drives much of the allocation of resources and energy within the ELCA.[3]

The CNLC faced a difficult series of decisions in attempting to bring about a merger of the Lutheran Church in America, the American Lutheran Church, and the Association of Evangelical Lutheran Churches (a group formed out of dissidents who left the Lutheran

2. See Clifford Nelson, *The Lutherans in North America* (Philadelphia: Fortress, 1975).

3. CNLC, *Report and Recommendations of the Commission for a New Lutheran Church to the American Lutheran Church, the Association of Evangelical Lutheran Churches, Lutheran Church in America, June 25, 1986.*

Church–Missouri Synod in the mid 1970s). The institutional cultures of the three denominations were different, especially the ALC and LCA, which had divergent ways of organizing congregations, synods/districts, and their national structures (although the issues were not always along straight ALC/LCA lines). Power flowed differently in the two denominations, and some compromise on these structures would have to be reached. There were also any number of divisive issues involved which have bedeviled American Lutherans for hundreds of years — the role of the congregation as it relates to the national denomination, questions of ministry and ecclesiastical theory and organization, and the ecumenical stance of the new Lutheran denomination.[4]

These matters were a source of intense debate and struggle within the merging denominations and in the CNLC during the 1980s, as the ELCA was coming into existence. It is clear in the actual formation of the ELCA, through the actions of the CNLC, that three important steps were taken. First, the congregations of the new denomination were more closely bound to the national church organization, a structure more like that of the LCA than that of the ALC. Although this was opposed by many in the ALC and some in the LCA, congregations in the ELCA have more restrictions and fewer freedoms than before. Second, there is in the ELCA structure more of an emphasis on the ordained ministry, especially as it exists on its own, so that it is not seen as being derived directly from the powers inherent in the local congregation. Although the LCA lost some practical issues here (pastors are not to be congregational presidents, and there are more "slots" for laypeople in governance), the structure is more "clerical" than many in the ALC had wished. Third, the constitution of the ELCA includes a strengthened emphasis on the new church's ecumenical commitments, chiefly through the addition to the constitution of language taken from the LCA constitution.[5]

Many areas of controversy were left unsettled, however, or the details of a solution were left to the young denomination to determine. The chief questions facing the nascent ELCA were the nature and doc-

---

4. Todd W. Nichol, *All These Lutherans: Three Paths toward a New Lutheran Church* (Minneapolis: Augsburg, 1986).

5. Edgar R. Trexler, *Anatomy of a Merger: People, Dynamics, and Decisions That Shaped the ELCA* (Minneapolis: Augsburg, 1991).

trine of its ministry, and the formation of its ecumenical policies and directions. The nature of ministry was a pressing issue, because the three merging denominations had different types of formally recognized (rostered) ministries. Historically, Lutheranism has insisted that there is only one form of ministry, the ordained pastorate, and that other professional church work must be seen in this light. The question, then, was not so much about pastors as it was about other rostered personnel; the merging denominations had deacons and deaconesses, commissioned teachers, associates in ministry, and other forms of certified lay professionals with which the new denomination had to deal. The AELC especially, with its commissioned teachers (a holdover from the LCMS), was worried about how to structure such ministries, but this was a problem that the CNLC did not solve. Another problematic question was the issue of Lutheran bishops; Lutherans had begun to title their synodical and district presidents as "bishops" in the 1970s, but the change brought out a number of complicated issues.

In 1988 the practical and theoretical questions concerning the ministry were given to a Task Force for the Study of the Ministry, which was given five years to bring to the ELCA Assembly a comprehensive solution to the ministry questions that vexed the new denomination. The task force did not, however, bring denominational peace, but rather plunged the new church into more controversy with its recommendations. Some had urged that instead of continuing the historical Lutheran pattern of a single ministry, the ELCA ought rather to adopt the threefold pattern of ministry (deacons, priest/pastors, and bishop), with a separate ordination for each level of ministry. Besides solving the roster confusion by making the lay workers ordained deacons, the proponents of this change saw this as a chance to "correct" the Lutheran understanding of ministry, and bring Lutherans closer to the historical pattern of Roman Catholicism, Anglicanism, and Orthodox Christianity. In 1993, the task force report did propose to the ELCA Churchwide Assembly (CWA) that lay professionals in the denomination should be ordained into a separate ministry of the diaconate, but this suggestion was rejected by the CWA, which instead approved a category of lay diaconal ministers. This issue was further clouded in 1994, when the ELCA Church Council narrowly approved a ritual of "consecration" for diaconal ministers, rather than "commissioning" them, the term used for other lay workers. Some saw this move by the Church Council as a way of moving toward a separate ordination for diaconal ministers, and as an end run around the 1993 decision of the CWA.

Another bit of unfinished business in the new ELCA involved the status of ecumenical relationships with the Reformed, Episcopal, and Roman Catholic denominations in the United States, relationships which had been the subject of previous and ongoing discussions ever since the 1960s. Although discussions with Roman Catholicism had produced some very interesting statements and resolutions, this dialogue was not regarded as bearing any immediate, practical changes in the relationship between these two groups. There were, however, more immediate possibilities brewing with the Reformed communion and Episcopal Church. The ALC, especially, had a significant relationship with the Reformed denominations in the United States, and ALC leaders pushed hard to have the CNLC adopt these understandings as a part of the new ELCA structure. There had also been two rounds of Lutheran-Episcopal dialogues (1969-1972 and 1978-1980), and a third round began in 1983. The goal of these talks, broadly speaking, was not merger or integration, but rather the mutual recognition of word and sacrament through Communion and pulpit fellowship (the interchange of pastors and communicants between the denominations).

Tensions over Lutheran-Episcopal Agreement

Although there were some lingering questions about the Lutheran-Reformed dialogues (concerning the nature of the sacraments and creedal subscription), the larger questions involved the Lutheran-Episcopal dialogues. Although Lutherans and Episcopalians have had a long history of relationship in the United States, the question of ministry was always problematic. As one of the core doctrines of their church, Episcopalians had insisted on the threefold ministry and pastors/priests ordained at the hands of properly ordained bishops, and this insistence was carried over to a similar demand for their ecumenical partners (an insistence that had stalled previous Lutheran-Episcopal discussions). When the third Lutheran-Episcopal dialogue (LED III) resumed in 1988, this stumbling block remained; there would be no official intercommunion or interchange of ministers without agreement on the threefold order of ministry.

By 1991, the participants of LED III had developed a plan, the "Concordat of Agreement," to bridge this difficulty. The Concordat called on the ELCA to formally adopt the Episcopal threefold ministry: bishops for life, properly ordained into the historic episcopate, would be the only ones to ordain pastors, eventually bringing the ELCA into line with the Episcopal Church on the question of ministry. The proposal was controversial from the start; although the Episcopal members of LED III voted for the agreement, the Lutheran participants were split 5-3.[6] The rejection of the ordained diaconate by the CWA later that year also suggested trouble for the proposal. Nevertheless, the Concordat was brought to the CWA at Philadelphia in 1997, where the Assembly failed by six votes to pass the agreement by the necessary two-thirds margin. The same CWA, however, approved an ecumenical agreement with the Reformed denominations (the Formula of Agreement), and also directed the ELCA to develop a new document for "full communion" with the Episcopal Church that would address the concerns of opponents, especially the issue of the imposition of the historic episcopate.

Although the main cause of the defeat of the Concordat at Philadelphia was the historic episcopate, in October 1997 Presiding Bishop H. George Anderson declared that this part of the agreement was "non-negotiable," because without it there could be no agreement on full communion with the Episcopal Church. The guiding term here is "full communion," which means a full and complete exchange of ministers and communicants between the various churches involved. Many Lutherans and Episcopalians had already been exchanging pulpits and taking Communion in each other's congregations since the 1970s through an interim agreement, which, though not to the level of full communion, had nevertheless guaranteed access between the two denominations. The idea of "full communion" had been brought into the ELCA in 1991, when the Churchwide Assembly had adopted a strategy for ecumenism in the guise of a document called "Ecumenism: The Vision of the ELCA." This document, which was rather noncontroversial at the time, committed the ELCA to seek out full-communion relationships with other denominations whenever and

---

6. William G. Rusch and William A. Norgren, eds., *The Implications of the Gospel: Lutheran Episcopal Dialogue, Series III* (Minneapolis: Augsburg, 1988).

wherever possible. The ecumenism document, however, called for the definition of full communion to allow for the greatest possible degree of flexibility, and not to bind the ELCA to any one particular structure of ministry. That definition of full communion would be greatly strained in negotiations with the Episcopalians, who would insist on the historic episcopate as a precondition for full communion.

In November of 1997, the Lutherans and Episcopalians each selected three people to serve on a drafting team to revise the Concordat, which was to be presented to the ELCA Churchwide Assembly in 1999, and, assuming passage there, to the Episcopal Church, USA, in 2000. The drafting team did make many changes to the document: the ELCA would not have to adopt the threefold ministry (at least explicitly), Lutheran bishops would be "installed" rather than ordained, and would serve for terms rather than for life, and the Episcopalians would agree to suspend their ordinals concerning the historic episcopate, at least until the ELCA ministry came fully into line with their own. This revised document, entitled "Called to Common Mission" (CCM), was presented in rough draft form to the ELCA Church Council in April 1998; two of the Lutheran writers (Michael Root and Martin Marty) concurred with the document, while the third member of the team (Todd Nichol) dissented from the document.[7]

Because of the close decision against the Concordat in 1997, the modified version, CCM, was anxiously awaited by both Lutheran defenders and detractors. Although there had not been much widespread activity concerning the Concordat before the CWA in Philadelphia, CCM fell instantly into an ELCA that was becoming deeply divided about the historic episcopate and full communion with the Episcopalians. The presentation of CCM, and its public reading in the ELCA, led to a flurry of activity both for and against the revised agreement, and the document was discussed on all levels of the denomination. By November 1998, a further revision of CCM was presented, but these changes did very little to quell the storm of controversy that had met the first draft of CCM in the spring of 1998. Chiefly, the opponents

7. Division for Ecumenical Affairs, Evangelical Lutheran Church in America, "Called to Common Mission: A Lutheran Proposal for a Revision of the 'Concordat of Agreement,'" http://www.elca.org/ea/Relationships/episcopalian/ccmresources/ccmintro.html (August 16, 2002).

were opposed to the very concept of the historic episcopate itself, and felt that adopting such a system in the ELCA, under the pressure of the Episcopal Church, would be contrary to both the historical Lutheran understanding of the ministry and the Lutheran confessions themselves. Opponents cited as a basis for their rejection of CCM the Augsburg Confession, article 7, which reads in part:

> For the true unity of the church it is enough [satus est] to agree concerning the teaching of the Gospel and the administration of the sacraments. It is not necessary that human traditions or rites and ceremonies, instituted by men, should be alike everywhere.[8]

They claimed that this seventh article of the Augsburg Confession acted as a limiter, and that nothing more, including the historic episcopate, could be required for full communion. Proponents of CCM countered with a view of the Confession that saw it as a floor or basis for agreement; since, they argued, the ELCA was freely adopting the historic episcopate, and there was already agreement between the two churches on word and sacrament, the CCM in no way offended article 7.

The Roots of Word Alone

The development of opposition to CCM had its roots in a loose grouping of Lutherans who had gathered together initially in 1996 to oppose the passage of the Concordat. One interesting factor in this initial opposition was the use of the new electronic medium of the Internet as a means of communication and cooperation. In December 1996, about forty ELCA Lutherans began an electronic discussion group (an e-mail list-serve) to develop strategies and materials aimed at defeating the Concordat. This was a very new technology at the time, but it provided a means of instant communication that would be crucial in their fight against both the Concordat and, later, CCM itself. This was, perhaps, one of the first such usages of the Internet and its capacities in a

---

8. From article 7 of the Augsburg Confession (Latin version), in *The Book of Concord: The Confessions of the Evangelical Lutheran Church*, ed. and trans. Theodore G. Tappert (Philadelphia: Muhlenberg, 1959), p. 32.

denominational struggle; certainly, this was a novel experience for many ELCA Lutherans.[9]

Fueled by discussions both in print and on-line, opposition to CCM began to develop and coalesce through the summer of 1998, as the details of the new agreement began to become clear. A letter of petition against the current shape of the agreement, with over three thousand signatures, was directed to the ELCA Church Council in the fall of 1998, as were two public letters of dissent from ELCA leaders and academics, the so-called Reformation Day letter (November 1, 1998) and the Reformation Scholars' letter (November 3, 1998).[10] This public dissent did not dissuade the ELCA Church Council, however, which approved a revised version of CCM in November 1998, and forwarded it to the ELCA Churchwide Assembly for action in the summer of 1999. Opponents then intensified their efforts against CCM. Pastor Roger Eigenfeld of St. Andrew's Lutheran Church, Mahtomedi, Minnesota (a very large ELCA congregation in the suburban Twin Cities), invited CCM opponents to a meeting in February 1999, to organize and plan strategy. This meeting produced an alternative document intended for ELCA discussion and action, the "Mahtomedi Resolution," which presented a vision of ecumenical relations with the Episcopal Church, USA, but without the adoption of the historic episcopate in the ELCA.[11]

The composition of the opposition to CCM has been the subject of much debate, analysis, and downright stereotyping, especially among CCM advocates. The common stereotype of CCM opponents is that they were angry, ex-ALC Lutherans from the Upper Midwest, of a definite pietistic and congregationalist proclivity. This stereotype suggests that CCM opponents had been marginalized in the ELCA merger, were radical congregationalists, and were deeply distrustful of the rest of the ELCA. While there may well be examples of such indi-

9. Word Alone Network, "Who We Are — History," http://www.wordalone.org/who/who_history.htm (August 16, 2002).

10. "Reformation Day Letter, November 1, 1998," http://wordalone.org/archives/letters/reformation_day_letter.htm (August 16, 2002); "Reformation Scholars' Letter, November 3, 1988," http://wordalone.org/archives/letters/refscholars.htm (August 16, 2002).

11. "Mahtomedi Resolution," http://wordalone.org/archives/articles_by_title/mahtomedi_resolution.htm (August 16, 2002).

viduals within the dissenting movement, the stereotype is simply not true. There were prominent members of both the ALC and the LCA involved in the opposition to CCM, including the former president of the LCA, Robert Marshall, and the former president of the ALC, David Preus, both of whom presented speeches at the first Mahtomedi conference. Although a majority of opponents were from the Upper Midwest, it is important to remember that the majority of American Lutherans do live in the northwest quadrant of the United States, and so such a representation would be natural. There were representatives in the opposition from virtually every one of the sixty-five synods of the ELCA, and from many ELCA institutions, including active and retired bishops, administrators, college and seminary professors, and pastors.

As to the question of congregationalism, it seems clear that many in the opposition to CCM were seeking to defend the traditional Lutheran understanding of the congregation as it had been developed over the previous two hundred years of American Lutheran history. It has already been seen how in the formation of the ELCA the role of the congregation had been curbed by the authority of synodical and church-wide units, and this was a source of concern to many opponents. They thought that in CCM the role of the bishop would be enhanced, and that this would continue the tilt of the ELCA toward a more centralized ecclesiastical polity. But this does not mean that most of the opponents of CCM were radical congregationalists in nature, but rather that they sought to maintain the balance of powers between the congregational and larger church structures. Many opponents believed that some of the proponents of CCM sought instead to bring the ELCA into a truly Episcopal polity, rather than the modified form of Presbyterian (synodical) polity that has been the norm in American Lutheranism since the eighteenth century.

The opponents of CCM who gathered in Mahtomedi in February 1999 organized under a name taken from the previously established electronic list-serve, calling themselves the Word Alone Network. The strategy for the spring and summer of 1999 (prior to the Churchwide Assembly) was twofold: first, the dissemination of the anti-CCM viewpoint through various forms of publication (newsletters, journals, mailings, and electronic forums), and, second, the submission of the Mahtomedi Resolution to as many of the ELCA synodical assemblies as possible. The publication campaign was waged with intensity on both sides of the issue, although CCM opponents believed that official ELCA media was not only in favor of CCM but limited the access of opponents to equal time. The Mahtomedi Resolution was submitted to numerous synodical assemblies, and was passed as a substitute for CCM in twenty of the sixty-five synods; these twenty synods represented approximately 35 percent of the total of ELCA members. Twelve synods, representing 20 percent of ELCA membership, passed motions of support for CCM by over the two-thirds threshold, while another seven synods passed pro-CCM resolutions but by less than a two-thirds majority.[12] One analysis of votes in forty-seven of the sixty-five synods (some synods did not address the issue that spring) suggested that the popular vote on CCM at this time was running about evenly divided for and against the CCM document.[13]

Heading into the ELCA Churchwide Assembly at Denver in August 1999, opponents of CCM felt that although they had made a strong case against the document on the local and synodical levels, the CWA itself would be an uphill fight, for any number of reasons. First, the "voting members" of the CWA were repeatedly told by the officials of the ELCA that they were not bound by synodical votes on the issue, and thus were free to vote as they wished on the issue. Second, control of the CWA was firmly in the hands of the national church organization and the bishops, who were squarely behind CCM. Third, the composition of debate at the CWA was seen as being biased against the CCM opponents; one example of such bias was the now-infamous "hearings" at Denver, which though supposedly equal were structurally biased toward those who favored CCM. The debate on CCM at the Denver CWA was heated on both sides, but when the voting was tallied on August 19, 1999, the vote was 916 to 373, twenty-seven votes over the needed two-thirds majority.[14] In an intense campaign of two years between 1997 and 1999, with the allocation of a large amount of denominational resources, proponents of CCM and the historic episco-

12. Word Alone Network, "1999 Synod Assembly Results: Called to Common Mission," http://www.wordalone.org/synods.htm (June 29, 1999).

13. Bradley C. Jenson, "Results of 1999 Synod Assembly Votes on CCM/MR," Kenwood Lutheran Church, Duluth, Minnesota, 1999.

14. Martha Sawyer Allen, "Lutheran Group Approves Unity Pact with the Episcopal Church," *Minneapolis Star Tribune*, August 20, 1999; Gustav Niebuhr, "Lutheran Group Approves a Link to Episcopalians," *New York Times*, August 20, 1999.

pate had managed to swing a grand total of thirty-three votes, but those thirty-three votes were enough to carry the measure through.

The results of the Denver Churchwide Assembly were a blow to the Word Alone Network and its members, many of whom had worked passionately to defeat CCM. There was a range of opinions within Word Alone as to the next steps that should be taken, ranging from those who wanted to work to modify the effects of CCM in the ELCA, to those who saw no future in the ELCA after August 19, 1999. The Word Alone Network held a series of regional meetings during the fall of 1999, and decided to formally incorporate the network into an organization. On November 15, 1999, three hundred people came together at Roseville Lutheran Church, Roseville, Minnesota, to begin to create a formal organization to seek out reform and renewal in the ELCA.[15] The constituting convention of the Word Alone Network was held at St. Andrews, Mahtomedi, on March 26 to 29, 2000, and opposition to CCM and the historic episcopate was seen as the main work of the group, along with wider themes of renewal and reform.[16]

The passage of CCM, however, limited the options for opponents. There was little hope for a campaign to reverse the passage of the document, as the necessary two-thirds vote to overturn the constitutional changes imposed by CCM was widely viewed as being unlikely. The Episcopal Church was voting on CCM in the summer of 2000, but even though some Episcopalians were less than enthusiastic about the document, there was not significant opposition among Episcopalians to the plan (which passed handily). A group of twenty ELCA leaders, evenly divided between CCM opponents and proponents, met in Milwaukee in February 2000, to see what might be done to mitigate the effects of CCM on a badly divided ELCA. By a vote of 17 to 1, they endorsed a document known as the Common Ground Resolution, which called on the ELCA Church Council and ELCA Council of Bishops to allow for exceptions to the rule that bishops had to be "installed" in the historic episcopate, and to the rule that pastors would have to be ordained by bishops. They asked for a delay in the imple-

15. Martha Sawyer Allen, "Lutherans Form to Protest Called to Common Mission," *Minneapolis Star Tribune,* November 20, 1999.

16. Martha Sawyer Allen, "ELCA Leaders Try to Heal Rift over CCM," *Minneapolis Star Tribune,* February 26, 2000; ELCA News Service, "ELCA Bishops Discuss Aftermath of Proposal with Episcopal Church" (October 7, 1999).

mentation of CCM until after the 2001 Churchwide Assembly, to allow for these changes to be implemented. The ELCA bishops and Church Council would not consider the Common Ground Resolution, but did act on one idea, that a bylaw could be passed allowing the ordination of a pastor by another pastor, under a special set of carefully controlled circumstances. This bylaw was passed by the ELCA Churchwide Assembly in 2001, despite some Lutheran and Episcopalian protests that such a move would undermine the newly passed ecumenical relationship. With all of this long history of controversy and strife, the ecumenical agreement, Called to Common Mission, came into force officially on January 1, 2001.

Whether to Stay or Leave

Although there was great impetus among CCM opponents to form the Word Alone Network in 2000, there were significant internal tensions within the movement itself concerning strategy, tactics, and focus. One section of the CCM opponents saw the August 1999 vote by the Churchwide Assembly to approve CCM as the last straw in their relationship with the ELCA. They believed that any resistance or work for reform within the ELCA was ultimately futile, and that the best course of action would be to withdraw as far as possible from the ELCA, and to encourage others to do so, as well. The other section of opposition sought to remain in the ELCA, and to work for reform from within. These people believed that there were still ways to work for reform, or to weaken CCM, from within the organization, and they were greatly encouraged by the 2001 vote of the Churchwide Assembly to allow pastoral candidates an exemption from the requirement of being ordained by a bishop. Within the Word Alone Network the common reference was that the organization had two prongs, or emphases, one internal to the ELCA, and the other outside of it; people would identify themselves as being "prong 1" or "prong 2," depending on their orientation.[17]

For the first year or two of its existence, the Word Alone Network

17. Martha Sawyer Allen, "Word Alone Takes Lead in ELCA Dispute," *Minneapolis Star Tribune*, March 18, 2000.

(WAN) was seen as being tilted somewhat in the direction of those who sought to remain in the ELCA, especially as it struggled to work out accommodation and exceptions with the ELCA. Recognizing this division within the movement itself, Word Alone leaders began to implement a structural strategy that would institutionalize the needs of those who wished to leave the ELCA or have minimal contact with the organization. On October 26-27, 2000, WAN leaders met at Westwood Lutheran Church, St. Louis Park, Minnesota, to sketch out plans for a new organization separate from the ELCA and WAN, which would provide alternate ecclesiastical arrangements for pastors and congregations who wanted maximum independence from the ELCA; this organization was eventually named the Lutheran Congregations in Mission for Christ (LCMC). Much of the Word Alone Network's second convention in Phoenix, Arizona, in March 2001, was devoted to the practical issues behind the launch of LCMC: the formation of a new constitution, provisions for ordaining pastors, the development of pension and medical programs, and other such issues. Initially, the board of WAN was also the board for LCMC, but LCMC soon elected its own board and achieved independence from WAN. The two groups had simultaneous but separate conventions in April 2002, at North Heights Lutheran Church, Arden Hills, Minnesota, but future plans call for annual meetings to be held at different times and places from each other. There is some overlap between the two groups, and cordial relations, but a definite difference in focus.

Although it was founded to be a new type of umbrella organization, holding together pastors and congregations both in and out of the ELCA, LCMC has moved forward aggressively with traditional denominational tasks, such as the ordination of pastors, foundation of mission congregations, and formation of pension plans. As of 2002, the LCMC consists of 60 congregations, as well as other congregations and pastors in an associated role. The Word Alone Network counts over 190 member congregations, and nearly 100,000 members in forty-five states, and drawn from almost every ELCA synod; they have an executive director and offices in New Brighton, Minnesota.[18]

---

18. Word Alone Network, "Who We Are — History," http://www.wordalone .org/who/who_history.htm (August 16, 2002).

Word Alone and LCMC — Reconfiguring Lutheran Institutions?

Both organizations, however, do face significant challenges in the future. The Word Alone Network seems to be searching for its role within the ELCA, a role that is more tightly prescribed now that the constitutional provisions of CCM have come into effect. The internal, political, and institutional reform that WAN envisions within the ELCA is tough, slow work, and has not always proved successful; at times, such a strategy can seem rather disheartening. There are other renewal groups within the ELCA, such as the Great Commission Network and the Fellowship of Confessional Lutherans, but they have not proved to be very successful in altering the course of the ELCA itself. The Lutheran Congregations in Mission for Christ face the very real danger that they will not be able to realize the goal of being a new kind of paradigm of American Lutheran organization, and that they will simply become another small Lutheran splinter group, of which there are at least a dozen. Both groups also face the lingering effects of unfocused anger and resentment remaining from the fight over CCM; the battle within the ELCA left a very sour taste in the mouths of many activists, and a distrust of ecclesiastical leaders and organizations in general that has sometimes haunted the new structures and their leaders.

Both WAN and LCMC were born out of opposition to something — to the general leadership and direction of the ELCA, and, more specifically, to the CCM proposal. It can be quick and easy, at times, to unite disparate individuals against a common enemy or threat, but the real trick comes in turning that negative energy in a positive direction. Both WAN and LCMC need to struggle to find a positive direction and message as to what they stand for, what they represent, rather than just what they oppose. As well, both groups seek a new paradigm of leadership — a grassroots, bottom-up type of power structure, in opposition to what they see as the increasingly hierarchical, centralized, and bureaucratic ELCA. This is perhaps a laudable vision, but it will take a great amount of patience to make this vision a reality.

That being said, however, it is still true that WAN and LCMC are significant forces in the ELCA and in American Lutheranism, and will be for some time to come. ELCA leaders will have to be mindful of these two groups and the large number of ELCA pastors and members that these groups represent. The WAN has been very influential in modifying the course of the implementation of CCM within the ELCA itself, having an important role in shaping the Common Ground Resolution and the 2001 bylaw that allowed for exceptional, non-episcopal ordinations, in the face of significant ELCA opposition. LCMC has accomplished a great deal of new activity in a short period of time, and has attracted some large congregations out of the ELCA, most noticeably the Lutheran Church of the Master, in Omaha, Nebraska. Both organizations seem well supported by their base constituencies and capable of mobilizing energies in a particular direction, if the need arises. Should additional divisive issues flare up in the ELCA, such as the Study on Human Sexuality or something equally controversial, these organizations could play an important role. ELCA bishops, especially those in the Upper Midwest, know that their actions are being closely scrutinized, and that promises and assurances made to mollify opponents to CCM will need to be carried out.

The ELCA itself has generally survived the CCM controversy intact; there have been no large-scale defections, and no immediate and dramatic drop in funding. The 1999 vote by the Churchwide Assembly may, however, turn out to be a pyrrhic victory in the long run, increasing a sense of alienation toward the national and synodical church structures in a significant number of Lutheran pastors and congregations. In the formation of the ELCA, congregations were bound more closely to the national church structure, making it more difficult for congregations to leave the denomination. This may have unintended negative consequences, however, as it forces disaffected congregations, with all their negative energy and drive, to remain within the denominational folds. Pastors, with a significant professional stake in the denomination, and with concerns about pensions, benefits, and mobility, may also have to stay in a denomination they dislike and distrust, with similar results. As a relatively young denomination, the ELCA needed a time of peaceful transition and growth to mature as an organization, but with divisive controversies over the structure of ministry, the nature of ecumenical relationships, and its stance on issues of human sexuality, the young denomination has had instead a series of polarizing controversies. It is almost as though the ELCA has chosen the most divisive and destructive controversies to fight at a time when what it needed most was to pull together and coalesce. And the ELCA has also jumped into the organizational and ecumenical models of

American mainline Protestantism just at the very time when it was becoming acknowledged that such paradigms were, at best, ineffective and impotent.[19]

Given this scenario, both the Word Alone Network and the Lutheran Congregations in Mission for Christ may well have a significant role to play in the future of the ELCA and of American Lutheranism. They do indeed represent new models and new ways of ordering church life in twenty-first-century America, and if they remain vital and active they could provide direction for the ELCA itself, as it faces the continuing decline of the Protestant mainline, and the significant challenges of an increasingly pluralistic and diverse American society.

BIBLIOGRAPHY

Division for Ecumenical Affairs, Evangelical Lutheran Church in America, "Called to Common Mission: A Lutheran Proposal for a Revision of the 'Concordat of Agreement.'" Http://www.elca.org/ea/Relationships/episcopalian/ccmresources/ccmintro.html.

Lagerquist, L. DeAne. *The Lutherans.* Westport, Conn.: Praeger, 1999.

"Mahtomedi Resolution." Http://wordalone.org/archives/articles_by_title/mahtomedi_resolution.htm.

"Milwaukee 'Common Ground' Resolution," 2000. Http://wordalone.org/archives/articles_by_title/milwaukee-common_ground_rez.htm.

Nelson, Clifford. *The Lutherans in North America.* Philadelphia: Fortress, 1975.

Nichol, Todd W. *All These Lutherans: Three Paths toward a New Lutheran Church.* Minneapolis: Augsburg, 1986.

"Reformation Day Letter, November 1, 1998." Http://wordalone.org/archives/letters/reformation_day_letter.htm.

"Reformation Scholars Letter, November 3, 1988." Http://wordalone.org/archives/letters/refscholars.htm.

Rusch, William G., and William A. Norgren, eds. *The Implications of the Gospel: Lutheran Episcopal Dialogue, Series III.* Minneapolis: Augsburg, 1988.

Tietjen, John H. *Which Way to Lutheran Unity?* St. Louis: Clayton Publishing House, 1966.

19. Randall Balmer, "United We Fall," *New York Times,* Saturday, August 28, 1999.

Trexler, Edgar R. *Anatomy of a Merger: People, Dynamics, and Decisions That Shaped the ELCA.* Minneapolis: Augsburg, 1991.

Word Alone Network. "Who We Are — History." Http://www.wordalone .org/who/who_history.htm.

The Evangelical Catholics:
Seeking Tradition and Unity
in a Pluralistic Church

RICHARD CIMINO

Sitting in his office at Immanuel Lutheran Church in New York City, Pastor Gregory Fryer seemed exasperated over the question of whether evangelical catholic Lutherans could be a force for renewal and reform in American Lutheranism. "It's like trying to reform a reform movement," he finally said. Fryer and other evangelical catholics have traditionally raised their sights to grander visions, viewing Lutheranism itself as a reform movement within the catholic tradition and eventually within all of Christendom.

The tensions over the purposes and strategy of evangelical catholicism in Lutheran churches were evident among most of the pastors and church members I interviewed who were involved in this loosely defined movement (twenty pastors and fifteen laypeople in the New York and Chicago areas from 1998 to 2002). Evangelical catholics seek to recover the liturgical and confessional heritage of Lutheranism in continuity within the broad catholic tradition ("catholic" is not capitalized to stress that the term is not the sole province of the Roman church) that includes Anglicans, Roman Catholics, and the Eastern Orthodox.[1] Such an attempt of recovery illuminates the dilemma of seeking unity and orthodoxy within the pluralistic world of contemporary Lutheranism.

---

1. Richard Cimino, *Trusting the Spirit* (San Francisco: Jossey-Bass, 2001), chap. 3.

Recovering the Confessions and the Church

The evangelical catholic movement is based on the teaching that Martin Luther and the early reformers did not intend to jettison the historic liturgy, church order, and other traditions of the historic church, much less establish Protestantism. Luther was a Catholic monk who fought primarily to reassert the biblical teaching of justification by faith as central to the faith. When this doctrine was rejected by Rome and Luther was excommunicated, the split that resulted in Western Christianity was a "tragic necessity," but one that would eventually be mended.

But Lutheranism developed distinctive teachings and practices apart from Roman Catholicism as it swept across Northern Europe and was eventually transplanted in North America through early settlers and mass immigration in the nineteenth and twentieth centuries. In the United States, much of Lutheranism was distinctly Protestant in worship and belief, even if it was embellished with liturgical overtones. While some Catholic practices and traditions in Europe were preserved (in Lutheran Sweden crucifixes, bishops and priests, and other Roman Catholic holdovers are the norm), it was mainly in the mid twentieth century that theologians and clergy made strides toward introducing into Lutheran congregations and denominations liturgy and practices seen to be in continuity with the pre-Reformation church.

ALPB and the Liturgical Resurgence

The American Lutheran Publicity Bureau (ALPB), one of the leading centers of the evangelical catholic movement, can serve as a case study on how this reform movement has shifted between marginal and mainstream roles in Lutheranism. Like evangelical catholicism itself, the ALPB never intended to become a reform group in Lutheran denominations. The organization was founded in New York in 1914 to help immigrant German Lutherans make the transition to American church life, including the use of English in parishes. As its name implied, the bureau also served as a public relations vehicle for Lutherans to communicate with the wider American society about their faith and traditions. It was this concern to overcome parochialism and reach a wider public with the theology of Martin Luther that led the ALPB and its magazine, the *American Lutheran* (later to be renamed the *Lutheran Forum*), to include evangelical catholic liturgical renewal in its coverage on American Lutheran life.[2] During the mid twentieth century, the ALPB was not alone in broaching the topic of liturgical reform. Within both the Lutheran Church–Missouri Synod and the United Lutheran Church (a predecessor body to the Lutheran Church in America), organizations such as the Liturgical Society of St. James and the Society of St. Ambrose were formed to foster a greater appreciation and usage of classical Western catholic liturgical sources, especially stressing weekly communion.[3]

The Lutherans were also not the only ones to experiment with liturgical renovations and reform. The evangelical catholics were influenced in the nineteenth and early twentieth century by what became known as the liturgical movement. During this period, there was high interest in the worship patterns of earlier — usually pre-Reformation — eras, mainly as a response to the emphasis on individualism and rationalism, on the one hand, and on religious experience or pietism, on the other, found in many Protestant churches. Liturgical reformers proposed a third way based on a corporate religious life and the "catholicity" or universal character of the church. All this is related to returning to the sources of a tradition — in other words, to the idea that believers need to return to the founding vision or original mission of a tradition and dust away the accretions and distortions that have accumulated with time. The Oxford movement in England, in which Anglicans sought to return to pre-Reformation forms of worship and piety, was a major example of liturgical reform. At the same time, more American influences were part of liturgical renewal, such as raising the level of participation among worshipers.

By the 1960s, such subjects as the importance of baptism and communion, as well as coverage of broader trends in worship and liturgy, were prominently featured in the *American Lutheran* and subsequently in *Lutheran Forum*. All this was new to most Lutheran congregations and

2. A. Graebner and A. P. Klausler, "50 Years of the ALPB," parts 1-5, *American Lutheran* (August 1963, pp. 14-17; September 1963, pp. 14-15; October 1963, pp. 14-15; November 1963, pp. 20-23; December 1963, pp. 6-21).

3. James B. Bittner, "On the Societies of St. Ambrose and St. James: A Study in Liturgical Critique," *Bride of Christ* (July 2002): 18-23.

their members, since communion was more often celebrated monthly or quarterly and preaching was the central focus of every service. Evangelical catholic reformers argued that the Lutheran confessions and Luther himself, not to mention the historic Catholic tradition, had favored more frequent reception of the sacrament.

During this same period, there was a new impetus for Lutheran unity in the United States. The force of assimilation made ethnic differences fade into the background, while such issues as inner-city ministry, social action, ecumenism, and new currents in theology received attention. Ironically, the call for unity came at a time when new theological fault lines were developing in American Lutheranism. During most of the 1960s, evangelical catholics were prominent in the conservative Lutheran Church–Missouri Synod, with their influence strongly felt in the plans of that body's 1965 convention to create a common Lutheran liturgy and hymnbook. These plans for a common service book would come to fruition with the creation of the *Lutheran Book of Worship* in 1977, although by that time Missouri had withdrawn from involvement in Lutheran unity plans due to its concern about the other church bodies' liberalism. By then a conservative change of guard had taken place in the Missouri Synod after a lengthy battle with more liberal members in the 1970s. Although the ALPB was primarily geared to the Lutheran Church–Missouri Synod in its early years, the organization and its publications began to take a broader approach, not least because many of its leaders were part of the more liberal or "moderate" wing that left the Missouri Synod during this controversy.

In the early 1970s, the bureau started publishing *Forum Letter*, a newsletter that became known for its feisty and independent commentary and coverage of Lutheran affairs, particularly under the editorship of Richard John Neuhaus, then a young pastor and activist in a largely black parish in Brooklyn. The 1970s was a time of growing engagement with American and international Lutheranism for the ALPB. Although the ALPB retained a strong evangelical catholic identity, theologians, lay leaders, and clergy from diverse perspectives were featured in its publications. The bureau sponsored intra-Lutheran conferences featuring such scholars and leaders as church historian Martin Marty and sociologist Peter Berger.

All in all, the ALPB and Lutherans in general viewed their future with cautious optimism during the 1970s and much of the 1980s. Such evangelical catholic liturgical innovations and recoveries as weekly communion, the celebration of the Saturday Vigil before Easter (a practice that the evangelical Catholic journal *Una Sancta* had a large part in introducing), and common liturgy drawing on Western catholic forms of worship through the new cooperative Lutheran text, the *Lutheran Book of Worship*, found their way into the Lutheran mainstream.

All this was taking place as the Second Vatican Council had not only opened Catholicism to the outside world but also to its "separated brethren" among Protestants. Observers of Vatican II note that Lutheranism had a good deal of impact in these Catholic reforms: the use of the vernacular in the Mass, and the greater role for the laity and the use of the Bible in the church, all had their roots in debates unleashed by Luther four hundred years earlier, as well as being influenced by more modern Lutheran theologians. The new friendliness between Lutherans and Catholics resulted in a historic dialogue between the two traditions that later produced a 1999 joint statement on the doctrine of justification by faith, in which both traditions claimed new convergences on this doctrine even amidst continuing differences.

A New Church and New Struggles

The merger of the American Lutheran Church, Lutheran Church in America, and the Association of Evangelical Lutheran Churches in 1988 was the largest church merger to take place in decades in American Christianity. Overnight, two moderate-sized denominations and one small one had consolidated to become one of the largest Protestant churches in the United States, with approximately five million members and over eleven thousand clergy. Whereas many thought the birth of a united Lutheran church would extend their influence, the evangelical catholics associated with the ALPB claimed that the newly merged denomination marginalized them, driving some of their most important leaders out of Lutheranism altogether.

To these evangelical catholics and other conservative critics, concerns were apparent months, even years, before the merger. An affirmative action policy that stipulated that minorities and women make up a third of leadership was bitterly opposed by evangelical catholics and other conservative Lutherans. Such a policy was viewed as enforcing a "pseudo-catholic" church structure that placed more value on political power relations than leaders chosen by the gifts and guidance of the Holy Spirit. The quota system was part of a general program of inclusiveness, trying to diversify the church from its northern European base to include particularly African-American, Asian, and Latino minorities. This was seen in the church-wide drive to raise the minority membership of the denomination to 10 percent within ten years. Related to the emphasis on diversity were feminist concerns over inclusiveness not only in membership but in liturgy and theology.

Issues of sexuality were ever-present in the conflict between evangelical catholics and the ELCA. In 1994 the ELCA issued a statement calling for liberalization on sexuality, including on its positions on premarital sex and homosexuality. (Later, in the face of protests, this was modified.) But the twin issues of ordination of practicing homosexuals and the approval of conducting same-sex blessings became a major point of contention in the ELCA (as in other mainline bodies) later on in the late 1990s and the early years of the new millennium. The generally pro-life evangelical catholics, at least as they were represented by the ALPB, also registered fervent protests against the ELCA for providing abortion coverage in employee and clergy health plans. As the ELCA moved closer to other mainline bodies, there was also widespread concern the church was moving Lutheranism away from its mission of being a reforming movement in the catholic tradition — in Anglicanism, Roman Catholicism, and Eastern Orthodoxy. For many, this was confirmed in the 1997 agreement with the Presbyterian church, the United Church of Christ, and the Reformed Church in America to enter into "full communion." The agreement, allowing the churches to celebrate communion together and allowing the churches' pastors to preach in congregations of the other denominations, was criticized for giving short shrift to the Lutheran teaching of the real presence of Christ in communion and for pandering to a lowest-common-denominator brand of ecumenism.

Resistance and Opposition

The recent history of the ALPB, specifically the *Lutheran Forum*, provides a documentary account of how external forces turned a broad and open theological and liturgical movement into a more self-contained and oppositional renewal group. The writers and others gathered around the *Lutheran Forum* freely admit that the evangelical catholic movement changed after the formation of the ELCA. Upon assuming the post of editor of the *Lutheran Forum* in 1993, Leonard Klein wrote that the

> publications of the ALPB have been a lively voice for moderate confessionalism. . . . In the past, that viewpoint meant the freedom to be a cheerful, high-spirited gadfly, tweaking torpid and overly cautious church leaders, arguing for renewal in liturgy, education, stewardship and evangelism. . . . [E]xcept for some rare bad moments the relationship to the denominations and the institutions of the church was a friendly one.

Klein then added that

> I assume the editorship in a different climate. The last generation has been a disaster for anything like moderate confessionalism. . . . And so our little journal has found itself much farther out on a limb and more critical for the Lutheran future than ever before. No longer a progressive gadfly to stodgy denominationalism, we now find ourselves at the head of the effort to reclaim any kind of confessionalist center in American Lutheranism.[4]

The increasing reference to the confessions (as found, for example, in the Augsburg Confession) conveyed basic Christian doctrine as well as Lutheran teachings on the gospel and the sacraments, providing a source of Lutheran identity to those unsure of their leaders' orthodoxy.

That the *Lutheran Forum's* paid circulation declined from 5,200 in the late 1960s to about 2,700 by 2001 illustrates how the magazine changed from a pan-Lutheran publication that covered a wide range of issues appealing to most Lutherans into a more polemical mouthpiece for a segment of evangelical catholics. The number of articles in the magazine written by or for laity also dropped sharply during this period. Only about 20 percent of the subscribers to the *Lutheran Forum*

---

4. Leonard Klein, "The Role of the Lutheran Forum," *Lutheran Forum* (Advent 1993): 4.

are now laypeople. Considering that there are approximately sixteen thousand clergy in the ELCA and the Lutheran Church–Missouri Synod, the ALPB's literature and publications are reaching only about one-fifth of its potential clergy base.

From the 1960s to the late 1980s, *Lutheran Forum* served as an open forum of contemporary American Lutheranism, discussing issues from a wide variety of perspectives. After that period a particular liturgical and confessional aspect of Lutheranism was highlighted. The change could be seen in the advertising in the magazine. Books on a wide range of theological subjects — from liberation theology to popular evangelical titles — were once advertised. The scope was narrowed in the post-ELCA phase to advertising books and other products in sync with evangelical catholic sensibilities.

The change in the *Lutheran Forum* was evident enough on its own masthead. In the 1970s, a Statement of Policy by the American Lutheran Publicity Bureau published in the *Lutheran Forum* had emphasized the role of unity in Lutheran identity. The statement read, "We believe that a united approach by Lutherans to their joint mission is crucial to the growth and strength of the Lutheran Church. . . . The discovery and expression of our unity in Christ must be a task of every generation."[5] By the 1990s, the mission statement of the ALPB still carried a message of unity, but it was set within the framework of confessional renewal. It reads, "Committed to an understanding of Lutheran tradition as evangelical and catholic, the ALPB affirms the Church's scriptural and confessional foundations in order to foster renewal not only within the present Evangelical Lutheran Church in America, the Lutheran Church–Missouri Synod and Evangelical Lutheran Church of Canada, but also Lutheran churches abroad and the wider ecumenical community."[6]

The signs of a more oppositional stance stared out at the reader from almost every page of the *Lutheran Forum.* It was not only that the bureaucracy was drastically losing the faith; seminaries with their strong feminist programs were also breathing in this air and becoming adversely influenced. A frequent target of *Lutheran Forum* writers was the church growth movement and the way congregations involved in

5. *Lutheran Forum* 1973.
6. *Lutheran Forum* 1998.

the effort to use contemporary music and discard the traditional liturgy were losing their Lutheran identity. The polemics reached a fever
pitch with a sustained attack on Protestantism: the problem was not
that Protestantism was distorted or had become apostate; rather, the
problem was Protestantism itself and the way it cut itself off from catholic tradition to embrace individualism and freedom from any authority. Much of this critique dovetailed with Leonard Klein's indictment
of the ELCA for its policy of paying for abortions in its health plan, as
he charged that "real churches don't kill babies."[7]

This does not mean that the ALPB and evangelical catholics did
not also have concrete ideas about denominational reform. Before the
formation of the ELCA, both the *Lutheran Forum* and the *Forum Letter*
devoted many articles to the future structure and ministries of the new
denomination. Aside from discarding quotas and scaling down the
bureaucracy, the most commonly heard proposal involved (and still
involves) increasing the voting influence of bishops and clergy and de-
creasing the voting power of the laity to less than its 60 percent majority. There is the prevalent view that majority voting and democratic
procedures should not decide questions of doctrine and practice. In
such matters, a "magisterium" or a central teaching authority consist-
ing of bishops should be the ones to decide such crucial questions.

Evangelical catholic critics also add that it is not so much fear of
the laity that is behind such proposals as it is the realization that most
of the lay delegates are selected by political criteria, such as quotas. Yet
in the *Lutheran Forum* and other evangelical catholic strongholds, there
is the common sentiment that the ELCA, and the Missouri Synod for
that matter, are not going to be changed anytime soon by political
means. Rather, reform will most likely take place among pastors and
parishes.

As these developments unfolded and alarmed evangelical catholics, the mood of discontent and dissent about the fledgling ELCA became more widespread. Usually, such dissent came more in the form of
critiques than grassroots activism. In 1992, a "free theological conference" was organized sponsored by the ALPB, with other independent
Lutheran publications, to hash out the discontent and protests surrounding the ELCA. A unique feature of the conference, held at St. Olaf

7. Leonard Klein, "Editorial," *Lutheran Forum* (Lent 1996): 10.

College in Northfield, Minnesota, was that the organizers tried to build bridges between the various "confessional Lutherans" critical of the ELCA. The largest group of confessional Lutherans, aside from the evangelical catholics, were the denominational or "gnesio Lutherans" gathered around Luther Seminary in St. Paul. These Lutherans, largely based in the Midwest and West (while the evangelical catholics are often the strongest on the East Coast), adhered closely to Luther's theology but saw the Reformation more as a declaration of independence from Rome, not as simply being intended to reform Catholicism. Represented by such theologians as Gerhard Forde and James Nestingen, this camp was critical of the liberal tendencies of the ELCA, while also none too pleased with the fondness of evangelical catholics for pre-Reformation forms of church order or with their desire for ecumenical unity with Rome, Anglicanism, and Eastern Orthodoxy. While the conference and its critique of the ELCA were widely reported in both secular and church publications, the event also revealed that there was little likelihood of a strong coalition between evangelical catholics and other confessional Lutherans to enact widespread reforms. The divisions in both camps over ecumenism and ministry were too great for any unified platform for renewal to emerge. The divisions between these two camps would later haunt the ELCA on questions of ministry and church order, intensifying divisions in the denomination.

Alienation and the Search for Alternatives

In interviewing evangelical catholic pastors who support the ALPB, I found that their relationships with local leaders and bishops were often shaky, even in synods with relatively orthodox and evangelical catholic bishops. ALPB director Reverend Frederick Schumacher and other evangelical catholic pastors are engaged in a serious conflict with the Metropolitan New York Synod over its issuing of a statement called "Reconciled in Christ," adopted at the synod's 1998 annual meeting. The statement called for acceptance of gays in all congregations in the synod. Schumacher publicly challenged the statement, saying it was imposing an agenda of gay rights and eventual acceptance of homosexuality on the churches. While supporting the document's call to love and minister to all people, including "homosexual oriented persons," Schumacher said it divorced love from biblical teachings. He found little support for his protests and soon took another route: his congregation suspended benevolence giving to the synod and the ELCA, channeling money to orthodox Lutheran causes.

Another pastor said he has not been giving any money to the ELCA — either locally or nationally — for several years. Now he is taking a more radical step. He said he is opting out of the ELCA pension and health plan in order to protest the approval of abortion as an option in the denomination's health coverage. In April of 1999, *Forum Letter* editor Russell Saltzman wrote a short article giving readers details about how they could opt out of the ELCA health plan and transfer to the plan of a new smaller orthodox Lutheran denomination.

The formation of the ELCA and subsequent controversies have also wrought changes within evangelical catholicism. Some of the issues that evangelical catholics targeted as signs of dilution of the Lutheran tradition were present in American Lutheranism before the ELCA formed. Liberal theological programs and professors and a downplaying of the importance of liturgy and the sacraments, for example, have been prevalent throughout American Lutheran history. Evangelical catholics in the post-ELCA period have put a much stronger emphasis on the role of tradition and a magisterium (or teaching authority) in safeguarding catholic doctrine. The concept that the "church is part of the gospel" gained greater currency during this time to drive home the point that the sacraments, historic church structure (such as the historic episcopate, the practice of bishops passing on their authority to each other in a line of succession from the apostles on down to the present), and creeds and teachings of the early church fathers cannot be divorced from the gospel, the "good news" of Christ's death and resurrection for the forgiveness of sins. The fact that one of the previous editors of the *Lutheran Forum* from the 1970s, Richard Koenig, strongly criticized this concept — as it might make church structures more resistant to reform — suggests this is a recent development among many post-ELCA evangelical catholics.[8] During the 1990s, the use of the term "catholic" often came to mean exclusively "Western Catholic" — Roman Catholic and possibly Anglican — along with deference paid to Eastern Orthodoxy.

8. Richard Koenig, "Letter to Richard Neuhaus on His Conversion," *Christian Century* (October 3, 1990): 860.

Protestantism and Catholicism were played against each other as incompatible entities that could not be reconciled.

This tendency to stress the catholic nature of Lutheranism to the exclusion of Protestantism emerged at a time when there was a small migration of evangelical catholic ELCA (and, to a lesser extent, Missouri Synod) clergy to Roman Catholicism and Eastern Orthodoxy. Starting in the early 1990s, the converts included such eminent evangelical catholics as Richard John Neuhaus and Robert Wilken (to Roman Catholicism) and Jaroslav Pelikan (to Eastern Orthodoxy), as well as many clergy increasingly alienated from the ELCA (former *Lutheran Forum* editor Leonard Klein converted to Catholicism in 2003). Neuhaus's conversion caused the greatest controversy, particularly as he stated upon his reception into the Catholic church that the Lutheran Reformation had achieved its purposes in reforming Catholicism, especially after Vatican II and the papacy of John Paul II, and that the existence of a separate Lutheran church was no longer necessary. In other words, the place for evangelical catholics was now in uppercase "Catholicism."

Clergy, Laity, and the Liturgy

Historian Christa Klein writes that throughout American Lutheran history, the liturgical movement has been

> largely clerical. Because the liturgy is a corporate, public event at which an ordained minister presides, lay people have been dependent on the clergy for their exposure to western catholic forms of worship. . . . Thus the catholic strain of piety, although officially present in Lutheranism, is only slowly and selectively coming to the laity.[9]

Those clergy I interviewed who were brought up in the Lutheran church said they always considered Lutheranism as a liturgical church that had more in common with Roman Catholic than with Protestant worship and teachings. Those who converted to Lutheranism said they adopted the church because of its liturgy and catholic identity.

9. Christa Klein, "Lutheranism," in *Encyclopedia of the American Religious Experience*, ed. Charles H. Lippy and Peter W. Williams, 3 vols. (New York: Scribners, 1988), 1:431-35.

Pastor Wayne, a forty-seven-year-old pastor, grew up in the Wesleyan Church, which is an evangelical church stressing the born-again experience and preaching. It was during high school when he did a report on Martin Luther and the Reformation that he became curious about the Lutheran church. "When I attended a Lutheran service, I thought the liturgy was catholic. Someone from a pietist background could see that this was obvious." Reading the *Lutheran Forum* and such evangelical catholic theologians as Arthur Carl Piepkorn reinforced this view of Lutheranism, he said.

Another pastor in his early forties would like to see evangelical catholics accepted as a new order in Roman Catholicism. "We should busy ourselves for this particular destiny [of being an order within the Roman church]. If you look back at church history, you'll see other examples of this, such as the Franciscans or Dominicans," the pastor said. These pastors represent a younger generation of evangelical catholics who often find closer bonds of unity with Roman Catholics, Orthodox, and Anglicans than with fellow Lutherans. The older generation (those older than the baby boom generation) tend to believe that there will most likely always be an orthodox Lutheran church, even if it is no longer in the ELCA. As one younger pastor said, "You'll find that the younger generations of evangelical catholics will speak of 'the Tradition' [meaning the church fathers and other Catholic sources], where the older generation doesn't."

Only a small minority of the laity I interviewed had knowledge of the evangelical catholic criticisms and concerns about the ELCA or the Missouri Synod. It is not that the members disagreed with their pastors' stance on various issues, but, rather, they had not thought much about the national expressions of their faith. Most said they rarely heard their pastors speak about their denominations and came to their conclusions about such matters as gay rights, quotas, and feminism after I first pointed out church statements on these issues. This may seem surprising given the fervent protests and criticisms of the denominations by many evangelical catholic clergy. The hesitancy to speak on controversial denominational issues from the pulpit was voiced by one pastor in Chicago when he said, "I have a passion to preach the gospel and administer the sacraments. I never wanted to use the worship service as a setting to be wrestling with these church issues. . . . It may be that I've taken the cowardly path of not talking [about such matters]." It may be part of the evangelical catholic ethos that they don't bring up the more political and divisive denominational issues, given their concern about the primacy of worship and liturgy in the life of the church.

Most of the pastors interviewed readily admit that members have often resisted the liturgical changes they have introduced into parishes. The struggles that evangelical catholic pastors experience range from conflicts about introducing weekly communion to the introduction of the paschal candle (the candle lit during the Easter season to symbolize Christ's resurrection). Even when liturgical renewal is fully implemented in churches, there is often a gap between clergy and laity in their views on the importance of such rituals.

Jack and Eileen are a couple in their mid sixties who have been deeply involved in church and denominational affairs since their youth. Jack took a leadership role in committees and organizations in his local Lutheran church and in Lutheran men's organizations on a national level. But their involvement in their small ELCA congregation in New York has become more problematic since a new evangelical catholic pastor arrived. She introduced a number of changes that bother Jack and Eileen and some other members, both young and old. In contrast to the informal services, more liturgy and weekly communion at all services has become the rule.

Under the new pastor, making the sign of the cross is encouraged. The pastor planned to dispense ashes on Ash Wednesday until she met with protests from members. "Having communion every service cheapens it. It becomes rote, once it becomes a habit. You don't think about what it means. . . . It's all these ceremonial and symbolic things — the robes and liturgies. Now some churches are calling their service Masses. It's catering to the Catholics," Eileen says. Both Jack and Eileen are particularly troubled by the undemocratic way that these innovations have been brought into the life of the congregation. "They're trying to make all the churches alike. . . . It's pressure from above," Jack said of the local synod of the ELCA.

Those more receptive to evangelical catholic renewal, including its commitment to sacrament and liturgy, often received their initial exposure to Christianity in such liturgical settings. Matthew, a forty-four-year-old New York investment analyst, was raised in the Wisconsin Evangelical Lutheran Synod, a strongly conservative denomination that forbids fellowship with other Lutheran churches, not to mention non-Lutheran denominations. Matthew eventually became involved in planting a Wisconsin Synod congregation in New York. When that project fell through, he gravitated to an evangelical catholic ELCA parish. He was used to a less liturgical and sacramental form of Lutheranism; growing up, the minister wore a black gown and parishioners would never cross themselves or use kneelers, because those things were too Catholic. But he started studying the liturgy and church history and found that Lutheranism "was part of the Western catholic tradition." Today, he feels that his church's link to other historic communions, such as Roman Catholicism and Eastern Orthodoxy, has made his faith "more universal and less provincial," in contrast to his Wisconsin Synod beginnings.

Throughout my interviews it was evident that even though evangelical catholic practices may become accepted as "traditions" in a church, members do not necessarily understand or agree with the theological underpinnings pastors provide. One businesswoman in her forties who has also been involved with the ALPB says that there is a split between the pastors who have strong catholic attachments and sensibilities and laypeople who define themselves as Protestant. While supporting the ALPB and evangelical catholic efforts at reform, she sees some evangelical catholics as "[Roman] Catholic wannabes. . . . There's nothing wrong with the Lutheran tradition. We don't need to become more Roman Catholic or Eastern Orthodox. We just have to be Lutheran."

Obstacles to Evangelical Catholic Reform

The evangelical catholics gathered around the ALPB, as well as most other conservative renewalists, would be the first ones to admit the problems they have in extending their influence in their denominations. Because the ALPB and other evangelical catholics sought to avoid the factionalism of forming the caucuses and parties found in Anglo-Catholicism in the Anglican tradition, they don't have the alternative structures and sources of support that such groups can provide in pluralistic denominations. This lack of organizational focus may be due to the prevailing view (suggested by Gregory Fryer at the beginning of this chapter) that the Lutheran church itself should be a renewal movement within Western catholicism. If Lutheranism is not seen as the primary target for renewal and reform by such Lutherans, it is not surprising that evangelical catholic strategies lack influence in the ELCA and LCMS. When one asks these renewalists about their future in their denominations, the answers are far from upbeat. Many see increasing marginalization and opposition of their ministries; some in the back of their minds may be hatching escape plans to greener pastures, even as they express allegiance to their current tradition and congregations. In one way, they are right. Attempting to change structures and denominational leaderships often involves a recourse to politics and "culture wars" that end up being more divisive than effective. In short, the evangelical catholics gathered around the ALPB realize that ELCA Lutherans (and, to a lesser extent, Missouri Lutherans) have fallen victim to what sociologist Robert Wuthnow has termed the "restructuring of American religion," where serious divisions often run within denominations as much as between them.[10]

One solution to this dilemma is to encourage new informal and formal networks of association. When Paul Hinlickey was editor of the *Lutheran Forum* during the stormy years of the early 1990s, he urged the formation of an ecumenical alternative synod that would gather together orthodox believers of a catholic orientation from many denominations. Even if such a synod does not become a separate church, he wrote that Lutherans should treat their own "denominational machinery as lacking ecclesial density, as nothing more than a mechanism for pensions, charity and other necessary temporal goods and services."[11] The hope for such an alternative confessing synod materialized in 2002, when the Evangelical Lutheran Confessing Fellowship was founded. The fellowship seeks to draw together all orthodox Lutherans in an attempt to renew the ELCA along confessional lines. At the same time, participants admit that the group may be the launching pad of a new Lutheran denomination, particularly if liberal measures to ordain gays and lesbians and approve same-sex unions are passed at the ELCA's 2005 Churchwide Assembly. In its statement of faith, the

10. Robert Wuthnow, *The Restructuring of American Religion* (Princeton, N.J. Princeton University Press, 1988).

11. Paul Hinlickey, "Editorial," *Lutheran Forum* (Reformation 1993): 5.

fellowship stresses issues and points of doctrine that are in contention in the ELCA, such as heterosexual marriage as the sole institution for sexual expression, and the traditional Trinitarian formula in opposition to inclusive language for God.[12]

In the ELCA, the commitment to quotas and the policy of inclusiveness makes it difficult for those who come from outside this "system" to make significant changes or form new caucuses with wide influence. Many evangelical catholic Lutherans and others of a similar persuasion have come to the conclusion that it is better to concentrate on fellowship and cooperation with like-minded believers wherever one finds them, and on nurturing one's own congregation, rather than expending their resources and energy in attempting to reform denominational structures. The formation of the Society of the Holy Trinity in 1997 represented a major effort to form a counterculture of clergy adhering to the Lutheran confessions, evangelical catholic liturgy, and the disciplines of prayer and spiritual direction. The society seeks to provide Lutheran pastors (the organization is open to ELCA and LCMS pastors) oversight and accountability (for instance, providing pastors with the rite of personal confession and absolution) that it sees as lacking in the Lutheran denominations. The society has also acted as a support system for clergy resisting non-orthodox directions in their particular synod or district (such as gay rights initiatives), as well as a means of referring and matching up evangelical catholic pastors to like-minded congregations, thus overriding in some cases the usual procedure of synods advising congregations on available clergy prospects.[13]

But despite the sharp polemics and anti-ELCA positions of many evangelical catholics associated with the ALPB, I found that the negativity was not being returned at church headquarters. "The evangelical catholics have an important part to play in the ELCA," the Reverend Randall Lee, former executive assistant to the Secretary of the ELCA and currently director of ecumenical affairs for the denomination, said during an interview I had with him. Reverend Lee said that he views the ELCA leadership as being "in dialogue" with the evan-

12. Evangelical Lutheran Confessing Fellowship, http://www24.brinkster.com/newsitedesign.elcf/

13. Cimino, *Trusting the Spirit*, chap. 3.

gelical catholics gathered around the ALPB and the *Lutheran Forum,* and that he sees the evangelical catholic influence running in opposing directions to the church growth–seeker movement in the denominational leadership. The division is expressed in the more evangelical catholic influence found in the church's Division of Worship, and the evangelical church growth influence in the ELCA's evangelism office. This means that while the evangelism offices may be providing material on contemporary and seeker services, the worship division may issue liturgical statements drawing on Roman Catholic and Anglican sources.

Reverend Lee's receptivity to the evangelical catholics suggests that the movement's appeal is far broader than simply the readership of the *Lutheran Forum.* It is not at all unusual to come across evangelical catholics who have never read the magazine and who arrive at theological positions that are far from conservative on such issues as abortion, social justice, gay rights, and gender-inclusive language. One thirty-eight-year-old pastor says that he represents the younger generation of evangelical catholics who are looking for an alternative to the ALPB. He is particularly critical of the conservative political and social positions found in the *Lutheran Forum* and other related publications. "I don't want to see evangelical catholicism equated with neo-conservatism. If you look at history, the catholic tradition offers a wide spectrum of different positions. These hard lines being drawn [on sexuality and other social issues] in the ALPB will be its death knell."

This pastor and others I interviewed with similar views had strongly positive views of their regional synods — in this case, the Metropolitan New York and Chicago synods — with one pastor from the South moving to New York so he could serve in the area known as the High Church "biretta belt" of Lutheranism. They were somewhat more ambivalent about the national ELCA body, believing that the merger papered over differences between predecessor churches that are unlikely to be resolved easily. But their support of the local and national church body was linked to their evangelical catholic position, believing that it provided the unity and diversity found in the catholic tradition. In fact, a level of anger was expressed by three pastors I interviewed regarding other clergy and church members who withheld offerings and support for the synod and national office in protest over issues such as gay rights and abortion. One thirty-seven-year-old pastor in a suburban New York church said, "It makes me so angry. I want to say to them: 'This is the church and you don't do that to the church.' They are whoring around with the church; it's whoring with the bride of Christ. It's treating the church as a voluntary organization, and it's a heretical understanding of the congregation. The local synod, the churchwide assembly, the ELCA, they're just as much the church as [the congregation]." As might be expected, those evangelical catholics in resistance to their synods and the ELCA national body do not view themselves as isolated congregationalists. One pastor whose inner-city ethnic German congregation does not give either to the national office or synod said, "We're giving to the wider church, just not channelling it through the ELCA." He cited the church's strong missionary involvement and connection to struggling area churches in his city as well as in the Middle East.

Escape, Loyalty, or Resistance?

From a historical perspective, the evangelical catholic effect in Lutheranism is impressive. The once "radical" practice of weekly communion in American Lutheranism has spread to many ELCA congregations — whether or not they call themselves evangelical catholic or agree with the *Lutheran Forum.* Approximately 25 percent of ELCA congregations now have weekly communion. With such texts as the *Lutheran Book of Worship* and *Lutheran Worship,* those with an evangelical catholic orientation have imparted their vision to the whole denomination. Other "innovations" such as the Easter Vigil, inner-city parish ministries, and ecumenical relations with Roman Catholicism and Eastern Orthodoxy have also spread far beyond the evangelical catholic enclaves in which they emerged.

Nevertheless, the top-down nature of liturgical renewal in parishes, flowing down from the liturgically trained pastor and assisting ministers to the untutored laity often raised on a different kind of piety, will continue to be a difficult and slow process. For confessional and liturgical renewal to survive and prosper, it is important that its teachings and sensibility find a place among the laity. The future of evangelical catholicism in Lutheranism depends on developments both within the movement and within the ELCA and the Missouri

Synod. As noted above, evangelical catholicism is not a monolithic movement, which is evident even within such strongholds as the ALPB and the Society of the Holy Trinity. We have seen that the evangelical catholics can play the roles of dissenters or loyalists. The dissenters, though they may shy away from protesting church decisions and moving outside of the denominational system, make their dissent evident through, for example, the practice of withholding offerings to the synods and national church, and some have now taken the further step of forming the Evangelical Lutheran Confessing Fellowship. The loyalists, on the other hand, help shore up the denomination by their emphasis on cooperation and connections with the wider church beyond the congregation.

These dissenters and loyalists will have a significant impact on the Lutheran future. Those who more strongly identify with an evangelical catholic identity rather than with a strictly Lutheran one (usually those of the younger generations) may continue to gravitate toward Roman Catholicism and Eastern Orthodoxy. This group is strongly ecumenical and is based around the Center for Evangelical and Catholic Theology and the journal *Pro Ecclesia*, edited by theologians Carl Braaten and Robert Jenson. But even among this group of theologians, clergy, and laity there is a hesitation to make the individual trek to Rome or Constantinople, believing it undermines the long-held ecumenical vision of corporate church unity between the Reformation traditions and the Western and Eastern historic churches.

Then there are the evangelical catholics strongly loyal to the ELCA. Although critical of some facets of the church (such as catering to the seeker-sensitive movement in the denominational evangelism department, and group-interest politics in the denomination), they see no ultimate conflict between church policies and liturgical renewal; moreover, they particularly value the national and international connections the ELCA provides. Such liberal evangelical catholicism may become a dominant and influential form of Lutheranism in the ELCA, particularly as several recent church agreements (CCM and the joint agreement with the Catholics on justification) have run in their favor.

Rather than accommodation to the denominational pluralism of the ELCA, the third group of evangelical catholics mainly associated with the ALPB calls for *resistance* to the continuing movement of the ELCA into the mainline Protestant orbit, particularly on issues of sexual ethics. These evangelical catholics may well leave the denomination (particularly if the ELCA decides to ordain gays and lesbians and approves same-sex unions in 2005), either for Catholicism and Orthodoxy or for new confessional Lutheran associations, such as the Evangelical Lutheran Confessing Fellowship, that will exist on the margins or even outside of the ELCA.

Finally, in addition to these three groups, mention should also be made of a growing segment of evangelical catholics in the Missouri Synod who are sharply different from those described above. Based at Concordia Seminary in Fort Wayne, Indiana, these strict evangelical catholics reject with few qualms both women's ordination and intercommunion with ELCA Lutherans.

Whatever routes are taken by evangelical catholics — escape, loyalty, or resistance — Pastor Fryer's and others' hopes for Lutheranism as a united reform movement within the Western catholic tradition will be complicated and confounded by the pluralism and restructuring of American Christianity taking place in the twenty-first century.

BIBLIOGRAPHY

Bittner, James B. "On the Societies of St. Ambrose and St. James: A Study in Liturgical Critique." *Bride of Christ* (July 2002): 18-23.

Cimino, Richard. *Trusting the Spirit*, chap. 3. San Francisco: Jossey-Bass, 2001.

Graebner, A., and A. P. Klausler. "50 Years of the ALPB," parts 1-5. *American Lutheran* (August 1963, pp. 14-17; September 1963, pp. 14-15; October 1963, pp. 14-15; November 1963, pp. 20-23; December 1963, pp. 6-21).

Hinlickey, Paul. "Editorial." *Lutheran Forum* (Reformation 1993): 5.

Klein, Christa. "Lutheranism." In *Encyclopedia of the American Religious Experience*, 3 vols., ed. Charles H. Lippy and Peter W. Williams, 1:431-35. New York: Scribners, 1988.

Klein, Leonard. "Editorial." *Lutheran Forum* (Lent 1996): 10.

————. "The Role of the Lutheran Forum." *Lutheran Forum* (Advent 1993): 4.

Koenig, Richard. "Letter to Richard Neuhaus on His Conversion." *Christian Century* (October 3, 1990): 860.

Wuthnow, Robert. *The Restructuring of American Religion*. Princeton, N.J.: Princeton University Press, 1988.

Goliaths in Our Midst: Megachurches in the ELCA

SCOTT THUMMA AND JIM PETERSEN

A Microscopic Look at a Megachurch

It's Sunday afternoon. Outside your hotel room, the temperature is 108 degrees and rising. Foot-weary from working the display booth at your company's national product convention and annoyed by the incessant ringing of slot machines in the hotel's casino, you decide to do something few folks even think about when they come to Las Vegas. You decide to go to church. You grab the telephone book and look in the yellow pages for an ELCA Lutheran congregation with a Sunday evening service. Incredibly enough, there's one just down the street.

After an early dinner, you climb into your car and head east on Tropicana Avenue, where you soon are confronted by yet another massive Las Vegas building. This one looks more like a corporate conference center than a church, but the sign in front says Community Lutheran, so you follow a string of cars along the marked route to the parking lot. As you pull into the lot you're thinking, "Surely this can't be right. This building is too big for a church. Besides, there are too many people coming here for a Sunday evening service." You wonder

The authors would like to thank Kenn Inskeep and Martin Smith of the ELCA research office for their willingness to provide us with lists of the largest churches and access to the congregational trend reports, as well as for their comments on earlier drafts. Likewise, we thank John O'Hara for providing us with the information about the large churches in the Lutheran Church–Missouri Synod.

what else is happening. Is there a wedding? A funeral? Seems unlikely at night, so you decide to take a chance and go on in.

As you climb out of your car, the couple who just parked next to you say hello. On the way to the door, you find yourself telling them about your reason for being here. Their response surprises you: "Oh, we get lots of people from the Strip. Many have been told about our congregation by a friend, neighbor, or person with whom they work. We're always surprised by how many people from all over the country send their friends to us when they're in town!" As you walk through the door, you're surprised by the kind of music you hear in the background. It's a country gospel song sung by a group you'll later learn is called the Honky Tonk Angels. "Honky Tonk Angels?" you think, "You've got to be kidding!"

When you walk into the church's spacious, well-lighted lobby, the first thing that catches your eye is a large area formed by a rectangle of skirted tables and labeled "Information." The person behind the tables is answering the questions of three others standing there listening. Obviously, you're not the only visitor tonight. As you approach, you see a large number of brochures, pamphlets, and other printed materials. In addition to the information area, there are signs everywhere. One says "Chapel." You wander into a worship space with room for 150 that would easily seat the Sunday worship attendance of half the ELCA congregations in America. You learn that the chapel is used for weddings, funerals, prayer services, mini-worship for children at the congregation's Christian day care center next door, and staff devotions. You again look across the lobby and notice the restrooms are clearly marked. Upon entering, you are a bit surprised, but also intrigued, to see framed prints of paintings on the walls. You think, "even the restroom is upscale!"

At the door to the worship space, an usher wearing cowboy boots introduces herself and asks the question, "Have we met?" You chat, then walk through the door. In front of you are roughly three to four hundred people seated in the theater-style worship area. The pastors are wandering up and down aisles, which slope toward the front of the worship auditorium so that everyone can have a good view. They're chatting with those seated in the pew chairs while the Honky Tonks sing and play the gathering music. The pastor nearest to you walks up and introduces himself. As the song ends, the pastors wander down toward the front and begin an announcement time in which they banter with each other, the musicians, and the crowd. There's much laughter. By now you're feeling warm and welcomed, but this is so far removed from the pre-worship experience at your home church that you ask yourself, "Is this Lutheran?"

The banter ends and worship begins with another song. When it ends, you explore the printed, stapled document you were handed at the door. You discover news of the congregation, ministry opportunities, sign-up and prayer sheets, and an all-in-one service outline. Though different from the one you're used to, this church does have a liturgy, Scripture and Gospel messages, a sermon, and Communion, so you must be in the right place. During the sermon you ponder how the minister knew your situation since it felt as if he were talking directly to you, about your own life and struggles. On this particular evening, new members are being welcomed "into community." You find it interesting that the people who first invited the new members to church are asked to come up front and stand with the new members, and then are applauded for issuing the invitation.

Later, while reading the newsletter you picked up at the information desk, you find that the new members are listed in the newsletter along with the names of the people who invited them or told them about the congregation. You learn that twelve of the twenty-four families and singles who joined were either invited or told about the congregation by friends or relatives, one of whom lives in Minnesota! Two of the remaining twelve learned of the congregation on the Internet, three came from the yellow pages, three discovered the congregation by driving by it, and another lived nearby. The comment that most interests you, though, comes from a couple who answered the question, "How did you learn about CLC?" with, "We have attended for ten years."

After the worship service you find yourself chatting with others in the relaxed, air-conditioned atmosphere of the lobby. You learn that the church has six weekend services with five distinct styles, only one of which is traditional Lutheran worship. You finally return to your hotel feeling so upbeat, refreshed, and renewed that you tell your entire convention team about the experience, concluding, "You missed something special. Next year, you've got to come with me to that church. That was an incredible experience!"

The reaction of this Las Vegas conventioneer is typical of many people who wander into a service at one of the several megachurches within the Evangelical Lutheran Church in America (ELCA) or its counterparts in other Lutheran denominations. It is not the only reaction these massive churches evoke, however. In our experience, there are two common responses to megachurches — either you love them or you hate them. Whichever your reaction, much can be learned from these massive enterprises. Likewise, whether you think these behemoths are cutting-edge Christianity or capitulation to secular society, they possess a level of influence and notoriety far beyond their numbers on the religious landscape. To many laity and a number of clergy, megachurches seem the epitome of congregational success. Before we engage in a discussion of their appropriate place in the religious world and assess their strengths and potential shortcomings, however, a description of the phenomenon, both within the Evangelical Lutheran Church in America and elsewhere, is in order.

Much of the information for this chapter comes directly from the ELCA's annual congregational reports. Additionally, data from several of the largest ELCA congregations was collected during the Faith Communities Today (FACT) megachurch survey.[1] This study, coupled with earlier research by author Scott Thumma on megachurches, provides the national picture of this phenomenon.[2] Anecdotal and other material comes from author Jim Petersen, who served as Executive Director for Ministries at Community Lutheran in Las Vegas and is presently Associate Director for Evangelism, Communication, and Networking for the ELCA's Division for Congregational Ministries. Additional information was gathered through nonsystematic interviews with clergy and extensive analysis of Lutheran and other written sources.

A Macroscopic Look at the Megas

Of the 10,816 congregations that make up the Evangelical Lutheran Church in America as it begins the twenty-first century, only seven are

---

1. Faith Communities Today Survey, Hartford Seminary, 2001. This survey can be accessed at http://hirr.hartsem.edu/org/faith_megachurches.html.
2. Scott Thumma, "The Kingdom, the Power, and the Glory: Megachurches in Modern American Society," Ph.D. diss., Emory University, 1996.

considered true megachurches, in which more than 2,000 people worship each Sunday. Six of these true "megas" are in Minnesota; the other
is in Arizona. In addition to the seven megachurches, ten others have an
average worship attendance of between 1,500 and 1,999 people each
weekend, and twenty-six more have between 1,000 and 1,499 at worship. In total, the ELCA has forty-three congregations with 1,000 or more
in weekly attendance. To obtain the broadest picture of the presence of
very large churches in the ELCA, these forty-three congregations will be
the focus of this chapter. They represent *only four-tenths of one percent* of
the total number of ELCA congregations, yet they are home to *almost five
percent* of Lutheran worship attenders — 72,790 persons — each week.

Although not a focus of this chapter, the Lutheran Church–Missouri Synod has four congregations that qualify as megachurches with
worship attendance of 2,000 or more. Additionally, they have thirty-
four churches with attendance between 1,000 and 1,999 persons. These
thirty-eight churches represent six-tenths of one percent of all the
LCMS congregations. Although a large number of these congregations
are found in Missouri and Michigan, these largest LCMS churches are
significantly more dispersed throughout the United States than are the
ELCA's largest churches.

Nationally, there are approximately seven hundred Protestant
megachurches with 2,000 or more in average attendance (roughly two-
tenths of one percent of the total number of Protestant churches in
America) and between three and four thousand more churches with
weekly attendance above 1,000 (around 1 percent of all Protestant congregations).

Megachurches are characteristically found in Sunbelt sprawl cities such as Los Angeles, Atlanta, Houston, Orlando, and Dallas. The
vast majority are also located in the newer suburbs of these cities. California, Georgia, Texas, and Florida are the states of residence for over
40 percent of all megas.

Though only 14 percent of the forty-three very large ELCA congregations are located in the desert Southwest, around Phoenix and in
Las Vegas, that represents a significant number for Lutherans. Prior to
World War II, only *one* Lutheran congregation existed in all of southern
Nevada and Arizona. Today, seven of the forty-three largest congregations are located there, in the ELCA's Grand Canyon Synod. Interestingly, the Grand Canyon Synod also had the largest percentage of

ELCA congregations that grew by over 5 percent between 1997 and 2000. It would be easy to conclude that the Southwest is a logical location for ELCA megas, since Minnesotans, Iowans, and Dakotans retire in Arizona and Nevada. This is not the case, though, since the overwhelming majority of attenders in these very large congregations are far below retirement age.

A look at the national megachurch trends shows that this Southwest anomaly makes sense — the vast majority of megachurch growth has taken place in the relatively newer cities of the South and West. This is not the pattern for the very large ELCA churches, however. It is, in fact, the presence of the large number of ELCA megas in the upper Midwest that is the aberration in the national megachurch scene.

The majority of these very large congregations — twenty-nine of the forty-three — are found in Minnesota, North Dakota, South Dakota, and Iowa, where the concentration of ELCA members in the general population is also the highest. Twenty are located in just two synods, Minneapolis Area and Saint Paul Area, a virtual hotbed for ELCA congregational growth. In these two synods almost half (40 percent) of all ELCA congregations grew by more than 5 percent between 1997 and 2000.

Perhaps the core anomaly for the existence of ELCA megas is simply their presence within a mainline Protestant denomination. Just 11 percent of Protestant megachurches are from mainline denominations such as the ELCA, the United Methodist Church, the Presbyterian Church (USA), and the Reformed Church of America. The vast majority of America's megachurches are nondenominational (23 percent), Southern Baptist (19 percent), or Assemblies of God (10 percent). Even given the large numbers of megachurches within these more theologically conservative denominations, it is important to note that for none of these groups is the percent of true megas in their midst larger than roughly half of one percent of all their churches.

Lutheran Megachurches — A New Phenomenon?

The United States has always been home to a few very large churches, but the appearance of hundreds of these congregations is a recent phenomenon. The best estimate identifies a handful of megachurches prior to 1970. By the mid 1980s there were roughly 350 megas. Fifteen years later there were at least twice that many.

Megachurches are also a relatively recent ELCA phenomenon. Among the forty-three largest ELCA congregations, 37 percent were organized prior to 1943, 63 percent were established following World War II, and 32 percent were founded after 1970. However, the growth of nearly all of these presently massive churches took place in the past twenty-five years. Just nineteen of the forty-three had attendance over one thousand prior to 1987, when three Lutheran church bodies merged to form the ELCA. The growth of these churches is all the more impressive when one recalls that the ELCA has lost over a half million members since 1970.

The seven largest ELCA churches were all founded prior to the mid 1960s, but most of these have relocated within the past twenty years. Interestingly, the vast majority of very large churches in the Minneapolis Area Synod were founded prior to 1961. The founding dates of the largest congregations in the Saint Paul Area Synod are scattered evenly across the past century, with 40 percent before 1950 and 40 percent after 1974. Nearly all the very large churches within the Grand Canyon Synod, however, have been founded since 1970.

In 2000 the membership of the ELCA as a whole declined by a half percent. This continues the general decline in membership over the past decade. Growth and decline rates, however, are never evenly shared by all congregations. In fact, from 1997 to 2000, 29 percent of ELCA churches grew by over 5 percent. The forty-three largest ELCA congregations stand out even among all growing churches, gaining an average of 37 percent in membership from 1993 to 2000. The growth rates of these very large churches are not, however, uniformly consistent across all forty-three of them. Fourteen percent of very large ELCA churches actually lost members. Another 11 percent experienced a modest growth rate of 10 percent or less. Thirty-two percent of these largest ELCA churches reported 11 to 40 percent growth rates, and nineteen congregations (44 percent) grew more than 40 percent during the past decade. Worship attendance growth rates in these congregations show an almost identical pattern.

Looking at these characteristics together, it becomes apparent that there is a strong relationship between year of organization and current rates of growth. Those very large congregations founded since

Worship Growth Rate by Founding Date

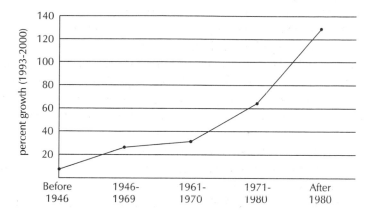

1970 grew more rapidly in the past eight years than those organized earlier, in terms of both overall membership and worship attendance. (See the chart above.)

This founding/growth pattern is part of the reason megachurches are most likely to be found in the newer suburbs of rapidly growing metropolitan areas. This is not to say that megas are only found in suburbia, however. Nationally, the FACT study found the locational distribution of megachurches to be 29 percent urban, 37 percent older suburban, and 34 percent new suburban.

ELCA megachurches also demonstrate a similar distribution across urban, older suburban, and the new suburbs of growing cities. This pattern of the distribution is most evident in the local Minneapolis area. The largest ELCA congregation — Mount Olivet Lutheran Church, with a weekly worship attendance of almost 6,000 — has been located in the heart of urban Minneapolis since its inception in 1920. Though its worship numbers have been relatively stable since 1994 — hovering around 6,000 — Mount Olivet has been the denomination's largest church for decades. Another mega, Prince of Peace Lutheran in Burnsville, Minnesota, is located in an older suburb of Minneapolis. Prince of Peace, just fourteen miles south of Mount Olivet, was organized in 1964. It grew roughly 5 percent in worship attendance between 1994 and 2001, from 4,000 to 4,200 per week. Less than five miles southeast of Prince of Peace and sixteen miles south of Mount Olivet, however, Hosanna Lutheran Church is a new megachurch in the new suburban area of Lakeville, Minnesota. Hosanna has exploded with growth in its short history. Organized in 1980, Hosanna crossed the 1,000-at-worship line in 1995 and by 2001 had 2,500 people at worship. These three ideally exemplify the pattern found throughout the megachurch phenomenon.

Characteristics of Participants: Whose Sheep Are Flocking In?

So what kinds of people are attracted to these congregations? The Faith Communities Today (FACT) survey of megachurches included in-depth survey research with five ELCA megachurches. The regularly participating adults profile from this survey of five megas showed that, on average, these participants are young (40 percent between eighteen and thirty-five years of age), middle-class, well-educated, and have household incomes in the fifty- to seventy-five-thousand-dollar range. In addition, three of the five churches report that 40 to 60 percent of their regularly participating adults are new to the church in the past five years. Some of these are lifelong ELCA members, but many are not.

The ELCA's Annual Report data bears this out. Of the 13,571 total members gained in 2000 by the forty-three largest ELCA churches, almost a third of the new members came from other ELCA congregations, close to another third came through adult and child baptisms, and slightly more than a third came either by affirmation of faith or from a non-ELCA church transfer. On the other hand, roughly half as many large-church members were lost to other ELCA congregations as were gained from them. (See Table 1 on p. 111.) However, Table 2 (also on p. 111) shows that this switching between ELCA churches was not uniform across all of these very large churches. A few of the largest congregations had significant net gains from sister churches while some actually lost more to other ELCA churches than they brought in from them.

Nearly all of these very large congregations are found in mixed residential/commercial-industrial areas where the local population (based on the zip code in which the churches were located) grew rapidly. In fact, the rate of population increase within a church's zip code area was highly correlated with the membership growth rates of these forty-three largest churches. Interestingly, the rate of population growth in the local zip code, however, was not statistically correlated

Table 1. Average Baptisms and Transfers Per Congregation in 2000

Category	Average Gains for the 43 Very Large ELCA Churches	Average Gains for All ELCA Congregations
Child baptisms	91	7
Adult baptisms	5	1
Affirmations of faith	63	6
Transfers from other ELCA congregations	101	7
Transfers from other Lutheran churches	22	2
Transfers from non-Lutheran churches	34	2
Members transferred to other ELCA congregations	56	6

Table 2. Net Change to and from ELCA Churches

	Percent of churches experiencing change
Net Loss	19
Gain 1-20	14
Gain 21-40	22
Gain 41-70	26
Gain 71-89	9
Gain 100 or more	12

to the rate of worship attendance growth. A possible implication of this finding might be that although a rapidly growing community context is a necessary component in attracting large numbers of members to these churches (there need to be a lot of fish in the sea), nevertheless, a growing region is not a sufficient cause to explain the rapid increase in worship attendance (or keeping them in the boat). Growth in worship attendance depends far more on internal dynamics (quality nets and skilled fishers) such as a pastor's qualities, innovative worship forms, warm and welcoming hospitality, and a vital congregational life in which people who attend feel their own lives being affected and changed than it does on neighborhood growth rates.

Clergy Leadership — With Vision and Purpose

In addition to their size, very large congregations have another crucial similarity — dynamic and gifted leaders. Of the five ELCA megachurches with two thousand or more attenders for which we have FACT data, four of these grew to their present large size during the tenure of the current pastor. In all five congregations polled, the senior pastors were male and, on average, were in their early fifties. These five congregations indicated on the survey that they strongly agreed they had a "clear sense of vision and purpose." Two of the five saw the church's stated vision and purpose as "the key source of congregational authority."

Though pastoral styles among very large ELCA congregations may be very different, it is clear that these pastors are self-confident, gifted leaders who talk about and model their own personal faith in effective ways. Leadership is shared among pastors, staff, and laity. The senior pastors in very large ELCA congregations are, for the most part, creative risk-takers. They have been able to articulate a vision and mission for their congregations that is powerfully compelling. They inspire the membership to embrace this vision and mission with enough conviction to allow them to grow past the traditional plateaus that cause congregations to "level off" in membership and worship numbers. Because of the magnitude of their ministries, these pastors have learned the importance of "giving away" the ministry — putting it into the hands of motivated leadership staff and laity.

Worship — Professional, Evangelical, and Expressive

The most significant programmatic component of a megachurch is its worship services. Without a doubt, members of megachurches more frequently praise their church's professional, high quality, and dynamic worship services than any other component of the church. Though some would claim that this kind of worship is more an entertainment spectacle than reverent worship, there is no denying its appeal. Nearly 80 percent of attenders in a study of one non-ELCA megachurch said the worship service was a major reason they stayed at the church. Worship is almost always a plural word for the Lutheran megachurches, being characterized by multiple services that often differ greatly in style and format. This pattern is also true of all megachurches, with 93 percent offering two or more services on Sunday morning and almost half having three or more services. Sixty-five percent have a Sunday evening service, and half of all megachurches nationwide have a service on Saturday, while 20 percent also offer a Friday service. Likewise, nearly half (48 percent) report that their multiple services differ considerably in style.

Flexibility, experimentation, and adaptation to contemporary styles also mark the worship of the largest ELCA churches. Four out of the five we surveyed changed their worship style during the past five years — with several of these making major changes in their style. An ever-present aspect of the constant modification is the use of high-tech equipment including computer and video projection, theater-style lighting, and surround sound, as well as dance, dramatic productions, and electronic instruments such as keyboard, guitar, drums, and bass. These are supplemented from time to time, or service to service, with strings, winds, other orchestral instruments, and even pre-recorded sound tracks. For example, at Community Lutheran, a worship attender might find traditional liturgical worship with hymns from the *Lutheran Book of Worship,* accompanied by organ, alongside music from the Catholic *Gather Songbook,* accompanied by keyboard, guitars, and drums; praise and worship with similar accompaniment; followed by country gospel with keyboard, guitars, drums, and a fiddle; and Christian contemporary music led by a band and vocal group.

Theologically, there is an inclination toward conservatism evident nationally for all megachurches. When asked to describe the theological character of their churches, FACT megachurch respondents characterized their congregational identity predominantly as evangelical (48 percent), although some theological diversity is evident (see Table 3 on p. 114). This religious identity pattern is paralleled in the five ELCA megachurches for which there is detailed FACT data. A clear evangelical theological perspective is evident in these churches, with four of five identifying with the "evangelical" label while the remaining congregation chose the "moderate" label. This theological identification is borne out in their worship and sermon characteristics as well.

Nevertheless, according to the survey information this group of five ELCA churches also exhibits a diversity of theological styles.

Table 3. FACT Megachurch Survey Respondents' Characterization of Congregational Identity

Evangelical	48%
Pentecostal	25%
Moderate	12%
Traditional	8%
Other	7%

Three say their sermons always focus on personal salvation. Two of the five also say they always or often focus on the Holy Spirit, with one of these being quite charismatic and the other somewhat charismatic. Three of the congregations say they always use creeds and two report they seldom do. All of the five claim to use personal stories and contemporary illustrations coupled with some doctrine and Scripture in the sermons.

One thing all megachurches have in common, regardless of theological inclination or denominational affiliation, is that all see their services as "spiritually vital and alive." Likewise, all five of the ELCA megachurches surveyed in the FACT study described their members as "excited about the future of their church." This vitality and excitement functions as a powerful stimulant for attracting others. Three in-depth marketing studies of Community Lutheran in Las Vegas and Community Church of Joy in Glendale, Arizona, done during the 1990s under the direction of one of the authors, showed that in both these congregations, more than 80 percent of those who come to worship find the experience so compelling they invite at least one other person to church every year, and around 60 percent invite three or more persons to come to church with them each year.

This evangelistic effort is not solely a natural outgrowth of enthusiasm; rather, there is a focused intentionality around inviting others that becomes an integral part of the congregational culture. This expectation of invitation greatly enhances the recruitment dynamic. At Community Lutheran, the process of asking "inviters" to stand up front with new members they invited and be acknowledged and applauded lifts up those who invite and reinforces the process. FACT information on the five ELCA megachurches showed that all of them had formal

evangelistic/recruitment programs and that their members were exten-
sively or moderately involved in recruiting new people.

At Community Lutheran, members have become so sophisticated at inviting others to church that they often take them to a weekend service with a different music style from their own. They might
tell their friends, for example, "We're going to take you to the 9:45
Sunday morning service. We don't go to that service, but we think
you'll like it best. We'll come with you a couple of times and introduce
you around; then once you've met some folks, we'll go back to our
own service."

Abundant Resources: A Benefit or Detriment?

Megachurches have in abundance one crucial resource that is lacking
in small churches — people. The average attendance of the forty-three
largest Lutheran churches (1,430 persons) is almost exactly ten times
the 145 persons in the average ELCA Sunday service. The average
weekend worship attendance of all megachurches (defined as having
over 2,000 in attendance) is 3,857 persons, with average membership
approaching 7,000. The size of these churches can in itself be an attrac-
tion. A congregation that consistently draws a thousand or more in attendance can become almost self-perpetuating. People are drawn to a
crowd. Once in church, these "curious onlookers" are intentionally
guided into contributing to the life of the congregation — in giving,
volunteering, and in ministry.

The monetary resources of megachurches are often envied, and
with good reason, since most have massive budgets. The total income
for these forty-three largest ELCA congregations falls between
$600,000 and nearly $8 million a year, with the average income being
$2.81 million. Expenditures in these churches are in most cases, how-
ever, virtually identical to their income, with the average for the group
at $2.67 million. Nevertheless, of the five megachurches for which
there is FACT data, three claimed in 1995 to be in excellent financial
shape, and in 2000 all but one claimed that category.

Likewise, the massive human resources of megachurches are often coveted by smaller struggling churches. The average staff of the
FACT-surveyed ELCA megas (paralleling the larger megachurch pat-

tern) includes approximately ten ministerial staff and twenty programmatic staff. These five congregations also report several hundred volunteer laypeople who give over five hours a week to church programs. Yet even with this volunteer army, there are nearly always gaps in positions of leadership. Nevertheless, three of five megas report that they have no problem getting leadership volunteers. Indeed, the larger Faith Communities Today study shows a strong positive correlation between the size of a congregation and the ease with which it can find volunteers, with 28 percent of those having one thousand or more regularly participating adults having the easiest time filling volunteer leadership slots.

Given this abundance it might be easy to conclude that these congregations are spilling over with wealth and lay leadership. To go back to the earlier fishing analogy, however, there is a vast difference between finding a stream full of fish and getting them to bite. There is no question that these massive numbers of people generate more excitement in the church and, when their lives are touched, tell more people of their church's strengths. With this flood of participants, however, come numerous unforeseen difficulties that make abundance a burden as much as a blessing.

Many of the people who come through the doors of megachurches are younger, often less-churched, and less likely to be cradle denominational members. These are people for whom the words "challenge" and "commitment" have little meaning. They are looking to be touched personally by God or even just entertained by the worship service. Because of these factors, church leadership must intentionally school them in a deeper understanding of the Christian lifestyle that includes how to serve others by giving of themselves through their time and money. This is typically a long-term process at which the megas must and do become skilled. Most megachurch pastors will tell you that it takes a lot of intentional effort and long periods of time to bring many of those attracted to megachurches into responsible Christian stewardship.

Likewise, because of their rapid growth, nearly all of these congregations occupy buildings that are insufficient for their needs. Only one of the five ELCA megachurches from the FACT study claimed to have sanctuaries, classrooms, and parking space adequate for the attendance. Nearly all of these five ELCA churches were in significantly smaller buildings (seating fewer in their sanctuaries) than the majority of national megachurches.

Most pastors of very large ELCA churches acknowledge in candid moments that even though they feel blessed that so many are coming, they believe there is at least as much stress in rapid growth as there is in decline. The rapid, sometimes chaotic expansion of staff and facilities almost always requires an initial budgetary leap of faith and trust in God to provide. At the outset of rapid growth, these congregations almost never have the money to pay for what they commit to in order to serve the influx of new members.

Intentional Ministries: Something for Everyone

Once these thousands of persons are in attendance, they must, as suggested above, be cared for. These large congregations are marked by a caring intentionality, not just of bringing people in, but more importantly of incorporating them into the life of the church. All the ELCA megachurches surveyed in the FACT study stated that new members were easily incorporated into the life of the church. All had programs to attend to new members' needs, including small groups, new members' classes, and formal channels to involve initiates in the ministries of the church. Two of the ELCA megas surveyed in depth had special visitor parking, and two also assigned "mentors" to shepherd new folks into the life of the congregation.

While on staff at Community Lutheran during the mid to late 1990s, one of the authors spotted an interesting trend that may be common to all the very large ELCA churches. It is best described by the new member's comment, "We have attended for ten years." When attenders were tracked through a database, the author was amazed to learn that although membership was around 3,200, there was an unacknowledged "shadow" congregation that included between 1,200 and 1,500 nonmembers at any given moment. This meant that the congregation's total pool of participants was actually nearly 40 percent larger than the membership record showed. This trend also seems to be developing through the entire denomination. In a survey of more than 43,000 ELCA attenders in congregations of all sizes, 5.3 percent said they were not members but regularly participated in the life of the congregation.

At Community Lutheran, faithful nonmembers were labeled "friends" of the congregation rather than "guests." These "less organizationally committed" persons could be seen as "free riders" — going to church for the benefits with few of the costs; but this conclusion would be somewhat inaccurate. Many in this group attended worship, and a number participated in activities and contributed money to Community Lutheran on a regular basis. Some even tithed! There is a simultaneous blessing and curse in this "shadow" congregation. Although they contributed their time, talent, and resources to the congregation, a comparison revealed that their contributions were less per capita than those of the members. At the same time, they took up just as much space and resources as fully participating members. And yet without them, the congregation might not be mega-sized, so this "shadow" did perform a valuable function.

Deepening the Faith: No Longer Spectators

Many very large ELCA congregations place strong emphasis on deepening the prayer life, devotional time, spirituality, and relationships of those who attend. This is accomplished through a variety of methods that include small groups, prayer and study circles, and service ministries; congregational councils and spiritual leadership groups (as opposed to operating committees, though this is not the case in all megas); and faith-deepening educational classes for adults and youth. For instance, in the entire group of forty-three large churches, the average church school attendance is 1,222 pupils and 168 educational leadership staff. What results from these efforts is the development of an expanded core of committed Christians within the congregation who choose to live out their faith by contributing time and talent to the church. As we've seen above, the FACT research shows that the typical megachurch has more than three hundred people who give five hours or more each week to their congregation. Other in-depth research by one of the authors showed that, additionally, many hundreds more members volunteered their time on a somewhat less regular basis, and over half the attenders were engaged in ministry outside the church itself.

Very large churches realize that within the gifts and dedication of their committed Christians, they also have the resources and means to make considerable contributions back to the community and the world. All megachurches have self-created, internally funded outreach ministry and mission programs from food pantries and clothes closets to health clinics and substance abuse recovery programs. Many also plan and run their own missionary efforts. For example, Community Lutheran goes to El Salvador each year to build a church building in a base community. In 2000, this congregation gave the Salvadoran Synod $400,000 in support. It has also built a school of natural medicine and supports several sewing schools in El Salvador. Locally, the church's thrift store funds numerous outreach efforts including its own prison and social ministries programs, in addition to contributing to Lutheran Social Ministries of Nevada and other denominational efforts.

An examination of the levels of mission giving of the forty-three largest ELCA churches reveals further interesting patterns of outreach giving. The giving to ELCA mission support for these congregations was just 3.6 percent of their income compared to nearly 6 percent for all ELCA churches. When one includes other specific denominational giving categories such as World Hunger Appeal, synod benevolence, missionary sponsorship, and designated giving, these forty-three largest Lutheran churches gave the denomination 7.4 percent of their income compared to 8 percent by all ELCA churches. If the very large churches' local community and other benevolence giving is also included in their total mission giving, however, they actually give 10.4 percent of their income compared to exactly 10 percent, on average, for all ELCA churches. Therefore, even though they are giving a smaller percentage of their income to denominational mission and service efforts, they are actually giving slightly more than the average ELCA church to mission efforts as a whole. It is also worth noting that these forty-three churches (less than .4 percent of all ELCA churches) contributed 4 percent of the total ELCA benevolence collected by the denomination in 2000.

ELCA Megachurches — How Denominational Are They?

The patterns of giving to the denomination found in the large churches raises the often unspoken question about megachurches: how denominationally loyal are they? To suggest an answer for this we must briefly examine the relationship between church size and denominational loyalty. When the FACT study looked at denominational identity across the total 14,300 congregations of all denominations, the rule of thumb was that the larger the FACT congregations were, the weaker their denominational identity. In addition, the overall study found no relationship between percent of growth in the past five years and denominational identity. The congregations of the Evangelical Lutheran Church in America, however, were the exception to both these findings.

The FACT data showed that ELCA congregations of all sizes not only had significantly higher identification with the denomination than did the rest of the mainline Protestant churches, but that this identity also created a distinctive growth dynamic. Denominationally strong ELCA churches were considerably more likely to be larger and more populated with persons who had come in the past five years than the rest of the mainline FACT denominational churches. Likewise, the highest denominationally identified congregations differed considerably from those less identified churches. The denominationally strong congregations more often described their worship as uplifting and inspirational. They saw their congregations as being vital and alive with a clear sense of mission and purpose at a greater rate than others. They were also more likely to be excited about the future of the congregation.

This optimistic picture of Lutheran identity and congregational size may be slightly less rosy for the very largest Lutheran churches, however. For the five large ELCA congregations in the FACT megachurch study, only one indicated that the phrase "having a strong denominational heritage" described itself "quite well"; three said "somewhat well," and one said the phrase fit "slightly well." In addition, none of these congregations used resources that were "solely" or "mostly" from denomination sources. In fact, a majority of these five created their own resources or went outside the denomination for them. These congregations were also more likely to engage in joint worship, nonworship programs, and cooperative social outreach with churches of other denominational traditions than they were with congregations of the ELCA. As seen above, the forty-three largest Lutheran churches give a smaller percentage of their income to denominational mission funds, but more to outside mission efforts. Likewise, many of the largest Lutheran megas have undertaken efforts to create networks of information and identity around themselves. Three of the five ELCA megas studied by FACT sponsor church-based ministerial conferences, and four of the five congregations have planted either one or two new churches. Two have radio programs and one has been on television.

A Bioscopic View of Megachurches

Early in this chapter we implied that not everyone held these very large congregations in high esteem. The opinions of average Lutherans regarding these megachurches are considerably mixed, and can best be expressed as, "It depends on who you ask!" In a recent unsystematic, and admittedly nonrepresentative, survey of over a dozen ELCA pastors and lay leaders attending a conference on transformational leadership, we found considerable diversity of opinion. A majority of those (although not everyone) we spoke to expressed rather positive impressions of megachurches, which included comments about their innovative and exciting worship, their effective ministries, and the belief that they are the "yardstick by which all congregations are measured." On the other hand, most of these interviewees also reported that many of the comments they hear from others are less than flattering; for example: "Megachurches are only about entertainment"; "They don't participate well with others"; and "They are just another sales pitch." Likewise, nearly all these persons assessed the relationship between megas and the denomination to be suspicious at best, and often downright tense. When asked whether they thought there was an implicit desire on the part of smaller churches to "be like the megas," the responses were also quite mixed. Finally, nearly all those questioned were certain that a theological stance of "bigness equaling God's blessing" was incorrect. Rather, they saw "God's hand and blessing on all sizes of churches," or, in the words of another interviewee, "We can get larger by getting smaller congregations and get larger by getting larger congregations."

Thus, even from this unsystematic sampling, it is apparent that opinions are mixed regarding the very large churches in the ELCA. Perhaps there is less animosity than in previous years, but misconceptions and prejudices still remain. Megachurches have much to teach smaller churches about intentional discipling of new members in small group ministries and the components of quality worship and innovative programs. On the other hand, smaller churches can be instructive to the megas in how to care for individuals and, especially, how to contribute to joint cooperative ventures without always being the center of attention. Faithfulness to the mission of Christ as it is lived out by deepening both faith and relationships to God and others, not size, should be the measure of congregational vitality. With that as the standard, churches in both categories, and every size in-between, can benefit and learn from each other.

The Future of Megachurches

What, then, is the future of the megachurch in the ELCA? Between 2000 and 2001, two more congregations crossed the thousand-at-worship line. Likewise, there is little indication in the larger American culture that the idea of "bigger is better" will diminish anytime soon. Over the past thirty years the total number of megachurches in the United States has continued to increase. Although still a minute percentage of all churches, in recent years megas have inordinately captured the attention of the clergy and the press alike. For the foreseeable future, therefore, these large churches are here to stay, and their ranks are more likely to swell than decline.

A look at the overall ELCA denominational figures portrays a distinctively different reality from that of the national megachurch picture, however. A recent report, *Ministry Needs and Resources in the 21st Century,* showed that from 1988 to 1998 the number of ELCA churches with average worship attendance of fifty or fewer increased by 21 percent. In 1998, over one-third of all ELCA congregations had seventy-five or fewer attenders and 50 percent had a hundred or fewer in attendance each Sunday. Likewise, attendance records from 1997 to 2000 showed that nearly 42 percent of ELCA congregations declined in attendance by 5 percent or more and another 30 percent had stagnant membership figures.

Given these facts, what then ought to be the role of ELCA megachurches in an increasingly downsized and small-church dominated denomination? What should the relationship be between megas, who can sometimes act as though they are synods-unto-themselves, and the ELCA synods and denomination? What and how should smaller congregations learn from these giants? Conversely, what is the most appropriate way for megas to contribute to the denomination? What might it mean for the denomination or for the collective psyches of ELCA churches and congregational leaders that over 10 percent of the growing congregations are the very large ones? Where will the denomination focus its resources, and what examples will it raise up as vital and effective congregations?

We don't have answers for these difficult questions. They remain for the denomination and clergy in congregations of all sizes to wrestle over. These are not, however, questions that can be answered by a "David versus Goliath" mentality toward megas. Nor can the denomination come to an adequate resolution if the understanding is that the "true Christian expression of church" can be found only in a particular size of congregation. Rather, like the different parts of the body, each size of congregation — mega, moderate, and small — contributes gifts and functionality to the whole body of Christ.

BIBLIOGRAPHY

Faith Communities Today Survey, Hartford Seminary, 2001. This survey can be accessed at http://hirr.hartsem.edu/org/faith_megachurches .html.

Miller, Donald E. *Reinventing American Protestantism: Christianity in the New Millennium.* Berkeley: University of California Press, 1997.

Pritchard, Gregory A. *Willow Creek Seeker Services: Evaluating a New Way of Doing Church.* Grand Rapids: Baker, 1996.

Schaller, Lyle E. *The Seven-Day-A-Week Church.* Nashville: Abingdon, 1992.

———. *The Very Large Church.* Nashville: Abingdon, 2000.

Thumma, Scott. Database of Megachurches in the U.S. Http://hirr. hartsem.edu/org/faith_megachurches_database.html (accessed September 13, 2002).

———. "Exploring the Megachurch Phenomena: Their Characteristics and Cultural Context." Http://hirr.hartsem.edu/bookshelf/thumma _article2.html (accessed September 19, 2002).

———. "The Kingdom, the Power, and the Glory: Megachurches in Modern American Society." Ph.D. diss., Emory University, 1996.

————. "Megachurches Today: Summary of Data from the Faith Communities Today Project." Http://hirr.hartsem.edu/org/faith_megachurches_FACTsummary.html (accessed August 10, 2002).

Vaughan, John N. *Megachurches and America's Cities: How Churches Grow.* Grand Rapids: Baker, 1993.

Lutheran Charismatics — Renewal or Schism?

ROBERT LONGMAN

When the charismatic movement began in the late 1960s, it seemed such a small thing — a few college fellowships, or a congregation here or there, where the experiences that were once thought of as belonging to "Holy Rollers" were being lived out by people in the mainstream churches. And church people wondered if this would grab a few headlines and go away, or grow and become a full part of church life. By the time the 1970s came, the charismatics were clearly here to stay. The new question was, would my congregation be ripped apart by it? (Unfortunately, for some, the answer was yes.) By the end of the 1970s, just about every major denomination had a charismatic movement within it, Lutherans included. In some denominations, such as Catholicism, Methodism, and Anglicanism, these movements found a home — not always a comfortable home, but a home nonetheless. For a while, it seemed that this would be true of Lutherans, too, as the movement grew in prominence and to a lesser extent in numbers. But some time in the 1980s, the engines stalled. A lot of it had to do with the way Lutherans do things. Lutherans think and study, and then act in an orderly fashion, while charismatics live in experiences that have reshaped them, showing in their relationships surprises and quick moves. Problems have come both from the attitudes of church leaders and seminaries and from the attitudes of those in the charismatic movement toward the rest of the church. And those with a sense of history remembered that Luther in his day fanatically opposed fanatics who bore some resemblance to many Pentecostalists.

Now we are in the twenty-first century. The questions are changing once again. And they are changing not just for the church as a whole, but also for the no-longer-young charismatic movements. The whole church faces a much more cynical world, where organized religions (including Lutherans and charismatics) have often acted in ways that make the cynicism grow. And we have all grown more cynical about each other, especially about our ability and willingness to listen, learn, change, and work together. So we have questions about each other: What is the state of the charismatic movement among Lutherans? Where is it heading? How does it affect the noncharismatic Lutheran churches? And is it helping to bring people in the general public to a robust faith in Christ?

Charismatics in the ELCA

The heartbeat of the American Lutheran charismatic movement is where it was twenty years ago, at North Heights Lutheran Church in Arden Hills/St. Paul, Minnesota. North Heights' old church building on Rice Street is home to the International Lutheran Renewal Center (ILRC) and Lutheran Renewal, directed by the Reverend Paul Anderson, with Dan Siemens as ministry coordinator and emeritus director Larry Christonson. The website contains links to their seminars and congregation-based renewal weeks. Updates are spotty and there is little information on an itinerary for their activity. There is not much material that would be helpful to a lay member or to someone trying to learn what a Lutheran renewal is like. Nor is there anything to indicate where one can find a congregation that identifies itself as "charismatic Lutheran." Most movements find it crucial to make those kinds of information freely available. There is also evidence that Lutheran Renewal has episodic problems raising money.

For the past fifteen years or so, the charismatic movement has represented no more than 5 percent of ELCA pastors and laity (based on an estimate of around 250,000 charismatics in the ELCA). Another 5 percent or so would not call themselves charismatics but share in much of what is happening among them. Most of these were from the predecessor American Lutheran Church (ALC), where congregational independence and a Lutheran pietism that valued faith experiences made charismatic ideas easier to accept. The charismatics' numbers haven't changed much since the late 1980s. They were never as big as they seemed to be in the early 1980s, when the charismatics were an active and growing group. But when well-known sympathizers such as Richard Jensen and Donald Matzat stepped away from the movement, it marked the end of its rise. Some members have "leaked out" into other churches, hoping to find a church that more fully treasures their experiences. Some switch to charismatic Episcopal and Methodist congregations. (The ELCA's growing involvement with the Episcopal Church may put it back in touch with these "leakers.") Many others leave for independent congregations — especially for startup missions that meet in old church or lodge buildings, school auditoriums, warehouses, and banquet halls.

The mainstream of the ELCA puts aside its movements the "mainline Protestant" way: it ignores them in hopes they will go away, and trains seminarians away from the movement. (This has been done against Lutheran pietism for several generations.) At the denominational level, charismatics are merely "there," left to themselves on the edges of the church. ELCA charismatics rarely take an active role in shaping church-wide pronouncements, policies, ministries, or activities. In the day-to-day life of the ELCA, charismatics do not give input, and ELCA leaders do not seek or want it from them. Beneath the veneer of diplomatic words there have been fifteen years of mutual avoidance and general disregard.

This situation, and the usual inefficiencies and stiffnesses of bureaucracy, have led Lutheran Renewal to develop a renewal support network, the Alliance of Renewal Churches (ARC). The ARC calls itself a "new wineskin," a network in which the member congregations and ministries give each other a full and fairly intensive level of support, sharing, and interchange. It does not ask or require that a congregation leave its denomination. But the stated reasons for the ARC question the whole idea of staying within the existing church bodies. For instance, on the Lutheran Renewal website's description of the ARC, it states:

> There was a bureaucracy with commissions and committees, and its constitution and bylaws were the product of past mergers of Lutheran bodies with all their historical concerns and compro-

mises. Missions, publications, and curriculums were directed by the central offices. These structures have proven less than optimal at serving their members during an unprecedented time of change.[1]

In the April 2002 Lutheran Renewal newsletter, church structure is likened to the human skeleton, which is only seen when it is broken. "A visible skeleton," it says, "is as grotesque as a church convention where feuds and voting procedures and platform speeches overshadow relationships, where the purpose for gathering is to do rather than to be. Many have quit attending these 'family functions.'"[2] And in the draft ARC proposal, it says, "When the form no longer fits, it needs to be put to rest, which means decisive, intentional, organizational change."[3]

Many Lutheran charismatic leaders, including those at North Heights, have concluded that being part of the ELCA is not worth the time and trouble. Hence the recent decision of North Heights to leave the ELCA, a decision that will be followed by several other congregations. They want to delve deeper into practices of what Peter Wagner terms the "New Apostolic" churches, such as modern prophecy during meetings and worship, ministries of deliverance from demonic harassment, spiritual warfare mapping, and leaders who are empowered to act in their sphere of responsibility. Nearly all ELCA officials and teachers find most of these practices to be suspect, but many charismatics see them as outgrowths of what they have believed all along. (For instance, deliverance ministries were discussed in Larry Christianson's book, *Welcome Holy Spirit,* published in 1987, but they were not nearly as important then as they are among many independent churches today.)

The charismatics want no part of the new sexual and medical moralities supported by the church-wide offices, and believe that in the new sexuality studies proposed by the ELCA leadership, the fix is already in. They see the starting of new congregations as a task for existing congregations and new support networks, not denominations. They have a growing belief that accountability and theology are less important than acting on what they believe are the leadings of the Spirit, with

1. This description can be found through http://www.lutheranrenewal.org.

2. The newsletter can be found at http://www.lutheranrenewal.org/archives/april2002/newsletter_4.html.

3. This proposal can be accessed through http://www.lutheranrenewal.org.

accountability brought in mostly after the fact through relationships with leadership peers. Lutheran charismatics are far from alone in their frustrations with denominational structures: the Word Alone opponents of the historic episocpate created the Lutheran Churches in Mission for Christ (LCMC) network, which sidesteps the ELCA much as the ARC does. (The LCMC does more in supporting ministers' benefits, while the ARC helps the congregation shape its daily ministries. Neither group asks the congregation to leave their denomination, but both lead people to ask, "why stay?" and give them support ministries if they do leave.) In a way, this hearkens back to the ALC, which was more congregational and personal than the ELCA. The ALC could officially say, "We freely enter into relationships with other congregations and voluntarily give a portion of our freedom to the church at large. Our pastors, district presidents, and congregations are a support system."[4] American culture rails against any kind of hierarchy or organization, whether it be a business, government, charitable bureaucracy, or religious denominational office, even as it creates the largest such institutions in history. Lutherans are proving not to be any different.

The draft ARC statement says that its "values and visions" will be more key to its operation than its Statement of Faith, in order that it can be "relationship-based and function/action-oriented" as well as "vision-directed."[5] But to say "Lutheran" is precisely to say that a vision for the future arises from a special way (or "theology") of approaching the Christian faith. It is not just the grace alone/faith alone/word alone formulas. It is also an incarnational and sacramental view of the life we lead and the world we live in: God's loving grace, presence, strength, and attention coming through the stuff and the people of this material world. The Lutheran vision is centered on the crucified Christ, whom we meet in the Eucharist and in Scripture. This heritage, and not what one pastor called "a jones for the new," is what guides a Lutheran's action.

Several charismatic ministers have expressed fear that due to the liturgical evangelical catholic movement, the ELCA is paying most of

4. Paul D. Opsahl, ed., *The Holy Spirit in the Life of the Church: From Biblical Times to the Present* (Minneapolis: Augsburg, 1978), p. 249.

5. See the "Questions and Answers about the ARC" section of the Statement of the Alliance of Renewal Churches, which can be accessed at http://www.lutheranrenewal.org.

its attention to the duties and powers of the clergy. "We're turning more clergy-oriented at the moment in history that the laity are best poised to lead," one said. This worries a charismatic movement that picks up many of its cues from lay members. Yet the movement itself has a train of thought that could eventually lead back to structure and authority: the idea that the Spirit selects leaders, and as they emerge, the rest of the church should see its role as carriers of the vision which the leader calls forth. The strengths and weaknesses of this approach have been shown in other Christian churches. If someone expresses strong doubts about the vision or course of action, he or she is often seen to be calling into question the Holy Spirit, who is presumed to be giving the main leader his or her vision. Such people are often labeled as naysayers and are asked to leave. That leaves less room for lay discernment and learning, and can create fear. When oversight peers do most of the discernment, a conflict of interest may evolve if the overseeing peers develop a stake in what their guidance helped create. This is only partially checked by calling on leaders to be servants and to empower others; in real life, leaders are more likely to serve and empower those who support them.

The appeal to a relationship-based structure is supported by likening the church to a family. And in many ways it is like a family, according to Scripture. But the church is not really a family as we know families here on earth. It's just too big, and we know too few of each other. Families don't bear witness so that outsiders can join the family; families tend to distrust outsiders. Earthly families often fall well short of the ideal — few fights are more brutal than those in a family. Trust sometimes seems betrayed when it is not; or, when trust is betrayed, the betrayal is often let slide for family's sake — at least until that betrayal births the next betrayals. The church may be called the family of God, but it is made of people, and the history of the charismatic movement is filled with congregations that split and fell apart because of the emotions of these family feuds. All "family" talk must keep such things in mind.

There is, however, a good structural question lurking under this leadership dialogue. Is it better for a congregation or synod to operate through layers of committees and councils (as now)? Or, if someone emerges who is clearly gifted in a certain ministry, is it best to give that person the authority to lead that ministry or do that task (as charismatics do), and let them just do it? The ARC is issuing the call, but how many will join into this high-commitment alliance? Outside of a couple dozen congregations, there does not appear to be much lay Lutheran interest in taking up the New Apostolic approach. In the early 1980s, the ILRC disappointed many would-be supporters by its openness to ideas from the Shepherding Movement of Ern Baxter and Derek Prince (stressing one-on-one mentoring in discipleship). Could Lutheran Renewal be doing it again? (The key presence of "prophet" Rick Joyner at their 2002 gathering suggests that possibility.) Or will the Alliance free them to be a creative force in the church universal?

Renewal in the Missouri Synod

The main organization of renewal in the Lutheran Church–Missouri Synod is Renewal In Missouri (RIM). Its director is Delbert Rossin in Wisconsin, and much of the apparent strength of RIM is in the Great Lakes area. The RIM's website posts some articles by Dr. Theodore Jungkuntz, mostly as an apologetic and theological polemic to answer RIM's critics. The RIM website is more forthcoming than the ILRC site about who is involved, in that member pastors and towns are listed (but not matched to congregations or addresses). The articles on the site are useful mainly to a visitor who is well-versed in LCMS theology and controversies. Thus the website fails to be helpful to lay members who are trying to find out about Lutheran charismatic faith and practice for themselves, or to a curious nonbeliever. Judging from descriptions given by interviewed ministers, Missouri Synod charismatics have the support of around 8 percent of pastors, about 4 percent of members. In the politics of a denomination, a group that small can usually be safely ignored, and in most districts it is ignored. Most charismatics tend toward the "moderate" side of LCMS controversies because of their interchurch contacts, and because their approach to worship is a special target of the "conservative" faction and most seminary professors. Their ideas sometimes show up church-wide in evangelism and church planting, but LCMS charismatic pastors often face opposition in their own congregations from more "traditional" members.

Nearly all of the rostered LCMS pastors interviewed for this chapter were very careful in what they said, even with the promise of anonymity. They gave a uniform pattern of response; this included handing out the official LCMS guidelines from 1972 and 1977, speaking in vague terms about how the gifts of the Spirit were given to all members as the Spirit sees fit, stating that their congregations use these gifts where they show up (they did not give specific examples), and repeating the refrain that "we follow Scripture."

It will take time to see how much more breathing room the new Missouri Synod president will give for RIM-oriented pastors. Most of the interviews for this chapter were conducted well after the new president was elected, but he was already under fire for supporting looser reins on district presidents. The official questioning of Dr. Jungkuntz's theology has lessened but could restart at any time. The interviewed pastors were still acting with great care to avoid conflict. "At least we will have less fear," said one pastor, "but will we have more freedom?"

Since the 1970s, the pace of developments from charismatics has been breathtaking: new styles and formats in worship and music; the Toronto and Pensacola revivals; the rise of Vineyard churches and large independent congregations that operate differently than traditional Pentecostal churches; the rise of small groups for fellowship, study, and prayer (these were always important to charismatics, but have since become common for all kinds of churches); a moving away from the "tongues required" approach by many Pentecostalist congregations and leaders; a new interest in tradition and spiritual disciplines among some charismatics and Pentecostalists; a rising interest in modern prophecy (especially during worship and small group meetings); strong disputes among charismatics over the offices of "prophet" and "apostle"; the men's ministry Promise Keepers; the Alpha Course; the televangelist scandals (most of these evangelists were far-end Pentecostalists); the boom in parachurch ministries (often supported or formed by Pentecostalists); the rise of a new approach to spiritual warfare, involving deliverance ministries and strategic mapping of neighborhoods and cities so that the centers of evil can be the subject of prayer; the attention some Lutheran charismatics have paid to their theological critics; the continuing relationship of mainline Protestant charismatics with independent and Catholic charismatics; scholarly studies by Finnish Lutherans on matters of the Spirit and on Reformation-era Lutherans; and the rise of Pentecostal urban churches that are very active and well-rooted in their neighborhoods.

Each of these teaches all of us something about how to be the church today, and each has implications for practice and theology that are simply not addressed in the 1972 and 1977 reports. The track record shows that charismatic churches actively create ministries and formats that benefit the day-to-day life of congregations and ministries of all kinds, including those in the LCMS. Such benefits grow from a view of church and of mission that is shaped more by action ("following the Spirit") than by theology or tradition (even their own). The LCMS reports dealt so much with theology and so little with the way charismatics live their faith that the reports seem out of touch with what they are describing, even for the 1970s. It could be helpful for Lutheran ministers and lay leaders to have a thorough, accurate, and up-to-date look at the impact on Lutherans of charismatic movements both inside and outside of Lutheranism, as they sort out the many crosscurrents that charismatics create. Such an investigation might only be credible, however, if it were led from outside of official circles.

Charismatic Renewal in Other Lutheran Churches

The American Association of Lutheran Churches (AALC) is a small denomination of churches that did not join in the ELCA merger. Originally made up of ALC congregations in the Midwest, it included early on several charismatic congregations. Trinity, San Pedro, California, which led Lutheran charismatics in the 1960s and '70s, is in the AALC. Most AALC churches show little interest in the more esoteric charismatic practices, but a renewal flavor comes through in most of what they do. The AALC contains many small congregations and newly planted churches that could benefit from some of what the ARC and other independent support networks have to offer. There is very little evidence that the AALC grows by members joining it from other Lutheran churches. Even a small leak of individual charismatics from the ELCA into the AALC (say, 0.1 percent of ELCA membership) would have a powerful impact on so small a denomination. So far, changes in total membership have come mostly as congregations join or leave the AALC.

The Association of Free Lutheran Churches (AFLC) is a group of highly independent pietist churches that arose from Lutheran Free Churches that did not join the ALC merger in 1962. Other churches joined it when the ELCA was created. They have many things in common with churches from the Word Alone/LCMC movement, but there is not much of a charismatic movement in the AFLC. This is not to say that these churches have escaped charismatic influences. They too sing songs and pray prayers differently because of the charismatics' influence. Several of the pastors are involved with Lutheran Renewal. And as pietists, they too stress experiencing the faith and personal commitment to Christ. For most of them, it adds up differently than for the charismatics, but there is much common ground.

There is no visible charismatic movement in any of the other splinter Lutheran churches, nor in the Wisconsin Synod.

Charismatic Influence across the Board

Though only a small percentage of Lutherans could be classified as charismatics, many Lutheran congregations have been affected by the charismatic movement in some way. When they sing a song such as "Shine Jesus Shine" or "Seek Ye First," they draw on charismatic music. When they hold an Alpha Course, they draw on Anglican charismatic education. When they string together praise and psalm songs in their "contemporary" worship services, they draw from Pentecostal worship. When they hold a men's group meeting, odds are strong it is a part of (or a response to) Promise Keepers, which was created by Pentecostalists. When they become part of a Cursillo activity, they draw on Catholic charismatic practices. When they attend a "Concert of Prayer" or get involved in a "city reaching" urban mission, they take part in movements started by Pentecostalists. These innovations didn't come from Lutheran charismatics. Time and time again, they came from outside the Lutheran church. In those other traditions, charismatics are always coming up with new ways to help the typical congregation fill the gaping holes in congregational life and personal devotions. These are things a congregation can choose to take up on its own, without the necessity of having outsiders come in to run a program, and without having to beg a bishop or district president for permission.

Perhaps the most broadly accepted theological influence on Lutherans is on the way we speak of the charisms, or gifts that the Spirit gives to all baptized Christians in order to build up the fellowship of believers, the church. Even die-hard anti-charismatics often use charismatic language on this subject. "I can't argue with Saint Paul," one professor quipped. Opponents argue about what kinds of gifts build up the church and what is still being given by the Spirit, but they do not argue against the fact of such gifting, nor do they disagree about how important it is for a congregation and a denomination to put those gifts to use.

Strangely enough, Lutherans are having an impact on Pentecostalists and charismatics in at least one way. In the past decade, many charismatic and Pentecostalist churches are showing a greater interest in liturgy, and especially in Holy Communion, sometimes even emphasizing Christ's presence in the elements of bread and wine. Those who are doing this cite not only Catholic, Orthodox, and Anglican sources, but also Lutheran liturgists such as Frank Senn and Philip Pfatteicher. But again, the pattern holds: the liturgists they cite are mainstream Lutheran liturgists who share few sympathies with charismatic Lutherans.

Prospects for the Future

Most of the Lutheran charismatic laity interviewed for this chapter (admittedly, from the Coasts and not the Midwest) sought to distance themselves from much of what has been happening in some of the more famous revivalist churches: barking like dogs, Jesus-Only baptisms, lack of Bible roots, prosperity gospels, self-styled "prophets," name-it-claim-it prayers, gold fillings, and "acting like there's a devil around every corner" (as one put it). They were not aware that a growing number of charismatic and independent congregations are also moving away from such behavior. The opportunity to discover some common ground with these non-Lutheran Christians may be lost because we don't know each other. Even more, Lutherans lack a strategy for relating to the unhierarchical independent congregations and congregational networks, even though there are many ways we can build each other up. Such a strategy would also prove helpful in relating to Baptist, Disciples of Christ (Christian), and United Church of Christ congregations, which have wide control over their own activities.

Most noncharismatic Lutherans queried for this chapter say they are open to pursuing new ways to live in the Spirit. Nevertheless, the track record is that they will adapt not from charismatic Lutherans but from non-Lutheran charismatics, and also from those in other liturgical churches. They look elsewhere for leadership and creativity. Noncharismatics don't even know what charismatic Lutherans are doing. They borrow much, but give back little that is new. "What can we give them?" one asked; "Potluck dinners?" There is much the Lutheran church culture and theological tradition can give to other Christians, but the laity interviewed for this chapter had no courage of conviction about it.

The most likely new arena for Lutherans to adapt from charismatics is on matters of prayer. C. F. W. Walther wrote, "our churches are in truth houses of prayer in which Christians serve the great God publicly before the world."[6] Some Lutherans (not just charismatics) are already starting to reshape Lutheran prayer life so that the churches can once again be houses of prayer. They are using Moravian-inspired prayer vigils, Eastern Orthodox breath prayers (such as the Jesus Prayer), and Celtic and monastic ways of listening for God in private devotion. Charismatics (again, mostly non-Lutheran ones) are also having an impact, especially on the corporate aspect of prayer, the prayers we do with our fellow believers. Lutherans are starting to borrow such practices as

- meeting with other churches of all kinds regularly, just to pray;
- creating prayer groups dedicated to intercessory prayer;
- prayerwalking the church and church grounds, to pray for each activity therein;
- prayerwalking the congregation's neighborhood, praying in specific places for specific needs;
- commissioning prayer leaders, assigned deacons, and gifted intercessors;
- designating a prayer team to pray during the pastor's sermon for the Spirit to move through the sermon (an idea that Pentecostalists preserved from nineteenth-century Baptist preacher Charles Spurgeon);
- prayer services for healing that dare to pray for more than just "comfort" or "inner healing";

6. C. F. W. Walther, *Essays for the Church*, vol. 1 (St. Louis: Concordia, 1992), p. 194.

- taking time during the worship service to pray in groups of three to five people on church and personal concerns;
- prayer as a central part of congregational decision-making, especially with committees and ministry groups that become prayer groups for their area of responsibility;
- designating prayer chapel rooms that are open for as many hours as is safe;
- prayer areas in gardens or on hills, especially for prayer at dawn;
- the use of "concert prayer," in which all offer their individual praises, thanks, and pleas aloud at the same time.

Will such changes take hold across Lutherandom? It may take a popular catalyst to accomplish this. Perhaps this may come from the new postmodern ministries, which are already reshaping their prayer practices from much the same sources. But once again, most postmodern ministries are from Pentecostalists such as the Vineyard Ministries and Assemblies of God. There are, however, a few Lutherans in such postmodern ministries, and they may teach the rest; there is still time for charismatic Lutherans to step forward and lead the mainstream on prayer, if they would choose to get involved enough with the rest of the church to do so.

A Crossroad

It appears that charismatic Lutherans are at a fork in the road. On the one hand, they can choose to be defined by their Pentecostal-charismatic experience. Those choosing that path have already discovered that they will not win over, or even be a major force in, the ELCA or LCMS. They are already coming to the conclusion that the only way to fully pursue this course is by stepping aside, and eventually away, from their denomination. This will leave them open to the same currents that bring some questionable practices into the New Apostolic churches. But perhaps their approach is so different that it is best (and most spiritually honest) that they part with official Lutheranism and make their mistakes so they can learn from them and develop into a mature church in its own right, one that has much to contribute to the rest of Christianity and especially to Lutherans.

On the other hand, they can choose to be defined by looking at their faith and the Bible through the lens of the Lutheran theological heritage. Within that framework, Pentecostal experiences and charismatic practices can come into play a lot more than most Lutherans think possible — though as part of an overall picture, not the picture itself. They would continue to have the same frustrations with their denomination that they have now: bureaucratic structures without real relationships, officials who are not gifted at what they do, traditions that harden into traditionalism, lack of support for personal or congregational mission, the synod's "party line," acceptance of a back-pew way of life. Nevertheless, their response is different than that of those who leave the denomination: for all its weaknesses, this denomination is where scriptural truth tells them they as followers of Christ can be most true to Christ and most helpful to others. It's not as weird and wonderful as some other places, but it may be more true and real and whole.

As times change, so do movements. New issues present themselves, and old responses prove not to be worth keeping. People try different ways to live their faith. It often starts shallow and childish, but some will learn to stand up, then walk, then run, then race. It takes time to learn what really builds up the body of Christ on earth, time to think through the consequences, time to see how (or even whether) something relates to the real-life faith of today. Each new thing feeds into others. Then something or someone comes along to catalyze these streams into a movement. Think here of how Martin Luther took up the many currents of change into a powerful call to reform the Roman Catholic Church, eventually leading to the creation of Protestantism. Or, perhaps, how Billy Graham catalyzed the currents of the 1950s into American evangelicalism. Long before such movements come together, people start doubting the status quo — at first not because of new ideas but because of the mounting failures of the old ideas.

Such a time seems to be on the horizon, seemingly far off but maybe as near as an instant. Some charismatics are moving away from behaviors and ideas that are out of touch with biblical faith. Most charismatic Lutherans are among them. But to move away from somewhere is to move toward somewhere else. That "somewhere else" is not the mainline-Protestant paradigm, nor is it the traditional Catholicism that Catholic charismatics are edging toward, nor is it the older

Protestant scholasticism that led to spiritual death in so many congregations. Is something new growing out of the Lutheran charismatic movement? And if so, what will catalyze it? Only the Spirit knows.

BIBLIOGRAPHY

Barr, William, and Rena Yocom, eds. *The Church in the Movement of the Spirit.* Grand Rapids, Eerdmans, 1994.

Christianson, Larry. *Back to Square One.* Minneapolis: Bethany, 1979.

———. *The Charismatic Renewal among Lutherans: A Pastoral and Theological Perspective.* Minneapolis: ILRC, 1985 [1976].

———. *Speaking in Tongues.* Minneapolis: Bethany, 1968.

———, ed. *Welcome, Holy Spirit.* Minneapolis: Augsburg, 1987.

Http://www.lutheranrenewal.org/ (the Lutheran Renewal website).

Http://www.lutheranrenewal.org/publications.html (Lutheran Renewal's newsletters).

Http://home.attbi.com/ gracelife/rim (website of Renewal In Missouri).

Http://www.nhlc.org/ (website of North Heights Lutheran Church, Arden Hills, Minnesota).

Http://www.bplc.org/ (website of Brooklyn Park Lutheran Church, Brooklyn Park, Minnesota).

Http://www.taalc.org/ (website of the AALC).

Jorstad, Erling. *Bold in the Spirit: Lutheran Charismatic Renewal in America Today.* Minneapolis: Augsburg, 1974.

Lindberg, Carter. *The Third Reformation?* Atlanta: Mercer University Press, 1983.

Opsahl, Paul D., ed. *The Holy Spirit in the Life of the Church: From Biblical Times to the Present.* Minneapolis: Augsburg, 1978. This work includes key official documents:

> The ALC's "The American Lutheran Church and Neo-Pentecostalism" (1975)
>
> The LCA's "The Charismatic Movement in the Lutheran Church in America" (1974)
>
> The LCMS's "The Lutheran Church and the Charismatic Movement" (1977)

Walther, C. F. W. *Essays for the Church,* vol. 1. St. Louis: Concordia, 1992.

II Trends and Issues in American Lutheranism

Pastors in the Two Kingdoms:
The Social Theology of Lutheran Clergy

JEFF WALZ, STEVE MONTREAL, AND DAN HOFRENNING

> *A potential crisis between theologically liberal Lutheran clergy and most lay members seems in its early stages. The bases for this schism already appear, and a more intense struggle seems ahead. The confrontation will be crucially important for the future of Lutheranism and Christianity.*
>
> Lawrence L. Kersten, *The Lutheran Ethic,* p. 217

Published in 1970, Lawrence Kersten's *The Lutheran Ethic* was a significant social scientific study that chronicled the growing divisions in American Lutheranism. Only a few years after the book's publication, the evangelical Lutheran Church–Missouri Synod (LCMS) was rent asunder by a schism at its St. Louis seminary that saw a walkout of many of its faculty to form an alternate seminary. As a result, the LCMS reestablished itself as a conservative, confessional church body. While affected by inner conflicts of their own, the Lutheran Church in America (LCA) and the American Lutheran Church (ALC) nonetheless merged in 1988 to form the Evangelical Lutheran Church in American (ELCA), a mainline denomination noted for its ecumenism. The Wisconsin Evangelical Lutheran Synod (WELS), meanwhile, has adhered to its strongly confessional nature, continuing to sit to the theological and political right of the LCMS in the American Lutheran church family.

We follow Kersten in this chapter by looking beyond these basic denominational differences and focusing on the identity today of one segment of American Lutheranism — clergy. Kersten noted divisions between clergy and laity within Lutheranism and differences among clergy in the LCA, ALC, LCMS, and WELS church bodies. It appears that at least in the ELCA, there continues to be a divide between liberal clergy and conservative members; this pastor-congregation ideological split is less evident in the LCMS and WELS. Kersten also described alternative identities among Lutheran pastors concerning political involvement. Our research confirms Kersten's view, suggesting that these Lutheran clergy divisions continue today, at least between the ELCA and LCMS. We found remarkable differences between these two clergy groups theologically, ideologically, and politically. Such differences portend a continuation of two separate groups of Lutheran clergy using different worldviews to pursue competing social agendas.

While many publications since 1970 have explored Lutheran theology, ethics, and church history, no social scientist since Kersten has conducted a thorough study of either Lutheran clergy or laity. Here we hope to begin to fill that research void by focusing on the political attitudes and activities of pastors within the ELCA and LCMS during the 2000 election year. Such an inquiry is crucial for at least four reasons. First, Lutherans make up a significant share of the American population, with the ELCA boasting 5.2 million members and the LCMS 2.6 million members. Second, there have been noteworthy political studies on clergy in other evangelical and Protestant camps,[1] yet very few on Lutheran pastors. Third, pastors who garner the respect of their parishioners can teach and encourage citizenship initiatives to a laity who, in Luther's words, should live out their vocations in society. Finally, American pastors are important political actors who have been crucial to the success of significant historical movements, such as the American Revolution, abolition, and civil rights.

Through a collaborative effort headed by Corwin Smidt at the Henry Institute of Calvin College, we compared and contrasted the political attitudes and activities of ELCA and LCMS clergy in the 2000

---

1. See, for example, James L. Guth, John C. Green, Corwin E. Smidt, Lyman A. Kellstedt, and Margaret M. Poloma, *The Bully Pulpit: The Politics of Protestant Clergy* (Lawrence: University of Kansas Press, 1997).

elections. (Unfortunately, no research team emerged to study WELS pastors.) Jeff Walz and Steve Montreal surveyed parish pastors in the LCMS, while Dan Hofrenning surveyed ELCA parish pastors. Each study used a random sample, with a sample size of approximately 1,500 parish pastors for each synod.

Lutheran Social Theology: The Two-Kingdoms Theory

The two-kingdoms theory of church and state is the central element in Lutheran social theology. H. Richard Niebuhr termed this model as "Christ and Culture in Paradox," the idea of allegiance to both heavenly and earthly kingdoms that is found in Luther's writings and in the Lutheran confessions. This model "best preserves and safeguards the Biblical tension" of rendering "therefore to Caesar the things that are Caesar's, and to God the things that are God's."[2] According to many critics, the greatest weakness of the two-kingdoms theory is in its "persistent passivity toward government," since government does not perform any gospel-based functions.[3] Though the ELCA and LCMS adhere to this common model in theory, the denominations diverge in applying this model to the twenty-first-century public square.

Indeed, there is significant agreement between the ELCA and the LCMS that the two-kingdoms theory should in principle provide a resource for political involvement. "Christians are simultaneously in the kingdom of the left hand, which includes the Law and secular reason, and the kingdom of the right hand, governed by grace and the Gospel."[4] To use St. Augustine's terminology, everyone is subject to two cities — the city of God and the city of man — that carry different expectations and responsibilities. The challenge is to separate spiritual righteousness from civil righteousness. The church embodies the city of God by its focus on things above. Below, civil governments blessed by God can be effective tools in creating and maintaining good and

2. *Render Unto Caesar . . . and Unto God: A Lutheran View of Church and State* (St. Louis: A Report of the Commission on Theology and Church Relations of the Lutheran Church–Missouri Synod, 1995), p. 33.

3. *Render Unto Caesar*, p. 33.

4. Angus Menuge, "Promoting Dialogue in the Christian Academy," Presentation for the CUW Faculty Retreat, Green Lake, Wisconsin (August 20-21, 2001), p. 3.

just societies. Christians can and should occupy civil offices and use them for society's good.

The problem, historically, has been that in practice the two-kingdoms theory leads to political passivity for some Lutheran church bodies and members. Afraid of being too sure of God's intent in a fallen world, LCMS pastors and parishioners have tended to defer to others on societal issues. Mark Noll notes[5] that Lutherans continue to be underrepresented in some aspects of the national political scene. No Lutheran has ever been president, and the highest national office filled by a Lutheran has been that of Chief Justice of the U.S. Supreme Court (William Rehnquist, 1986-present). Lutherans today, however, are actually over-represented in the 107th Congress, where twenty-one Lutherans reside in the House and Senate. While Lutherans comprise about 3 percent of the population — there were 8.57 million Lutherans in America in 1999, according to the Lutheran World Federation — the twenty-one members represent almost 4 percent of the 535 seats in the two Congressional chambers. The ELCA dominates this Lutheran membership; only two are Missouri Synod Lutherans (Representatives John Shimkus, R-Ill., and Doug Bereuter, R-Neb.). Some of this may stem from an LCMS denomination that has gone to great lengths to preserve its German theology and heritage, especially in the first half of the twentieth century. A larger piece of the puzzle, however, is social theology.

The LCMS, like other denominations, tries to avoid the extremes of becoming too politically apathetic or becoming overly involved, but it has tended to err on the passive side. Prior to his recent death, LCMS President Dr. A. L. Barry released a series of pamphlets on issues of importance to the church. In "What About . . . Pastors," Barry makes no mention of a public affairs component to clergy duties. "We must never allow other things to take priority over . . . key pastoral duties and activities."[6] On most issues, the church sees its impact through individual Christians pursuing their vocations in an indirect and unintentional influence, letting the Word speak for itself. The expectation is that individual Christians, in turn, will have "a transforming effect

5. Mark Noll, "The Lutheran Difference," *First Things* 20 (February 1992): 31-40.

6. A. L. Barry, "What About . . . Pastors" (St. Louis: The Lutheran Church–Missouri Synod, 2001).

upon the society in which they live."[7] Rather than a top down approach, with the church acting as an agent of societal change, the LCMS employs a bottom-up approach that sees its political influence coming through individuals.

The ELCA, on the other hand, has had fewer misgivings about entering the political arena. Unlike the LCMS, the ELCA as an institution has issued numerous positions on moral, social, and political issues of the day. For example, the ELCA issues social statements, messages, and social policy resolutions and statements that address a plethora of domestic and international issues. While the LCMS has focused on life and educational issues, the ELCA has concentrated on poverty and on environmental, women's, and racial issues. In any event, a Washington presence may best demonstrate the difference in political activity between the two synods: the ELCA has a Lutheran Office for Governmental Affairs (LOGA); due to budgetary constraints, the LCMS recently closed its Office of Government Information (OGI).

Part of the ELCA-LCMS political divide today — ELCA pastors are largely Democratic and LCMS pastors predominantly Republican — may have its roots in immigrant value systems.[8] Richard Jensen and Paul Kleppner suggest that in the nineteenth century, German Lutherans — the bulwark of what became the LCMS and what comprised much of the former LCA — subscribed to a ritualist model, while Scandinavian Lutherans — who form a foundation of today's ELCA — were pietist in their value systems and politics.[9] (The ELCA today has a sizable German block.)

Pietists encouraged government involvement at all levels to battle sin in its various forms, such as slavery, alcohol, and discrimination against women and immigrants. For much of the nineteenth century, the Republican Party upheld this activist model to which many Scandinavian Lutherans adhered. Today, it is the Democratic Party that believes in a more activist government. Ritualists, on the other hand,

---

7. *Render Unto Caesar*, p. 74.

8. Frederick C. Luebke, "Politics and Missouri Synod Lutherans: A Historiographical Review," *Concordia Historical Institute Quarterly* XLV, no. 2 (1972): 141-58.

9. See Richard Jensen, *The Winning of the Midwest: Social and Political Conflict* (Chicago: University of Chicago Press, 1971), and Paul Kleppner, *The Cross of Culture: A Social Analysis of Midwestern Politics, 1850 to 1900* (New York: Free Press, 1970).

were concerned with government intrusion into the personal rights of citizens, and were less likely to oppose slavery or alcohol. In fact, some ritualists believed that "to legislate morality was to threaten the authority of the church in spiritual matters."[10] Ritualists, including German Lutherans, wished to maintain traditional values through means outside of government, such as a system of parochial schools. The Democratic Party of the nineteenth century tended to be more receptive to this ritualistic agenda. Today, however, the Republican Party expresses more concern about governmental intrusion in citizens' lives. Thus, history may be a guide in explaining the roots of the Lutheran divide on the role of the church in society.

Another aspect of the Lutheran divide today is that clergy and laity relate very differently in the LCMS and ELCA. In the LCMS, the clergy and laity are much closer, theologically and politically, than in the ELCA. The LCMS, then, is a classic evangelical or orthodox church that focuses its mission on bringing the gospel — the good news of Jesus Christ as savior — to people worldwide. Involvement in political and social issues is of much less importance. The ELCA, on the other hand, has gone the way of mainline Protestantism, in which clergy tend to be more liberal, theologically and politically, than parishioners. Though focused on the gospel like LCMS clergy, ELCA pastors nonetheless exhibit a greater receptivity to and concern for the issues of this world.

Past Lutheran Divisions on Politics

The Kersten study cited above reinforces the central message of this chapter: LCMS pastors are aware of earthly problems brought on by human sin, but are fearful of allowing the kingdom of the left hand to dwarf the work of the kingdom of the right hand, the saving of souls for eternal salvation. ELCA pastors, on the other hand, are less fearful of engaging in a variety of political concerns that focus on a social justice agenda. Perhaps most importantly, Kersten noted denominational trends among clergy involvement in government and politics. Among both LCA and ALC clergy, "a theology of social reform and humanism

10. Luebke, "Politics and Missouri Synod Lutherans," p. 150.

seems to be replacing the traditional Lutheran emphasis on providing comfort in this world and soul-saving for the next."[11]

Kersten's work moved the frontiers of our understanding of Lutheran clergy politics forward. It emphasized the communitarian worldviews of the LCA and ALC clergy and the individualist worldviews of LCMS and WELS clergy.[12] As individualists, clergy on the Lutheran theological right continued to stress the "vertical" aspect of religion, including preaching the gospel and emphasizing personal morality.[13] As communitarians, clergy on the Lutheran theological left, while certainly not eschewing the gospel, put more emphasis on the "horizontal" aspect of religion, including the redemption of this world.[14]

Models of ELCA and LCMS Social Theology

In a contribution to Sue Crawford and Laura Olson's *Christian Clergy in American Politics*, James L. Guth presents a model of political activism among Southern Baptist clergy in 1996. Guth explains pastoral activity according to four theories of activism: personal resources, professional ideology, issue mobilization, and organizational activity. We use the outlines of Guth's model to explain the social theology of ELCA and LCMS clergy. *Personal resources* include factors such as socioeconomic status and psychological engagement, a pastor's propensity to be involved politically, political efficacy, and willingness to collaborate politically. *Professional ideology* encompasses a pastor's theological worldview, his view of the role of the church in the world, and what a pastor's specific political role should be. *Issue mobilization* is "the way in which political attachments, beliefs, and issues prompt

11. Lawrence L. Kersten, *The Lutheran Ethic* (Detroit: Wayne State University Press, 1970), p. 210.

12. David C. Leege and Lyman A. Kellstedt, eds., *Rediscovering the Religious Factor in American Politics* (Armonk, N.Y.: M. E. Sharpe, 1993).

13. George M. Thomas, *Revivalism and Cultural Change: Christianity, Nation Building, and the Market in the Nineteenth Century United States* (Chicago: University of Chicago Press, 1989).

14. Peter L. Benson and Dorothy L. Williams, *Religion on Capitol Hill: Myths and Realities* (San Francisco: Harper and Row, 1982).

people to become involved."[15] Finally, *organizational activity* taps areas such as denominational and congregational context, national political organizations, and campaign mobilization.

The levels of political activism of ELCA and LCMS pastors can be looked at in a couple of different ways. First is an additive index of the twenty-six questions that asked pastors whether they participated in any of a variety of political activities during the year 2000. As evidenced in Table 1, the average number of political activities engaged in by the LCMS pastors was 4.98, with a standard deviation of 4.46, while for the ELCA pastors the average number of activities was 5.91, with a standard deviation of 4.64. The average ELCA pastor commits almost one full political act more than the average LCMS pastor, a modest difference. Looking at the frequency distribution, one sees that 24.4 percent of the LCMS pastors reported no political activities for the year 2000, compared to 18.7 percent of the ELCA pastors. At the other end of the scale, 11.4 percent of LCMS and 17.3 percent of ELCA pastors participated in more than ten activities. Considering that the activity questions included items such as publicly (but not while preaching) taking a stand on some public issue, it is remarkable that so many of the pastors recorded no activity. Still, it is apparent from this data that ELCA pastors are indeed more politically active than their LCMS counterparts.

Table 1. Levels of Political Activity, 2000 (in percentages)

Number of Activities	LCMS	ELCA
More than 15	1.9	2.9
11-15	9.5	14.4
6-10	32.3	33.9
1-5	32.1	29.9
None	24.4	18.7
Mean	4.98	5.91
Standard Deviation	4.46	4.64

15. James L. Guth, "The Mobilization of a Religious Elite: Political Activism among Southern Baptist Clergy in 1996," in *Christian Clergy in American Politics,* ed. Sue E. S. Crawford and Laura R. Olson (Baltimore: Johns Hopkins University Press, 2001), p. 146.

Table 2 lists the different actions that comprise the index of activity. It is apparent that while there are some similarities in the types of activities pursued by the two groups of pastors, noteworthy differences do exist. Higher numbers of ELCA pastors signed petitions, organized a study group or an action group in their church, and were active participants in a local clergy council than the LCMS pastors. On eighteen of the twenty-six separate activities a higher percentage of ELCA pastors reported having engaged in that activity in 2000. It is safe to say that this is not a random pattern but further evidence of the higher levels of political involvement of the ELCA clergy.

A sizeable percentage of pastors said they actively supported their presidential candidate of choice in the last election: slightly over 28 percent of LCMS respondents chose to take an active role in helping their man get elected; the number was 22.5 percent for the ELCA. This action represents a much higher order of activism than many of the questions that make up the activism scale and does represent significant, if relatively narrow, engagement with the political system. In addition, there is evidence that all of these pastors would like to be more involved than they are, with high percentages of both ELCA and LCMS pastors expressing a desire to be more involved in social and political issues (56.2 percent and 46 percent, respectively).

Personal Resources

Education, social class, wealth, professional status, age — all of these contribute to a person's inclination and ability to participate in politics. Based on these characteristics, it would appear that Lutheran pastors would be well equipped to participate in politics, given their relatively high education levels (they all attend seminary after first earning a bachelor's degree) and mostly middle-class status. Holding leadership positions in an organization should also equip them with the requisite skills to be politically active. In fact, it may be argued that the longer a pastor has served in that capacity, the greater the ability to participate. In addition, the longer a pastor has been with a given church the higher his professional status, possibly making it easier for him to get involved politically without having to fear a backlash from the congregation.

Upon analysis, however, these pastors don't appear to match the

Table 2. Pastors Reporting Having Engaged in Political Activities during 2000

	% LCMS	% ELCA
Wrote letter	17	18
Signed petition	31	43
Contacted public official	33	40
Publicly (not from pulpit) supported a candidate in 2000	25	24
Publicly (not from pulpit) took stand on an issue in 2000	38	43
Boycotted a product	17	19
Endorsed a candidate while preaching	2	<1
Touched on political issue while preaching	43	51
Took a stand on issue from pulpit	22	20
Preached whole sermon on controversial issue	14	8
Participated in protest march	6	5
Practiced civil disobedience	.5	2
Organized study group in church	5	17
Organized an action group in church	4	12
Joined a national political organization	12	15
Ran for public office	<1	<1
Appointed to public office	4	6
Gave money to candidate, party, or PAC	22	24
Urged congregation to register and vote	52	50
Campaigned for party or candidate	8	5
Joined a local civic organization	17	21
Actively participated in a local clergy council	29	55
Prayed publicly about an issue	49	56
Prayed publicly for political candidates	32	33
Attended a political rally	9	10
Displayed a campaign button, sticker, or sign	12	16

theory. Older LCMS pastors are less participatory, but no correlation exists between age and participation for ELCA pastors. The correlation between years in the congregation and participation is slightly negative for the LCMS pastors and non-existent for ELCA pastors. In other words, there is a small tendency for those pastors who have served longer in a given congregation to participate in fewer political activities. So on these measures personal resources do not seem to be contributing to political activism. (A full listing of all of the reported correlation coefficients with the activism variable is presented in Table 3. It should be noted that the sign of the coefficient indicates whether it is a positive or negative relationship.)

Other personal resources that could contribute to an individual's propensity to participate in politics include the level of interest in politics and the willingness to compromise. Level of interest reflects the desire to acquire the necessary information and other resources needed to participate, while a willingness to compromise can be viewed as an acceptance of the give and take of politics and the necessity of working with others to achieve goals. The simple correlations here again provide mixed support for the hypothesis. Level of interest and activism are positively related (the higher a pastor's level of interest the more likely he or she is to participate) while willingness to compromise and activism are not related.

Professional Ideology

The LCMS-ELCA clergy divide may be seen most clearly in pastors' responses to a battery of theological statements, such as "Jesus will return to earth one day," "Jesus was born of a virgin," and "The devil actually exists." The higher the percent, the greater the level of agreement with these statements. For example, 99 percent of LCMS pastors and 72 percent of ELCA pastors agreed that "Jesus was born of a virgin." Consistently, LCMS pastors tended to agree with these questions at significantly higher levels than ELCA pastors. Remarkably, a full 70 percent of LCMS pastors had the highest score possible on the orthodoxy scale, compared to only 2 percent of ELCA pastors. This is a staggering difference between two groups of pastors, both of whom are in the Lutheran tradition, a difference that can be explained in part

Table 3. Correlations with the Activism Variable

	LCMS	ELCA
Age[1]	-0.12‡	-0.02
Years in congregation[1]	-0.11‡	-0.01
Years in ministry[1]	-0.08*	0.04
Level of interest[2]	0.24‡	0.24‡
Willingness to compromise[2]	0.06	0.05
Christian orthodoxy[2]	0.13‡	-0.03
Civic gospel[2]	0.09†	-0.11‡
Theological beliefs motivate political behavior[2]	0.20‡	0.26‡
Political beliefs motivate political behavior[2]	0.24‡	0.24‡
Republican strength[2]	0.13‡	-0.06
Democratic strength[2]	-0.10†	0.12‡
Group membership[1]	0.21‡	0.16‡
Religious group membership[1]	0.24‡	0.10†
Use of newspapers[2]	0.03	0.07*
Use of network television[2]	0.0^2	-0.03

1. Pearson's r correlation coefficients
2. Spearman's rho correlation coefficients
*$p < .10$; †$p < .05$; ‡$p < .01$

by the different approaches to Scripture taken by the different seminaries. LCMS seminaries teach and reinforce the literalness of the Bible, while ELCA seminaries have backed off from that stance toward a
more open and contextual interpretation.

We explored the relationship between activism and two concepts,
the Christian orthodoxy measure described above and a measure of belief in a civic gospel, or the theological meaning of American history
and politics, which included questions about the belief that the United
States was founded as a Christian nation, and whether there is only one
Christian view on most political issues. For the LCMS pastors, both of
these measures correlate positively, albeit weakly, with activism, and at

lower levels than for Guth's Southern Baptists. The findings for ELCA pastors differ, with no relationship existing between activism and orthodoxy alone, and a slight negative relationship between activism and civic gospel. These small correlations are not surprising given the two-kingdom theory that places emphasis on the vertical dimension of faith as the primary role for pastors, especially within the LCMS.

Another dimension of this area is whether a pastor's theological beliefs and/or political beliefs serve to motivate political behavior. Two questions on the survey were used to tap these beliefs. The first is a measure of how a pastor views the relationship between his faith and political action; the second is a measure of the relationship between a pastor's secular opinions and willingness to participate. The results of both correlated positively with activism, and both are relatively the same for each denomination.

Mobilizing Lutherans on the Issues

As they do in theology, the two groups of pastors diverge tremendously on political ideology and partisanship. Over 84 percent of LCMS pastors classify themselves as some form of conservative (somewhat, very, or extremely), while over 60 percent of ELCA pastors classify themselves as some form of liberal. This difference of course carries over into their party affiliations. According to our survey, Missouri Synod pastors are overwhelmingly Republican, with a full 47 percent identifying themselves as strong Republicans, while only 9 percent call themselves some type of Democrat. The ELCA pastors are at the other end of the spectrum with 23.5 percent calling themselves some type of Republican and over 65 percent identifying themselves as some type of Democrat. Table 4 shows the percentages.

Strength of partisanship has been shown to have consistent effects on motivating political behavior, including voting and working on campaigns. Highly partisan individuals exhibit strong emotional attachments to the party and the party's issues and representatives. Two measures were created to gauge the strength of a pastor's party attachments, one for Republican strength and one for Democratic strength, where a strong partisan was coded 3, a weak partisan was coded 2, an independent leaning toward the party was coded 1, and all others were

Table 4. Political Ideology and Party Identification (in percentages)

Political Ideology	LCMS	ELCA
Extremely liberal	0	1.8
Very liberal	1.1	21.3
Somewhat liberal	5.6	37.4
Moderate	8.9	17.1
Somewhat conservative	29.5	16.1
Very conservative	49.8	5.9
Extremely conservative	5.1	0.4
Party Identification		
Strong Democrat	3.9	28.7
Weak Democrat	1.7	12.9
Independent, lean Democrat	3.3	24.1
Independent	6.3	10.7
Independent, lean Republican	18.6	9.6
Weak Republican	18.3	7.1
Strong Republican	47.7	6.8

coded 0. For LCMS pastors the data shows that Republican strength is positively related to activism (the stronger the emotional ties to the Republican Party the greater the probability of engaging in political activity) but that Democratic strength is negatively related to activism; both of these are very weak, however. The situation is similar but reversed for the ELCA pastors: Democratic strength is positively, though weakly, correlated with activism, and Republican strength is negatively and weakly correlated. The motivational forces encouraging political activity that are provided by strong ties to a party do not appear to be influencing the Lutheran pastors in this study.

Organizational Activity

Although de Tocqueville characterized America as a nation of joiners, that does not seem to be true for the Lutheran pastors in this study. Of the interest groups or other organizations listed on the survey, which included religious groups as well as secular ones, almost 70 percent of LCMS pastors and 46 percent of ELCA pastors indicated they had not joined any of them; stated the other way, only 30 percent of LCMS pastors indicated membership in at least one group while 54 percent of ELCA pastors had joined a group. Of those who indicated membership, one fifth of LCMS and one fourth of ELCA pastors belonged to only one group. The numbers may not be out of line with joining levels in the general population, yet they are lower than we might have expected from a group of highly educated professionals such as clergy. Consistent with a two-kingdoms approach that is hesitant about remaking the world in our image, pastors are not rushing to join advocacy groups to accomplish secular aims, and the groups that they do belong to are not overtly political. More important, this reinforces noteworthy political differences between these two groups of pastors, with ELCA pastors acting more like "joiners" than their LCMS clergy colleagues.

Not surprisingly, the types of organizations that the two blocs of pastors are joining are quite different (Table 5). For LCMS pastors, the top four groups are Focus on the Family (16.7 percent), Habitat for Humanity (8.8 percent), a pro–gun rights group (7 percent), and the American Family Association (5.1 percent); only 1.3 percent belong to the Christian Coalition and less than 1 percent belong to some other Christian Right group. The top four groups for ELCA pastors are Habitat for Humanity (34.7 percent), Bread for the World (31.6 percent), the National Council of Churches (21.4 percent), and a pro-environmental group (16.1 percent). Even given the mobilization efforts many groups engage in, Missouri Synod pastors may not be afforded the same cues to activity as their ELCA brethren, though the low levels of political activity during the last presidential election year for both groups indicate that whatever motivational cues are being received are not producing much of an effect. This is, to be sure, of the pastors' own choosing: as a well-educated group they are ideally suited to obtaining information on and from these various groups, but their role orientations counteract this.

Those who are members of a group, however, are more active, and the impact seems to be greater for the Missouri Synod pastors. An index created by adding the memberships together is positively correlated, as is an index of predominantly religious groups: The more groups a pastor

Table 5. Membership by Type of Organization (in percentages)

	LCMS	ELCA
American Civil Liberties Union	0.2	2.8
American Family Association	5.1	0.4
Americans United for Separation of Church and State	0	1.0
Bread for the World	2.3	31.6
Christian Coalition	1.3	0.3
Christian Right group	0.7	0
Focus on the Family	16.7	2.8
Gay rights group	0	7.9
Habitat for Humanity	8.8	34.7
NAACP	0.3	1.8
National Assoc. of Evangelicals	0	0
National Council of Churches	0.5	21.4
Operation Rescue	0.8	0.8
People for the American Way	0	1.1
Prison Fellowship	4.9	1.3
Pro-environmental group	1.3	16.1
Pro–gun rights group	7.0	2.8

belongs to, the more politically active he is. For ELCA pastors the correlations are smaller but still positive. So while LCMS pastors belong to fewer groups on average than ELCA pastors, the impact of being in a group on activism is slightly greater for LCMS pastors.

Information Sources

Newspapers are the modal source of political news for both groups of pastors, with almost 57 percent of LCMS pastors and 69 percent of ELCA pastors reporting they rely on newspapers "a lot." Network television is not far behind with 42.5 percent of the first group and 54.8

percent of the second using network television "a lot." Interestingly, few in either group use Christian television or radio that much: of LCMS pastors a full 60 percent say they never use Christian television for their political news and 40 percent say they never rely on Christian radio, while the numbers for ELCA pastors are even higher with 83.8 percent saying they never use Christian television and 69.2 percent reporting they never use Christian radio. ELCA pastors are more likely than their LCMS counterparts to use public radio and public television "a lot": 56.3 percent to 27.8 percent for public radio and 42.2 percent to 22.9 percent for public television.

On the whole, the type of information source is not strongly related to activism. Newspapers and network television, despite being used by the pastors for information, are not related to activism at all for either group of pastors. The strongest correlations for LCMS pastors are listening to Christian radio, listening to commercial radio, and getting information from opinion magazines, though again all of these are weak relationships. No correlation exists for the ELCA pastors between information source and activism. Based on these correlations, those ELCA pastors who are content to get most of their news from the more "mainstream" information sources are not participating at higher or lower levels than anyone else.

Predicting Political Activism

Based on the discussion above, it is important to understand and gauge which of the various factors mentioned — age, partisanship, information source, etc. (the independent variables) — have the most impact on how active the pastors were in 2000 (the dependent variable). The initial models contained those measures that yielded significant correlations with the dependent variable; many of these relationships disappeared in the presence of other explanatory variables. Neither final model does a solid job at explaining the variance in political activism, but they do yield some interesting comparisons. Table 6 presents the models for both LCMS and ELCA clergy.

LCMS   Looking at the LCMS pastors first, age emerges as having a significant impact on the levels of activism: the older the pastor the

Table 6. Predicting LCMS and ELCA Activism

	Regression Coefficient	Beta
LCMS		
Strength of Republicanism	0.07	-0.016
Using commercial radio	0.498*	0.078
Using Christian magazines	0.568†	0.082
Level of interest in politics	0.525‡	0.150
Member Christian Coalition	3.47†	0.088
Member Focus on Family	1.81‡	0.150
Member pro-gun group	2.16‡	0.126
Theological beliefs motivate political action	0.468‡	0.109
Age	-0.044†	-0.096
Constant	0.194	

R2 =.140
F = 9.69‡
*p < .10; †p < .05; ‡p < .01

ELCA		
Orthodoxy	0.010†	0.098
Level of interest in politics	0.624‡	0.161
Political beliefs motivate political action	0.020‡	0.139
Theological beliefs motivate political action	0.720†	0.108
Member of Bread for the World	0.764*	0.076
Strength of Democratic attachment	0.249	0.065
Constant	-6.20	

R2 =.123
F = 11.73‡

fewer the number of political activities. It is the younger pastors who are getting more involved in politics; whether this is a trend that will continue is hard to say at this point, but if it does we may see more politically active LCMS pastors in the future. Being interested in politics is of course a determinant in the number of political activities undertaken: having the psychological propensity to follow politics leads pastors to get involved in politics. Related to this, those pastors who view their theological beliefs as encouraging their political involvement were more active in 2000. Pastors who see a connection between theology and the secular realm are taking actions in that realm in support of their theological beliefs.

We also found that members of Focus on the Family, a pro-gun group, or the Christian Coalition all committed more political acts than nonmembers of those groups. Pastors who are members of Focus on the Family committed an average of 1.8 more political actions in 2000 than nonmembers, those who belong to a pro-gun group committed an average of 2.2 more political actions than nonmembers, and Christian Coalition members participated in 3.5 additional acts on average over nonmembers. These findings are striking given the low numbers of individuals who belong to these groups. These groups are perhaps effective at mobilizing those pastors who are members to take actions at levels higher than that of those pastors who are not members. Finally, source of news does play a role. LCMS pastors who rely more on commercial radio and on Christian magazines for their political news were more politically active in 2000. Again, the finding for Christian magazines is interesting given that only 13 percent of pastors said they relied on that source "a lot" and 46 percent relied "some."

ELCA   Perhaps the biggest surprise in this full model is the strength of the Christian orthodoxy variable. Those pastors who scored higher on the orthodoxy scale were more politically active than those who had lower scores, controlling for other factors. Recall that there was no significant correlation or relationship between these two variables alone. This scale reflects a more literal interpretation of the Bible, so more literalist ELCA pastors are engaging in more activity. Conversely, more modernist pastors are less active, a significant finding that contradicts conventional wisdom. Many believe that it is the more liberal pastors, theologically, who are out trying to change the world; our data contradict this notion.

A pastor's level of interest in politics plays a large part in predicting activism, similar to the LCMS pastors. In addition, those who say their theological beliefs influence their political actions are more active; this too is the same for LCMS pastors. However, an ELCA pastor's political beliefs also lead to greater activity in the political sphere, and seems to have a greater impact on activism than theological beliefs. This variable had no impact on the activism of LCMS pastors. The last significant variable is whether the pastor was a member of Bread for the World. A pastor who was a member of that group committed on average about three-fourths of a political act more than nonmembers. This was the only membership-type variable that proved to have any impact on activism. And no variable representing information sources had a statistically significant effect on activism.

The Future of the Political Divide among Lutheran Clergy

This preliminary look at the political activities of ELCA and LCMS pastors in 2000 has produced some remarkable findings. Though ELCA and LCMS clergy come from a common two-kingdoms heritage, as groups they are very different theological and political animals. There are staggering differences in orthodoxy, with LCMS clergy placing much more belief in, for example, the authority of Scripture, the virgin birth, and the historicity of Adam and Eve, than ELCA clergy. There is likewise a huge gulf between these clergy in ideology and partisanship, with LCMS pastors strong conservative Republicans and a majority of ELCA pastors liberal Democrats. Differences exist too in political activity, though to a lesser degree than in orthodoxy, ideology, or partisanship. We now review these findings in the context of divisions in Lutheranism.

First, the ELCA clergy appear to be more politically active than their LCMS counterparts. Partial explanation for this may be the fact that ELCA pastors are motivated by their political beliefs as well as their theological beliefs to engage in political activity. This indicates that the ELCA has clearly moved toward mainline Protestantism. LCMS pastors, though they may have strong political convictions, are constrained by their role orientations from acting on those beliefs. The LCMS remains solidly an evangelical denomination.

Second, the wide difference between the two groups in their political orientations has several implications. Though not the subject of this chapter, these differences are evident in the issue positions taken by the two groups, with the ELCA clergy taking more consistently liberal views on issues and LCMS clergy taking more conservative positions. This gap is also discernable in the types of issue groups joined by these clergy. But in a surprising finding, those ELCA pastors who are more orthodox in their theological views were more active than those who are less orthodox, all other factors held constant. Further study to determine why this might be is certainly warranted.

Third, membership in certain organizations is clearly related to political involvement. Whether this is because of activities undertaken by the organizations or a connection between willingness to join a group and desire to get involved remains to be determined. Also, the overall explanatory power of both models is quite modest; much remains to be done to better explain why these Lutheran pastors are choosing, or not choosing, to engage in political acts.

Our findings suggest continuing schisms and divisions among Lutheran pastors on several levels. The most obvious division is between two groups of pastors, those in the ELCA and the LCMS. Very few areas of agreement exist on theological, ideological, or political questions, providing few opportunities for ecumenism or even discussion. Divisions are also evident within each denomination, particularly on ideological and political matters. Within the ELCA, pastors are divided on several theological questions, and the denomination includes a mix of liberals, moderates, and conservatives, and Democrats and Republicans. Within the LCMS — where pastors are overwhelmingly conservative and Republican — younger pastors are more likely to engage in political activity than their older peers. Furthermore, there continues to be discussion — if not division — within America's largest two Lutheran bodies on social theology, or the role of the church in society. Each synod continues to struggle with what role it should play in making the world a better place — a lynchpin of the two-kingdoms doctrine.

Further exploration needs to be carried out concerning the two-kingdoms doctrine and how these two groups of Lutheran pastors are living that doctrine. If pastors are not overly involved politically, what are they doing? How are the focus on spreading the gospel and concern for the individual translated into actions taken separate from preaching from the pulpit? These questions, as well as exploring the reasons for the widely divergent political viewpoints, offer researchers in this area opportunities for continued study.

BIBLIOGRAPHY

Barry, A. L. "What About . . . Pastors." St. Louis: The Lutheran Church–Missouri Synod, 2001.

Benson, Peter L., and Dorothy L. Williams. *Religion on Capitol Hill: Myths and Realities.* San Francisco: Harper and Row, 1982.

Djupe, Paul A., and Christopher P. Gilbert. "Leaders of the Flock or Lone Rangers: Clergy in Electoral Politics." Paper presented at the Midwest Political Science Association, Chicago, 2000.

Guth, James L. "The Mobilization of a Religious Elite: Political Activism among Southern Baptist Clergy in 1996." In *Christian Clergy in American Politics,* ed. Sue E. S. Crawford and Laura R. Olson. Baltimore: Johns Hopkins University Press, 2001.

Guth, James L., John C. Green, Corwin E. Smidt, Lyman A. Kellstedt, and Margaret M. Poloma. *The Bully Pulpit: The Politics of Protestant Clergy.* Lawrence: University of Kansas Press, 1997.

Jensen, Richard. *The Winning of the Midwest: Social and Political Conflict.* Chicago: University of Chicago Press, 1971.

Kersten, Lawrence L. *The Lutheran Ethic.* Detroit: Wayne State University Press, 1970.

Kleppner, Paul. *The Cross of Culture: A Social Analysis of Midwestern Politics, 1850 to 1900.* New York: Free Press, 1970.

Leege, David C., and Lyman A. Kellstedt, eds. *Rediscovering the Religious Factor in American Politics.* Armonk, N.Y.: M. E. Sharpe, 1993.

Luebke, Frederick C. "Politics and Missouri Synod Lutherans: A Historiographical Review." *Concordia Historical Institute Quarterly* XLV, no. 2 (1972): 141-58.

Menuge, Angus. "Promoting Dialogue in the Christian Academy." Presentation for the CUW Faculty Retreat, Green Lake, Wisconsin, August 20-21, 2001.

Niebuhr, H. Richard. *Christ and Culture.* New York: Harper and Row, 1951.

Noll, Mark. "The Lutheran Difference." *First Things* 20 (February 1992): 31-40.

Render Unto Caesar . . . and Unto God: A Lutheran View of Church and State. St. Louis: A Report of the Commission on Theology and Church Relations of the Lutheran Church–Missouri Synod, 1995.

Rosenstone, Steven J., and John Mark Hansen. *Mobilization, Participation, and Democracy in America.* New York: Macmillan, 1993.

St. Augustine. *The Political Writings.* Ed. Henry Paolucci. Washington, D.C.: Regnery Gateway, 1962.

Thomas, George M. *Revivalism and Cultural Change: Christianity, Nation Building, and the Market in the Nineteenth Century United States.* Chicago: University of Chicago Press, 1989.

Verba, Sidney, and Norman H. Nie. *Participation in America: Political Democracy and Social Equality.* Chicago: University of Chicago Press, 1972.

North American Lutheranism and the New Ethnics

MARK GRANQUIST

Most American Lutherans are descendants of immigrants who came to North America from northern Europe in the great trans-Atlantic migrations of the eighteenth and nineteenth centuries. Lutherans came from Germany and Scandinavia by the millions, and developed their own religious institutions in this new world, coming to dominate religious life in certain sections of the North American continent. But North American Lutheranism has never been solely about Germans and Scandinavians, and in the twentieth century this has become increasingly evident. Lutheran immigrants have arrived in North America from Eastern Europe, Africa, Asia, and Latin America.[1] Lutheran evangelistic efforts in North America have targeted non-traditional populations, such as African Americans, Hispanics, and Native Americans, to develop ethnic parishes. Lutheran congregations have also sponsored refugees from around the world, and some of these refugees have founded ethnic congregations of their own. In each of these three ways, North American Lutheranism has become a more diverse and multifaceted group, reflecting the full array of Lutheranism around the world.

1. E. Clifford Nelson, *The Lutherans in North America* (Philadelphia: Fortress, 1975); L. DeAne Lagerquist, *The Lutherans* (Westport, Conn.: Praeger, 1999).

New Ethnic European Lutherans

The great migration of North European Lutherans to North America came in waves. The eighteenth-century immigration consisted, for the most part, of German Lutherans to the Middle Colonies of the United States. Germans also dominated the early-nineteenth-century immigration to the United States and Canada, but they were increasingly matched and supplanted by Scandinavian immigrants by the middle and end of the nineteenth century. World War I, better economic conditions in Europe, and American controls on immigration all served to reduce this massive immigration to a trickle by 1924, and most North American Lutheran groups turned their attention to consolidation and acculturation to their new homeland. But beginning late in the nineteenth century there were also Lutheran immigrants from other areas of Europe — from Finland, Slovakia, Estonia, Latvia, Lithuania, and Hungary. These Lutherans too formed ethnic congregations and organizations wherever they gathered, and many of these groups still maintain a distinct ethnic presence in North America, often conducting some worship and activities in their immigrant languages even up to the present time. The Finns formed two separate groupings of congregations: one became a part of the Lutheran Church–Missouri Synod, and the other became part of the Evangelical Lutheran Church in America (ELCA).[2] The Slovak Lutherans did likewise, and there is still a nongeographic Slovak Zion Synod in the present-day ELCA.[3]

The presence of Eastern European Lutherans and Baltic Lutherans in North America was increased and refreshed by refugees escaping World War II and Communism in the 1940s and 1950s. The Soviet reoccupation of the Baltic states (Estonia, Latvia, and Lithuania), and the Communist takeover of Eastern Europe (including Slovakia and Hungary), brought a wave of refugees from these areas to Western Europe, and from there some of these refugees were admitted to the United States and Canada.[4] North American Lutherans played an im-

2. Jacob W. Heikkinen, *The Story of the Suomi Synod* (New York Mills, Minn.: Parta, 1985); Ralph J. Jalkanen, *The Faith of the Finns* (East Lansing, Mich.: Michigan State University Press, 1972).

3. John Adam, *A History of the Slovak Zion Synod LCA* (n.p.: Publications Committee of the Slovak Zion Synod, 1976).

4. Richard W. Solberg, *Open Doors: The Story of Lutherans Resettling Refugees* (St.

portant role in this process through the Lutheran World Federation efforts, and through their own organization, the Lutheran Immigration and Refugee Service (LIRS), a cooperative agency among various Lutheran groups in North America. Because these refugees were scattered among Europe, North America, and other countries (including Australia), they developed ethnic networks and church organizations that stretched around the world.

The Baltic Lutherans are a good example. There were scattered groups of Estonian, Latvian, and Lithuanian Lutherans who immigrated to North America during the late nineteenth and early twentieth centuries, and sporadic efforts were made by North American Lutherans (predominantly the United Lutheran Church in America and the Missouri Synod) to minister to them. Individual congregations were formed by these immigrants, and some affiliated with existing Lutheran denominations, while others remained independent. The majority of Baltic Lutheran congregations were formed by refugees who arrived after World War II, and often were affiliated with independent denominations, linked to other refugees around the world. Estonian refugees in North America founded the Estonian Evangelical Lutheran Church in 1954, as a part of the larger Estonian Lutheran Church in Exile, which has its headquarters in Stockholm, Sweden.[5] The EELC has twenty congregations in North America, with a total membership of nine thousand. The Latvian Lutherans also formed their own group, the Latvian Evangelical Lutheran Church in America, with forty-six congregations and sixteen thousand members. The Lithuanian Evangelical Church in Diaspora has six congregations and four thousand members.[6]

The experience of Eastern European Lutherans was similar to that of the Baltic Lutherans. Lutheran refugees from Slovakia were for-

Louis: Concordia, 1992); Frederick K. Wentz, *Lutherans in Concert: The Story of the National Lutheran Council, 1918-1966* (Minneapolis: Augsburg, 1968).

5. E. Theodore Bachmann and Mercia Brenne Bachmann, *Lutheran Churches in the World: A Handbook* (Minneapolis: Augsburg Fortress, 1989); Mark Granquist, "Estonian Americans," in *The Gale Encyclopedia of Multicultural America*, vol. 1 (New York: Gale, 1995), pp. 486-98.

6. ELCA, *Yearbook of the Evangelical Lutheran Church in America, 2001* (Minneapolis: Augsburg Fortress, 2001); Mark Granquist, "Lithuanian Americans," in *The Gale Encyclopedia of Multicultural America*, vol. 2 (New York: Gale, 1995), pp. 881-94.

tunate to have already existing Slovak Lutheran congregations in North America, and many refugees were able to be settled into these congregations. There were also existing Hungarian Lutheran congregations in North America. Some refugees from Hungary, both from World War II and from the failed 1956 uprising against the Soviets, came to the United States, and in 1957 there were nine ethnic congregations affiliated with the United Lutheran Church in America.[7] Although they did not form their own independent denomination, they did form a "Hungarian Special Interest Conference," which continues to exist and to publish its own materials, linking it with other Hungarian Lutheran congregations around the world. There were also Lutheran refugees from Poland and Yugoslavia, but they seem not to have founded their own general organizations. Since the collapse of the Soviet Union, the Lutheran Church–Missouri Synod (LCMS) has been very active in working with Lutherans in the former Soviet Union, many of whom are ethnic Germans who had settled in Russia and now are living in Russia, Ukraine, and the Central Asia republics.

African and Asian Lutherans in the United States

European and later North American Lutherans were active in the spread of Christianity to Africa and Asia, especially in the nineteenth and twentieth centuries. The results of this mission work are Lutheran congregations and denominations around the world; out of 63 million Lutherans worldwide, some 17 million Lutherans live in Africa, Asia, and Latin America. There are more Lutherans in Africa today (9.7 million) than there are in North America (8.5 million), and the growth rates for African and Asian Christianity are far outstripping those for European and North American Christian groups.[8] Although there has not been a large migration of African and Asian Lutherans to North America as of yet, there are scattered Lutheran congregations in North America worshiping in African and Asian languages, and this trend is

7. L. G. Terray , "Hungary, Lutherans in," in *Encyclopedia of the Lutheran Church,* ed. Julius Bodensieck, vol. 2 (Minneapolis: Augsburg, 1965), pp. 1059-64.

8. Gunther Gassmann, "Appendix: List of Lutheran Churches," in *Historical Dictionary of Lutheranism* (Lanham, Md.: Scarecrow, 2001), p. 359.

bound to increase in the twenty-first century. The ELCA yearbook lists congregations with active ministries in thirty-three languages, while the LCMS Yearbook lists over a dozen active languages in addition to the European ones.[9]

Lutheran missionary efforts began in the eighteenth century, when, under the influence of pietism, European Lutheran missionaries were sent to India and to native populations in North America. The nineteenth century, the "great" century of mission work, saw Lutheran activity expanded to include China, Indonesia, the Middle East, Latin America, and Africa, especially Tanzania, Ethiopia, South Africa, Madagascar, and Nigeria. The twentieth century saw further expansion to Japan, Korea, New Guinea, Brazil, and other countries. Today there are Lutheran congregations in more than one hundred countries around the world.[10] This expansion, and the growing strength of Lutheranism outside of North America and Europe, means that these world Lutheran groups will have an increased influence on Lutheranism in North America in the coming decades.

Immigration from Africa and Asia to North America was very limited during the nineteenth and early twentieth centuries. There was some immigration to the United States and Canada from China and Japan, but this was closely regulated, and mostly eliminated by a series of restrictive immigration laws in the United States. But immigration, especially to the United States, was greatly liberalized in 1965, and recent years have seen growing numbers of Asian and African immigrants to North America. Some are students and professionals who have come to study and work in North America; others are refugees fleeing war, famine, and social upheaval in their home countries. Some of these new immigrants to North America have come as members of Lutheran congregations in their home countries, while others have become Lutheran as a result of evangelistic efforts in North America. There are about 23,000 ELCA Lutherans who claim Asian/Pacific Islander heritage,[11] and there is an Association of

9. ELCA, *Yearbook of the Evangelical Lutheran Church in America, 2001;* LCMS, *The Lutheran Annual 2000 of the Lutheran Church–Missouri Synod* (St. Louis: Concordia, 2000).

10. Bachmann and Bachmann, *Lutheran Churches in the World.*

11. ELCA, "1988 to 2001 Racial/Ethnic Membership of the ELCA" (Evangelical Lutheran Church in America, 2002). This document can be accessed at http://www.elca.org/re/fyifacts.html (August 12, 2002).

Asians/Pacific Islanders–ELCA as an organized entity within the denomination.

The ELCA yearbook lists sixty-three congregations with ministries in a total of eleven different Asian languages, including Cambodian (one), Cantonese (seven), Hmong (five), Indonesian (one), Japanese (one), Korean (eighteen), Lao (five), Mandarin (twelve), Thai (one), Taiwanese (one), and Vietnamese (one). The LCMS yearbook lists seven different Asian-language ministries, including those in Cambodian, Cantonese, Hmong, Japanese, Korean, Lao, and Vietnamese. Since there are few, if any, established Lutheran churches in Southeast Asia, it is reasonable to surmise that those North American congregations with Southeast Asian ties were formed by evangelistic efforts among recent refugees, something that will be examined later. But the Chinese, Japanese, Korean, and Indonesian Lutheran congregations were formed in part by immigrants from Lutheran communities in Asia, and it is this immigration that should be examined first.

China was a center of intensive Lutheran missionary work beginning in 1846, and by World War II a dozen different Lutheran groups were involved in activities scattered around the country, with a total Chinese Lutheran population of approximately 100,000. The war and then Communist triumph in 1949 meant the destruction of much of this work, as foreign missionaries were expelled from China and indigenous Christians closely regulated. Some Chinese Lutherans became a part of the large Chinese diaspora in Asia, and the missionaries followed them to Hong Kong, Taiwan, Singapore, Malaysia, and other places. Of these "overseas" Chinese denominations, the Lutheran Church in Hong Kong, at about 50,000 members, is the largest. The Cantonese, Mandarin, and Taiwanese-speaking Lutheran congregations in North America can largely be traced to immigrants from the Chinese diaspora. Some of these Chinese congregations in North America have Lutheran roots that can be traced back for several generations in Asia. The Evangelical Lutheran Church of Hong Kong, for example, has cooperated with the ELCA in the establishment of a Chinese-language congregation in Toronto, Canada.[12] The ELCA lists twenty Chinese-speaking congregations, while the LCMS shows thir-

---

12. Bachmann and Bachmann, *Lutheran Churches in the World.*

teen active Chinese pastors serving twenty-eight congregations and missions.[13]

Lutheranism in Japan goes back to 1892, but the end of World War II and the expulsion of missionaries from China in 1949 were the impetus for more intensive Lutheran activities in Japan. There are about 30,000 Lutherans in Japan, and both the ELCA and the LCMS list at least one Japanese-speaking Lutheran congregation on their rosters. Former missionaries to Japan, such as the Reverend Paul Nakamura, were active in California in the 1940s and 1950s, working with Japanese immigrants and Japanese-American citizens.[14] The situation in Korea is similar to that of Japan, as Lutheran activities in Korea are recent, and the Lutheran presence in Korea is small. The ELCA lists a total of eighteen Korean-speaking congregations, however, which would seem to indicate an extensive outreach to the Korean-American community. The LCMS has shown dramatic increases in its Korean ministries, rising to forty congregations currently, up from eleven congregations just five years ago.[15]

The origin of Southeast Asian Lutheran congregations in North America has also resulted from the same dynamic of war, upheaval, flight, and refugee resettlement. Since there are virtually no Lutheran denominations on the Southeast Asia peninsula, it is clear that all these efforts have been developed in North America to serve Southeast Asian refugees, who have left behind the war, civil strife, and Communist oppression of their homelands. With the United States' withdrawal from South Vietnam in the mid 1970s, and the Communist capture of that area, some Lao, Hmong, Cambodian, and Vietnamese left their home areas for refugee camps in Thailand, or took to the seas to try and reach Hong Kong or the Philippines. LIRS, along with other refugee agencies, began to assist these refugees, seeking congregations to sponsor and provide for refugees to be resettled in North America. Besides the populations in California and Texas, there is also a large settlement of Southeast Asians in the Upper Midwest, due in large part to the sponsorship of refugees by individual Lutheran congrega-

13. LCMS, "Pentecost 2000+" (Lutheran Church Missouri Synod, 2002). This document can be accessed at http://www.pentecost2000.com/USworldnotes.htm (August 12, 2002).

14. Lagerquist, *The Lutherans.*

15. LCMS, "Pentecost 2000+."

tions. Several Southeast Asian men and women have become Lutheran pastors in both the ELCA and LCMS in the last few decades, and they continue this outreach ministry to Southeast Asian immigrants, with the support of Lutheran synods and districts.[16]

Of all the Asian Lutheran groups, the Protestant Christian Batak Church is the largest, with over 2.9 million members. Located primarily on the island of Sumatra, Indonesia, the Batak Church began with Lutheran mission efforts in 1861, and grew quickly. Most Batak Christians, however, remain in Indonesia (only 1.8 percent live outside of the country), so immigration to North America is limited; there is only one ELCA Indonesia-language ministry listed in North America, in California. Similarly, large Lutheran groups are in Papua New Guinea and India, but immigration from these areas has been limited, as well. There is a century of Lutheran mission work in Pakistan, and though Lutheran work in that country has been consolidated into the ecumenical Church of Pakistan, there is a single ELCA congregation that has a mission in Urdu, the official language of Pakistan.

It could also be noted that Lutheran missionary efforts in Jordan and the West Bank have produced the Evangelical Lutheran Church in Jordan, and it is from this group that the existence of five Arabic-language Lutheran congregations in the United States can be traced. The continuing tensions in the Middle East, and the rise of Islamic fundamentalism in the area, have caused many Arab Christians to leave the area, and many of these have immigrated to North America. There is an Association of Lutherans of Arab/Middle Eastern Heritage in the ELCA.[17]

Africa is the continent where Lutheranism is growing most quickly, and if there are only yet a few North American Lutheran congregations of direct African background, this is a situation that is bound to change in the coming century. In Africa, the largest Lutheran populations are in Ethiopia (2.6 million), Tanzania (2.5 million), Madagascar (1.5 million), South Africa (850,000), Nigeria (800,000), and Namibia (750,000), almost all of whom became Lutheran in the twentieth century.[18] Nine ELCA congregations have ministries in African languages: there are congregations using Amharic (six), Oromo (two),

---

16. LCMS, "Pentecost 2000+."
17. ELCA, *Yearbook of the Evangelical Lutheran Church in America, 2001.*
18. Bachmann and Bachmann, *Lutheran Churches in the World.*

and Yoruba (one). The LCMS lists congregations worshiping in Ethiopian, Sudanese, and Tigrinya. Outside of the single congregation worshiping in the Yoruba language of Nigeria, the rest of these congregations worship in the languages of the Ethiopia-Eritrea-Sudan area of Eastern Africa — Amharic, Oromo, Tigrinya, Ethiopian, and Sudanese. Many immigrants have come to North America since 1980 as war, famine, and economic instability have seriously affected this region of Africa. Lutheran efforts in Ethiopia go back to the end of the nineteenth century, and the church that resulted from this mission, the Ethiopian Evangelical Church Mekane Jesus, is the largest Lutheran denomination in Africa.[19] Ethiopia has struggled in the last twenty-five years through a socialist revolution, civil and regional wars, and massive famines that have destroyed much of the infrastructure of the country. Lutheran relief agencies from Europe and North America have been active in efforts to rebuild this part of Africa, and Lutheran Immigration and Refugee Services has settled refugees from Ethiopia in North America, resulting in these ethnic congregations. The LCMS has sixty-five preaching stations to serve approximately two thousand African immigrants in North America.[20]

Ministry to American Minorities

Although much of the Lutheran work in North America centered around ministry to European immigrants, there have also been numerous attempts (often sporadic and underfunded) to reach out to minority populations in North America, especially Native Americans, African Americans, and Hispanics. There is, in fact, a long history of such efforts among European and North American Lutherans, some of which have had lasting results, though many efforts failed.

Mission work among the Native Americans was often one reason cited for sending European missionaries to North America, and often a pretext for colonization.[21] In the seventeenth century, the short-lived

---

19. Gassmann, "Appendix: List of Lutheran Churches," p. 359.

20. LCMS, "Pentecost 2000+."

21. Henriette Lund, "Indigenous Americans, Lutheran work among," in *The Encyclopedia of the Lutheran Church*, vol. 2, pp. 1119-22.

colony of New Sweden on the Delaware sponsored the work of Johan Campanius among the Delaware tribe, and in the eighteenth century German pastors such as Conrad Weiser Jr. and John C. Hartwick worked for a time among tribes in Pennsylvania and New York. As Lutherans expanded into the interior of the continent in the nineteenth century, mission work was undertaken by many different synods and groups. The Pennsylvania Ministerium and the Missouri Synod supported work among the Chippewa and Dakota peoples in Michigan and Minnesota, while the Iowa Synod sent missionaries among the Crow tribe in Montana, though these workers were killed.

In the twentieth century, the United Evangelical Lutheran Church operated the Lutheran Indian Mission in Oklahoma among the Cherokees, which eventually developed into a social service agency. Two of the longer-lasting missions, still operative today, were begun among the native tribes in the Southwest: The Wisconsin Evangelical Lutheran Synod developed the Apache Indian Mission in Arizona at the beginning of the century, working on the San Carlos and Fort Apache reservations, and the synod still maintains an active presence there. The Navajo Evangelical Lutheran Mission at Rocky Point, Arizona, was developed in 1960, and still provides active service to the Navajo people in northern Arizona; its congregation, House of Prayer Lutheran, is listed as the only Navajo-speaking congregation in the ELCA.[22] The LCMS has ten full-time and several part-time workers who serve native American populations.[23]

Other Lutheran efforts have focused on northern Canada and Alaska. In 1894 a Norwegian pastor, T. L. Brevig, was assigned to Alaska to serve Norwegian Lapps who had been brought to Alaska to assist with a program to introduce reindeer to the Native population. Soon Brevig was also ministering to the Native populations, founding the Teller Mission, which brought the Lutheran message and medical care to the area.[24] Today the ELCA has five Inuipait-speaking congregations in Alaska that are the result of this missionary work. Also serving diverse populations in Northern Canada and Alaska is a pan-

---

22. ELCA, *Yearbook of the Evangelical Lutheran Church in America, 2001.*
23. LCMS, "Pentecost 2000+."
24. E. Clifford Nelson and Eugene Fevold, *The Lutheran Church among Norwegian Americans* (Minneapolis: Augsburg, 1960), vol. 2, p. 95.

Lutheran organization called LAMP, Lutheran Association of Missionaries and Pilots. Begun in 1970 by Les Stahlke, this organization now works with Native populations in Canada and Alaska, with long- and short-term mission workers serving scattered Arctic communities.[25]

There have been a number of other efforts by Lutherans to work among Native Americans, both on the Native reservations and among Native American populations off the reservations, many of which are locally developed initiatives. In the ELCA there is an American Indian/Alaska Native Association formed to advance the interests of Native Americans within that denomination.

The story of African-American Lutherans parallels that of the Lutheran efforts among Native Americans. Though there have been African-American Lutherans since the seventeenth century, Lutheran denominations in North America have not always been consistent or helpful in encouraging the growth of this population of Lutherans. There have been many efforts to extend African-American Lutheranism, but far too often these efforts have been sporadic, and they have sometimes failed for lack of long-term interest and planning. There are, however, significant pockets of African-American Lutheranism that continue not only to exist but to thrive in North America.[26]

The initial history of African-American Lutheranism begins in colonial New York and New Jersey, when occasional African Americans (free and slave) joined local Lutheran congregations and relied on Lutheran clergy for various pastoral functions. As early as 1669, an African American named Emmanuel was baptized and taken into the membership of a New York Lutheran congregation by the Reverend Jacob Fabricius. It was, however, among southern Lutherans that a substantial population of African-American Lutherans was developed, although most of these came from slaves owned by white Lutherans. Lutherans migrated to the southern colonies of Virginia, North Carolina, South Carolina, and Georgia beginning in the eigh-

25. LAMP, "A History of LAMP" (Lutheran Association of Missionaries and Pilots, 2002). This document can be accessed at http://lampministry.org (August 12, 2002).

26. See Richard C. Dickinson, *Roses and Thorns: The Centennial Edition of Black Lutheran Mission and Ministry in the Lutheran Church–Missouri Synod* (St. Louis: Concordia, 1977); Jeff G. Johnson, *Black Christians: The Untold Lutheran Story* (St. Louis: Concordia, 1991).

teenth century; one of the most notable of these early groups was the Salzburg Lutherans in Georgia, who began arriving in that colony in 1734. Although the Salzburger settlement in Georgia was intended originally to be free from the use of African slaves, this initial determination was soon discarded, and slavery became common among southern Lutherans. The Lutheran ownership of slaves, however, brought with it all the common questions that surrounded slavery and religion in the southern United States: could and should slaves be baptized and made Christians, and, if so, what was their place in southern Lutheran congregations? Some African Americans were baptized and admitted to local congregations during the colonial period, although these efforts were sporadic, and sometimes controversial. During the nineteenth century, southern Lutherans began to actively seek to Christianize both slave and free African Americans, though they carefully sought to maintain a distinction between the races. African Americans such as Jehu Jones, Alexander Payne, and Boston Drayton studied at American Lutheran seminaries, and Jones founded the first African-American Lutheran congregation, St. Pauls Colored Lutheran Church, in Philadelphia, in 1832.[27]

Just prior to the Civil War, southern Lutheran synods had substantial African-American populations, estimated at from 10 to 25 percent of total membership. But the emancipation of the slaves after the Civil War led to a quick decline in these numbers, and southern synods exacerbated this exodus by requesting that African-American Lutherans form separate congregations and synodical organizations, a move that effectively excluded many African-American Lutherans from membership. Beginning in 1877, there was a series of Lutheran initiatives begun with African Americans in the South, organized by the Synodical Conference and Joint Synod of Ohio, which resulted not only in African-American Lutheran congregations and pastors, but also training schools and colleges in the South.

In the twentieth century, North American Lutheran denominations have made repeated efforts to increase their African-American membership. The focus of much of this work also shifted in the twentieth century with the massive African-American migration to the urban areas of the northern United States; as a result, urban missions largely

27. Johnson, *Black Christians.*

replaced the rural South for much of this work. By the time of the Civil Rights movement of the 1950s and 1960s, Lutheran denominations had begun to push for integrated congregations, especially in urban areas, and to actively seek out African-American members, although such programs often varied, and were at times uneven. The late twentieth century also saw the rise of African-American Lutherans as pastors, bishops, denominational officials, and college and seminary professors, with a visibility within national denominational circles.

Another area of significant African-American presence for North American Lutherans is among Africans in the Caribbean area, notably the Virgin Islands of the United States and the countries of Suriname and Guyana. In these areas, mission work has been long-standing, and the initial mission efforts with free and slave populations have given way to substantial indigenous and independent African Lutheran churches. In turn, African immigrants from these areas to North America have added to the diversity of the Lutheran denominations here.

The Virgin Islands in the Caribbean were initially a colony of Denmark (the Danish West Indies), and it was through the efforts of Danish Lutherans in the eighteenth century that African slaves there were baptized and made Lutheran.[28] Beginning in the 1740s and 1750s, the Danish Lutherans began systematic attempts to reach the African population of the islands, but it was not until the work was shifted from Danish to the Creole language of the slaves that much success was had. By the end of the eighteenth century, African Lutherans (free and slave) outnumbered the Danish Lutherans, and the colonial government had embarked on a program to establish schools and congregations for them. African Lutherans in the Danish West Indies created a truly indigenous African Lutheran culture on the islands, one of the first successful attempts to accomplish this in a non-European culture.

When Denmark sold this colony to the United States in 1917, the Lutheran congregations and institutions there came under the control of the United Lutheran Church in America, which eventually constituted these Lutherans with others from Puerto Rico as the Caribbean

---

28. Benjamin H. Pershing, "Virgin Islands," in *The Encyclopedia of the Lutheran Church*, vol. 3, pp. 2443-44.

Synod of the ULCA in 1952. But Lutherans from the Virgin Islands had already been coming to the United States, as early as the 1870s, to find economic advancement and to escape the poverty of the islands. Several North American Lutheran congregations, most notably Transfiguration Lutheran Church in Harlem, New York City, were founded by Lutherans from the Virgin Islands. Lutherans from the West Indies also contributed early African-American Lutheran leaders, such as the Reverend Daniel Wiseman, the first African-American pastor to be formally trained, and deaconesses Emma Francis and Edith Prince, who served both in New York and in the Virgin Islands.[29]

The stories of African Lutherans in Guyana and Suriname parallel those of the Virgin Island Lutherans: in other words, a colonial ministry to slave and free populations grew into an indigenous church. Although these two countries have become independent, there are significant ties between them and Lutherans in North America. In Suriname, white Lutheran congregations established in the eighteenth century began in 1791 to baptize slaves.[30] This led in turn to the formation of a native Lutheranism of African and Creole background, and worship in the language of the people. Several African Lutheran congregations were formed in Suriname, and have continued to exist even through long periods of isolation and the antipathy of the dominant Reformed Protestantism of the colonial government. In the twentieth century, North American Lutherans, especially the Lutheran Church in America, worked closely with Surinamese Lutherans to strengthen their congregations and programs.

Lutheranism in Guyana traces a similar history. European Lutherans, mainly Dutch, began congregations in what was then British Guiana in the eighteenth century, but racial attitudes and suspicions hindered evangelism with slaves and free Africans until the 1830s.[31] The Reverend Mr. Junius began a practice of baptizing Africans and Creoles at this time, and laid the foundation for African Lutheran congregations in the country. The Lutheran congregations eventually came under the care of the United Lutheran Church in America in 1915, but when Guyana became independent in 1966, so did the Lu-

29. Johnson, *Black Christians.*
30. Johnson, *Black Christians.*
31. Johnson, *Black Christians.*

theran Church of Guyana, although many ties continued to exist between this church and North American Lutherans.[32]

Out of nearly 9 million North American Lutherans, there are approximately 105,000 African-American Lutherans, a figure that both the ELCA and the LCMS are actively seeking to increase. As of 2001, the Evangelical Lutheran Church in America had over 120 pastors and nearly 53,000 members who were African American,[33] and although the new denomination's goal of a 10 percent membership of persons of color (or those whose primary language is not English) has proven elusive so far, the ELCA has continued to stress the importance of this goal. In the Lutheran Church–Missouri Synod, as of 2001, there were 100 pastors and nearly 54,000 African-American members.[34]

Both denominations have active organizations in place to further African-American Lutheranism: the ELCA has a Commission for Multicultural Ministry and an African-American Lutheran Association, while the LCMS has a Board for Black Ministry Services. Both denominations have worked to produce worship materials for African-American Lutherans, as well as other materials of a historical and devotional nature. The history of Lutheran efforts among African Americans has shown time and again, however, that simply having organizations and materials in place is not enough to ensure the success of such ministries, and that local and independent efforts are often equally as important.

Hispanic Lutheran Missionaries and Missions

Much of what can be said about African-American Lutherans parallels the experience of Hispanic Lutherans in North America, although Lutheran contacts with the Hispanic world are of much more recent origin, beginning mostly in the twentieth century. Until the last century the official status of Roman Catholicism in the Latin American world,

32. Bachmann and Bachmann, *Lutheran Churches in the World.*

33. ELCA, "1988 to 2001 Racial/Ethnic Membership of the ELCA."

34. Board for Black Ministry Services, LCMS, "LCMS Black Ministry: What is Black Ministry?" (Board for Black Ministry Services, Lutheran Church–Missouri Synod). This document can be accessed at http://blackministry.lcms.org/whatis.html (August 12, 2002).

and Protestant sensibilities about "sheep-stealing," had limited most Lutheran efforts in Latin America to the organization of small European expatriate or ethnic congregations, especially in Brazil and Argentina. In the twentieth century three elements combined to increase Hispanic Lutheranism: growing opportunities for Protestant work in Latin American countries, the acculturation of expatriate and ethnic Lutheran populations to Hispanic cultures, and a large-scale immigration of Hispanics into North America itself.

On the heels of the Spanish-American War, a young Swedish-American pre-seminary student, Gustav Swenson, went to Puerto Rico and established a bilingual congregation there in 1898. He was followed shortly after by Lutheran pastors from the General Council in 1899, and a series of North American Lutheran missionaries soon came to work in Puerto Rico, most notably Alfred Ostrom of the Augustana Synod, who worked on the island from 1905 to 1931.[35] Beginning in the 1920s, native Puerto Rican pastors were trained at Lutheran seminaries in North America, and by 1952 the Lutheran congregations on the island were combined with the congregations on the Virgin Islands to create the Caribbean Synod; there are currently twenty-six congregations and 5,200 Lutherans in Puerto Rico.[36] As with the congregations on the Virgin Islands, the heavy immigration of Puerto Ricans to the United States (especially after World War II) has drained the strength of Puerto Rican congregations, but there are Lutheran congregations (especially in the New York area) that have benefited from this migration. There were other scattered Lutheran missions throughout the Hispanic Caribbean, including congregations in Cuba developed by the LCMS beginning in 1911, and small congregations on other islands.

Probably the largest part of the Hispanic population in North America has resulted from immigration from Mexico, while a smaller part has come from the countries of Central America. Most of the Lutheran efforts in these countries are fairly recent, and most do not extend back further than the post–World War II period. The Evangelical Lutheran Church of Mexico (ELCM), for example, is an offshoot of the

35. Benjamin H. Pershing, "Puerto Rico," in *The Encyclopedia of the Lutheran Church*, vol. 3, pp. 1991-92.

36. ELCA, *Yearbook of the Evangelical Lutheran Church in America, 2001*.

Latin American Lutheran Mission (LALM), which was organized in 1946 as the result of scattered efforts from a decade earlier.[37] The LALM has its base in Laredo, Texas, and supports the efforts of the ELCM, which is located just across the border in Nuevo Laredo, Mexico. The LCMS has similar ties to two smaller Mexican Lutheran denominations, as well as a long-running radio ministry to Latin America, a Spanish-language version of the "Lutheran Hour," whose roots go back to the 1940s.[38]

The bulk of Hispanic Lutherans in the United States, however, do not come as a result of immigration from the small Hispanic Lutheran denominations of Latin America, but as a result of outreach by Lutheran congregations and agencies among Hispanic immigrants to North America. The vast majority of Hispanic immigrants to North America come as Roman Catholics, but some are nominal adherents, or they are estranged from the Roman Catholic Church. Some are attracted to Protestant denominations in the United States, and up to 25 percent of North American Hispanics are now Protestant. The training of Spanish-speaking pastors and church workers, who found Hispanic congregations in North America, is key, and some Lutheran seminaries, such as the Lutheran Seminary Program in the Southwest, in Austin, Texas, have Spanish-language programs. The ELCA has 180 congregations that list worship in Spanish (including the congregations in Puerto Rico), with a Hispanic membership of 39,000, up 45 percent since 1988.[39] There is in the ELCA an *Asociacion Luterana de Ministerios Hispanes de la Iglesia Evangelica Luterana en America* (Association of Hispanic Ministries in the ELCA), which organizes and promotes Hispanic ministries. The LCMS lists 120 Hispanic congregations in North America, with "96 Hispanic workers" on its rolls, and has an "LCMS Hispanic Conference" that has met regularly since its formation in 1976.[40] Both the ELCA and LCMS produce hymnals, devotionals, and theological materials in Spanish for the use of these growing ministries.

37. Bachmann and Bachmann, *Lutheran Churches in the World.*
38. LCMS, "10th LCMS Hispanic Conference Seeks Autonomy," *LMCS News*, no. 44. This can be accessed at http://concordtx.org/missions/hisp.htm (August 12, 2002).
39. ELCA, "1988 to 2001 Racial/Ethnic Membership of the ELCA."
40. LCMS, "10th LCMS Hispanic Conference" and "Pentecost 2000+."

The Present and Future of Ethnic Ministry
in American Lutheranism

The work of the Lutheran Immigration and Refugee Services organization should be mentioned, as its effort has led, at least indirectly, to the growing ethnic diversity of North American Lutheranism.[41] Although LIRS settles refugees in North America without regard to religion, and although its main purpose is not to "Lutheranize" the refugees, the fact that they work through the structures of local Lutheran congregations means that the refugees are often provided with the supportive atmosphere of a Lutheran fellowship, and this has much to do with the growth of Lutheranism among certain refugee populations, most noticeably the Southeast Asian community, where Lutheranism is historically unknown.

The future would seem to suggest the increasing ethnic diversity of North American Lutheranism, although perhaps not to the degree, or with the rapidity, which its most ardent supporters might wish. The major North American Lutheran denominations are still predominantly white and European in background; the ELCA, for example, is still 97 percent white. Both the ELCA and the LCMS have set aggressive goals for diversity, of which they have, unfortunately, fallen short. In 1988 the newly formed ELCA suggested that its goal was to reach the point of being 10 percent "people of color or those whose primary language is not English," but this goal seems elusive, even though a large number of mission starts are funneled in this direction. In the LCMS, the Black Ministry Services board declared its desire to double the number of black Lutherans (in the LCMS) to 100,000 "by the early dawn of the New Century," and the World Mission Department declared its intention to start one thousand new cross-cultural ministries by 2000;[42] though these goals were not met by the desired dates, and have not yet been met, they are still the stated intentions of the denomination itself.

The drive to increase ethnic diversity of North American Luther-

---

41. See Richard W. Solberg, *Open Doors: The Story of Lutherans Resettling Refugees* (St. Louis: Concordia, 1992).

42. LCMS, "Pentecost 2000+"; Board for Black Ministry Services, LCMS, "LCMS Black Ministry: What is Black Ministry?"

anism can, however, lead to tensions and problems. The slow pace of diversification has sparked anger within minority Lutheran communities, who suspect that the denominations are not as committed to these goals as they say they are. A glance at the history of such efforts shows that some of these suspicions have had, in the past, a basis in reality. On the other hand, the progress toward these goals has not always seemed to match the resources devoted to the work, and critics feel that funds spent to begin and sustain struggling ethnic congregations are yielding very meager results. They worry that general efforts for evangelism and mission starts are being shortchanged in favor of ethnic ministries, and that this is a cause of the slow shrinkage of the denominations. In the ELCA, the goal of 10-percent minority representation is institutionalized in quotas for synodical and national positions; this has led not only to hard feelings on the part of some, but a very real fear that an already thin minority leadership (lay and clergy) is being diverted and misused.

Whatever the tensions and problems, it is clear that North American Lutheranism is slowly becoming more ethnically diverse. Perhaps the history of Lutheran work in North America among non-European populations could be a corrective and a lesson, as it seems that the growth of Lutheranism in North America among ethnically diverse groups is as much or more a result of initiatives from the local level as it is a result of the actions of boards, commissions, programs, and well-intended goal-setting. The history of such efforts is clearly uneven, as time and money are expended in bursts, with periods of shifting, neglect, and even abandonment in between. The most effective ways to reach ethnically diverse populations have been, it seems, efforts that are local, continuous, and based within the local cultures themselves, efforts that have led to the slow diversification of Lutheranism in North America up to this point in time.

BIBLIOGRAPHY

Adam, John. *A History of the Slovak Zion Synod LCA.* N.p.: Publications Committee of the Slovak Zion Synod, 1976.

Bachmann, E. Theodore, and Mercia Brenne Bachmann. *Lutheran Churches in the World: A Handbook.* Minneapolis: Augsburg Fortress, 1989.

Board for Black Ministry Services, LCMS. "LCMS Black Ministry: What is

Black Ministry?" Board for Black Ministry Services, Lutheran Church–Missouri Synod. Http://blackministry.lcms.org/whatis .html (August 12, 2002).

Dickinson, Richard C. *Roses and Thorns: The Centennial Edition of Black Lutheran Mission and Ministry in the Lutheran Church–Missouri Synod*. St. Louis: Concordia, 1977.

ELCA (Evangelical Lutheran Church in America). "1988 to 2001 Racial/ Ethnic Membership of the ELCA." Evangelical Lutheran Church in America, 2002. Http://www.elca.org/re/fyifacts.html (August 12, 2002).

————. *Yearbook of the Evangelical Lutheran Church in America, 2001*. Minneapolis: Augsburg Fortress, 2001.

Gassmann, Gunther. "Appendix: List of Lutheran Churches." In *Historical Dictionary of Lutheranism*. Lanham, Md.: Scarecrow, 2001.

Granquist, Mark. "Estonian Americans." In *The Gale Encyclopedia of Multicultural America*. Vol. 1, pp. 486-98. New York: Gale, 1995.

————. "Lithuanian Americans." In *The Gale Encyclopedia of Multicultural America*, vol. 2, pp. 881-94. New York: Gale, 1995.

Heikkinen, Jacob W. *The Story of the Suomi Synod*. New York Mills, Minn.: Parta, 1985.

Jalkanen, Ralph J. *The Faith of the Finns*. East Lansing, Mich.: Michigan State University Press, 1972.

Johnson, Jeff G. *Black Christians: The Untold Lutheran Story*. St. Louis: Concordia, 1991.

Lagerquist, L. DeAne. *The Lutherans*. Westport, Conn.: Praeger, 1999.

LAMP (Lutheran Association of Missionaries and Pilots). "A History of LAMP." Lutheran Association of Missionaries and Pilots, 2002. Http://lampministry.org (August 12, 2002).

LCMS (Lutheran Church–Missouri Synod). *The Lutheran Annual 2000 of the Lutheran Church–Missouri Synod*. St. Louis: Concordia, 2000.

————. "Pentecost 2000+." Lutheran Church–Missouri Synod, 2002. Http:/ /www.pentecost2000.com/USworldnotes.htm (August 12, 2002).

————. "10th LCMS Hispanic Conference Seeks Autonomy." LCMS News, no. 44. Http://concordtx.org/missions/hisp.htm (August 12, 2002).

Lund, Henriette. "Indigenous Americans, Lutheran work among." In *The Encyclopedia of the Lutheran Church*. Vol. 2, pp. 1119-22. Minneapolis: Augsburg, 1965.

Nelson, E. Clifford. *The Lutherans in North America*. Philadelphia: Fortress, 1975.

Nelson, E. Clifford, and Eugene Fevold. *The Lutheran Church among Norwegian Americans*. Vol. 2. Minneapolis: Augsburg, 1960.

Pershing, Benjamin H. "Puerto Rico." In *The Encyclopedia of the Lutheran Church*. Vol. 3, pp. 1991-92. Minneapolis: Augsburg, 1965.

————. "Virgin Islands." In *The Encyclopedia of the Lutheran Church*. Vol. 3, pp. 2443-44. Minneapolis: Augsburg, 1965.

Solberg, Richard W. *Open Doors: The Story of Lutherans Resettling Refugees*. St. Louis: Concordia, 1992.

Terray, L. G. "Hungary, Lutherans in." In *Encyclopedia of the Lutheran Church*. Vol. 2, pp. 1059-64. Minneapolis: Augsburg, 1965.

Wentz, Frederick K. *Lutherans in Concert: The Story of the National Lutheran Council, 1918-1966*. Minneapolis: Augsburg, 1968.

Multiculturalism and the Dilution of Lutheran Identity

ALVIN J. SCHMIDT

Lutheran immigrants arrived in America from Germany and the Scandinavian countries. Some came as early as the 1630s and 1640s, and many more arrived in the first half of the eighteenth century. They soon experienced countervailing forces to their Lutheran theology and heritage. A major problem was the virtual absence of Lutheran pastors to shepherd these immigrants in the hinterlands of Georgia, the Carolinas, Pennsylvania, and New York. Another was not being well-grounded in Lutheran doctrine and corresponding convictions. Thus, Lutheran immigrants were highly vulnerable to the prey of various Protestant clergy who, espousing a generic Protestantism, often asked them to join non-Lutheran churches, and frequently many did.

In 1742 Pastor Henry Melchior Muhlenberg arrived in America from Halle, Germany. In the 1740s and 1750s he kept Lutherans from becoming an extinct species in the New World as he traveled on horseback to primitive outposts, visited countless families, and conducted divine services in houses and barns; he worked faithfully to bring the gospel of Jesus Christ to shepherdless Lutherans who had little or no Lutheran identity. By 1748 he, as the principal mover, and several other Lutheran pastors formally organized the Pennsylvania Ministerium, a synod of German-speaking Lutherans. The founding of the Pennsylvania Ministerium was a noteworthy landmark in preserving Lutheran doctrine, practice, and identity in America's expansive Protestant environment. To give added substance to its goal of preserving historic Lutheranism, the ministerium adopted a uniform Lutheran liturgy for use in divine services. It was largely a facsimile of the liturgy used in 1694 by St. Mary's Lutheran Church of Savoy in London, England.[1]

Approximately a hundred years later, Lutheran doctrine and identity in America were seriously threatened for the second time. This time the threat came from within Lutheranism's own confines as Samuel S. Schmucker, president of Gettysburg Lutheran Seminary, sought to Americanize Lutheran churches by introducing his *Definite Synodical Platform* (1855), a document that found fault with the Unaltered Augsburg Confession of 1530, the Magna Carta of the Lutheran church. Schmucker especially disagreed with the Augsburg Confession's affirmation of baptismal regeneration and the real presence in the Lord's Supper.[2] He therefore tried to conform Lutheran doctrines to America's generic Protestantism.

Today, 250 years after Muhlenberg rescued Lutherans from the culture of generic Protestantism, and a century and a half after Charles Porterfield Krauth and C. F. W. Walther, in opposition to Schmucker's objectives, gave Lutheran churches in America a confessional posture, Lutherans are once again facing a serious challenge to their confessional, biblical theology. That challenge is coming from multiculturalism, a powerful and pervasive phenomenon that, in various ways, has already deeply penetrated the theology, structure, and polity of the Evangelical Lutheran Church in America (ELCA), and, to some extent, has also made inroads into the Lutheran Church–Missouri Synod (LCMS) as well as the Wisconsin Evangelical Lutheran Synod (WELS).

The Nature of Multiculturalism

Multiculturalism. We hear and see its effects virtually every day. To many its name sounds suave and sophisticated. Some think it is chic and trendy. Yet countless people, including many Lutherans and their

---

1. Abdel Ross Wentz, *A Basic History of Lutheranism in America* (Philadelphia: Muhlenberg, 1955), p. 41.

2. David A. Gustafson, *Lutherans in Crisis: The Question of Identity in America* (Minneapolis: Fortress, 1993), p. 19.

pastors, do not know what this phenomenon really is. All too often people think it means learning about other cultures. Some Christians think it means bringing the Christian gospel to various societies and ethnic groups who have different cultural customs and practices. These and other misunderstandings of multiculturalism are seen in examples like the following: A congregation of the conservative WELS in Seattle, Washington, announced that "Grace [Lutheran] Church became a multicultural mission. . . . [W]here 25 different languages are spoken in a five-block radius, the church has become a prime location for spreading the Word among immigrants."[3] In 1994, speaking about the need for other societies to hear the gospel of Jesus Christ, Alvin L. Barry, president of the LCMS, wrote, "[W]e are truly being called to be a multicultural church body and all that implies."[4] In their contexts, both of these statements erroneously see multiculturalism as bringing the message of Christ crucified and risen to other cultural groups. But that is not multiculturalism.

The current phenomenon of multiculturalism, as I have documented with numerous illustrations in *The Menace of Multiculturalism: Trojan Horse in America*,[5] is not about appreciating and learning about other cultures. Quite to the contrary, it is a radical sociopolitical ideology that sees all cultures, and their beliefs, values, mores, and institutions, as essentially equal. It ignores cultural practices of non-Western societies that are truly oppressive and often even cruel and inhuman. Consider the veiling of women, the curtailing of women's freedom, and the subjection of young girls to clitoridectomy, practices found in many Islamic societies (especially in numerous African countries), as well as using children to perform adult labor in Mexico, West Africa, Bangladesh, and other regions. Multiculturalism sees no culture as superior or inferior to any other. Cultures are merely different. Criticism of other cultures, or any of their practices, especially if directed toward non-Western cultures, is labeled "insensitive" or "bigoted." Such criticism is "politically incorrect," and the sociopolitical force of political correctness seeks to get nonconforming individuals to conform and ac-

3. Julie K. Tessmer, "The Changeless Gospel in a Changing Congregation," *The Northwestern Lutheran* (December 1997): 10.

4. Alvin L. Barry, "From the President: A Convention Overview," *The Lutheran Witness* (August 1994): 26.

5. Westport, Conn.: Praeger, 1997.

cept the values, norms, and practices of multiculturalism. Under this system, there is only one culture that one is not urged to accept; the Euro-American culture, with its numerous Christian underpinnings, not only may be criticized but is also frequently accused of racism, sexism, classism, and imperialism.

Multiculturalism has its roots in cultural relativism, a concept which holds that every culture is to be judged relative to its own standards, and not from the outside by people of another culture. This radical concept can be traced to the German philosopher and court preacher Johann Gottfried von Herder (1744-1803). Cultural relativism gave rise to the idea that not just culture but the moral activities of another culture are also relative. After World War II this concept, often couched in the words of "truth is relative," was taught to millions of Americans and imbibed by them in high schools, colleges, and universities across the nation. Soon this notion expanded from not judging cultural practices from the outside to not judging behavior, by individuals or groups, within one's own culture. This belief has now filtered down to the average man and woman in America, as well as in some other countries. If, for instance, one says sexual relations outside of marriage, bearing children out of wedlock, homosexual behavior, same-sex unions, and abortion on demand are wrong or immoral, it is not uncommon for that person to be called bigoted or insensitive. And given that most Americans do not want to be labeled negatively, multiculturalism, with its accent on tolerance and pluralistic values, has silenced many individuals. In the process it has made great inroads into today's cultural fabric, especially during the last decade.

Multiculturalism Seeps into Lutheran Publications

Given the present American infatuation with multiculturalism, it is not surprising to see that the Zeitgeist of multiculturalism has also found its way into the life of American Lutheranism. One place that it has surfaced is in some Lutheran publications. Thus, in January of 1999, for example, an article appeared in *The Lutheran*, the official publication of the ELCA, titled "Celebrating Diversity." Consistent with the ideology of multiculturalism, the article lauded an emphasis on diversity and saw no problems with this phenomenon.[6] Yet one must ask: Does diversity also include approving and promoting the practice of Islamic women wearing veils? What about clitoridectomy for young girls? And is it acceptable to bring back, as some have recently tried, the Hindu custom of *sati* (widow burning) in India, which the British outlawed in 1829?[7] These and related questions are never raised by the proponents of multiculturalism. Nor have they been addressed by *The Lutheran*, which frequently promotes multiculturalism in its issues. Still another article in *The Lutheran* put a positive spin on homosexuality, an item on multiculturalism's agenda.[8] The fact that homosexual behavior has been condemned from the earliest of biblical times as being contrary to nature and displeasing to God does not seem to deter this publication from promoting it. Admonitory letters from some ELCA members also make no difference. For instance, writing in response to a recent article in *The Lutheran* that approved same-sex unions, one reader warned, "The ELCA is wandering into a tinderbox and scattering burning matches along the path it's traveling on. Sooner or later, the tinderbox will explode and with it, the ELCA will be consumed by the flames."[9]

Although multiculturalism has emerged in the Missouri Synod (as shown below), this has occurred primarily outside of its official organ, *The Lutheran Witness*. One finds it in other contexts, however. For example, in 1993 the synod's Board for Parish Services published a twelve-page manual titled *Black History Multicultural Materials*, designed for use in the synod's parochial schools. The manual indicates various ways in which students might be made aware of different multiculturalist concerns. Much is made of Harriet Tubman, but nothing is said about Law and Gospel or any other noteworthy Lutheran doctrine. Were it not for the Board for Parish Services' address on the front page and one reference to the Lutheran Church–Missouri Synod in the manual's introduction, one would not know from any of the manual's exercises that it is a Lutheran publication prepared for Lutheran pupils.

6. Sonia C. Solomonson, "Celebrating Diversity," *The Lutheran* (January 1999): 36.

7. "Fire and Faith," *Time* (September 29, 1987): 41.

8. Margaret Farnham, "What About Same-Sex Unions?" *The Lutheran* (September 2000): 36.

9. Gavin L. Helme, "Same-Sex Unions," *The Lutheran* (October 2000): 57.

Political Correctness Enters Lutheran Church Services

One of the areas of Lutheran church life that is experiencing the invasion of political correctness and multiculturalism is the Sunday morning service. Lyrics of many hymns and other elements of the church service are being adapted to suit political correctness. The hymnal supplement *With One Voice*, published by ELCA's Augsburg Fortress Press in 1992, changed the Virgin Mary's use of the masculine pronouns in the "Magnificat" to second person pronouns. These alterations, as one observer has noted, have drastically changed the character of the song: "Instead of witnessing to others about God's mighty acts, it is now addressed directly to God as a song of praise."[10] This hymnal has also made numerous other changes. For instance, the first line of the "Brief Order for Confession and Forgiveness" has been radically changed from "Father of mercies and God of all consolation," as it appears in the *Lutheran Book of Worship* hymnal, to "God of all mercy and consolation." Lack of space does not permit noting other changes found in *With One Voice*, many of them manifestly influenced by multiculturalism's pro-feminist thinking, which has made deep inroads into the life and theology of the ELCA.

In 1993 the ELCA traveled even further down the road of multiculturalism when it ignored the biblical foundations of the historic Lutheran liturgy by using an American Indian "smudging" ritual as part of the worship activities at its national convention in Kansas City. This rite used smoldering sweet grass, sage, and cedar, an American Indian version of incense. In addition, a radical feminist clergywoman preached on "inclusiveness." She castigated the ELCA's Euro-American members for being afraid of "losing [their] denominational and ethnic identity."[11]

Making hymns and related elements in church services politically correct is not confined to the liberal-minded ELCA. One even finds this practice in the conservative Wisconsin Synod. In 1993, it published its new hymnal, *Christian Worship: A Lutheran Hymnal*. The producers of this hymnal, knowingly or unknowingly, acquiesced to the spirit of multiculturalism's political correctness in tampering with

10. James Culver, Jr., "With One Voice," *Lutheran Forum* (February 1996): 46.
11. "Religious Scapegoats," *Forum Letter* (October 1993): 3.

Martin Luther's well-known hymn, "A Mighty Fortress Is Our God." The committee altered the words "And take they our life, goods, fame, child, and wife," as they appeared in *The Lutheran Hymnal* (1941), and replaced them with "And do what they will — Hate, steal, hurt, or kill." It should be noted that the former wording is essentially a literal translation of Luther's original composition. Evidently, the words "child and wife" were seen as sexist, so they were changed to comply with today's political correctness.

Another change in the Wisconsin Synod's new hymnal is even more clearly influenced by the values of political correctness. The words of the Nicene Creed that say God became incarnate in Jesus Christ as he "was made man" have been changed to "became fully human." To be sure, this translation can in part be justified on the basis of what the original version says in the Greek, namely, *anthropos* (meaning "man"), and the translations of Latin *homo factus* and the German *Mensch* grammatically also permit such a translation. But it is difficult to believe that the Zeitgeist of multiculturalism's political correctness did not influence this change. This seems to be equally true of the clause in this hymnal that changed the Nicene Creed's words "for us men" to "for us." If asked, individuals in the Wisconsin Synod who made these changes would likely say that today's political correctness had nothing to do with the changes. But it is highly inconceivable that such changes would have been made a generation or two ago, before the advent of multiculturalism and political correctness.

When one takes a look at the LCMS, the influence of multiculturalism is also evident in its church services. The LCMS, similar to the ELCA and WELS, has in recent years had an increasing number of its congregations on Sunday morning jettison the historic Lutheran liturgy as it has been used in *The Lutheran Hymnal* since 1941 or *Lutheran Worship* since 1982. One of the primary vehicles used to aid and abet pastors and congregations in replacing the traditional liturgy is the publication known as *Creative Worship*, a publication produced and sold by the Missouri Synod's Concordia Publishing House.

Creative Worship materials come in printed form or on computer disks. Both can be reproduced verbatim or adapted for Sunday morning bulletins, which typically replace the hymnal. The reported popularity of these materials cannot be fully understood without taking into account the spirit of multiculturalism that so widely pervades

American society today. We need to remember that multiculturalism asserts that all cultures and their practices are essentially equal, and that the values of all cultures or subcultures must be honored. From this belief it is but a small step to say that all forms of worship are also equal, and so it is quite appropriate to supplant the historic Lutheran liturgies. Thus, *Creative Worship*, reproduced and printed in Sunday bulletins, commonly replaces the historic *Gloria Patria*, the *Kyrie*, the *Gloria in Excelsis*, and the *Sanctus* with something new and different every Sunday.

Eliminating the historic liturgies on Sunday morning and replacing them with various improvisations is quite consistent with multiculturalism, given its underlying relativism. Such changes imply that the new elements used in a Sunday morning service are as good as any historic liturgy, and also reveal the extent to which many pastors believe they need to appeal to people of different subcultures in our society. Jettisoning the traditional liturgy, however, and then calling the improvisations "creative worship" or "service of praise" is a definite rejection of what Lutherans for five hundred hundred years have understood by the concept of *Gottesdienst* (Divine Service), namely, that when Christians go to church, it is God serving them with his word and sacrament. They merely respond out of thankfulness for what he has given and continues to give (serve) them through his Son, Jesus Christ. In fact, the phrase "word and sacrament," a common Lutheran expression, makes sense only in light of the *Gottesdienst* concept. Unfortunately, the English word "worship," something that *people* do, leads members to think that the primary reason they go to church is to serve God. So they see it as their service, not God's. This makes for spiritual self-congratulation. Hence, it is not surprising that the ELCA calls its present hymnal *Lutheran Book of Worship* (published in 1978), and the Missouri Synod's counterpart is similarly called *Lutheran Worship* (published in 1982). A title like *Divine Service Book for Lutherans* or *A Lutheran Divine Service Hymnal* evidently had no appeal, even though such a title would have been a true reflection of traditional Lutheran theology.

In 1992, when multiculturalism had already made significant inroads in American thought and also in Lutheran circles, Concordia Publishing House of the LCMS produced a new songbook called *All God's People Sing*. Although this book of songs was not intended to replace the *Lutheran Worship* hymnal or *The Lutheran Hymnal* in LCMS congregations, its foreword does not rule out its use in Sunday morning services. It states that the book "can be used in almost any setting in which Christians gather."[12] Many of its songs are devoid of Law and Gospel content, a doctrine that has always been at the core of Lutheran theology. One section, "We Shall Overcome," filled with songs popular during the American Civil Rights movement of the 1960s, not only falls outside the rubric of Law and Gospel but also makes no reference to sin, repentance, forgiveness, or Jesus Christ. It belongs exclusively in the arena of political correctness.

Another example of multiculturalism's presence in the LCMS and the ELCA is the 1999 publication *This Far by Faith,* a hymnal designed for Lutherans who are black Americans. Initially, this hymnal was to be published by Concordia Publishing House of the LCMS, but the Doctrinal Review Committee of the synod did not approve the doctrinal content of this hymnal, and so the synod declined to publish it. After this declination, the ELCA's Augsburg Fortress Press published it. But it is worth noting that while the LCMS declined to publish and officially approve this hymnal, it did not advise its 6,200 congregations to refrain from using it. In fact, the sixtieth regular convention of the LCMS (July 2001) passed a resolution saying: "That congregations using *This Far By Faith* be encouraged to evaluate its contents on the basis of Holy Scripture and the Lutheran Confessions . . . [and] guidelines being prepared by the Commission on Worship, so that it may be used responsibly."[13] Members of the LCMS are probably unaware of how the societal presence of multiculturalism prompted the convention to adopt this resolution, which reveals a theological compromise, if not a contradiction, relative to the synod's historic emphasis on purity of doctrine. One need only look at the constitution of the synod, which in Article VI:4 states that all congregations are to make "Exclusive use of doctrinally pure agendas [and] hymn books."[14] Many of the hymns in *This Far By Faith* clearly fall short of a "doctrinally pure agenda."

The influence of multiculturalism can be seen throughout this

12. *All God's People Sing* (St. Louis: Concordia, 1992), p. 4.

13. "To Encourage Responsible Use of *This Far By Faith,*" Convention Proceedings, 60th Regular Convention, The Lutheran Church–Missouri Synod (2001), p. 130.

14. "Conditions of Membership," *Handbook of the Lutheran Church–Missouri Synod* (1998), p. 11.

hymnal. Its marriage rite, for example, has a section that suggests the use of a *kente* cloth that may be "unfolded and held around the couple and over their heads."[15] In addition to many of the book's hymns being devoid of Law and Gospel, it devotes two pages to the holiday of Kwanza, which was created in 1966 by Maulana (Ron) Karenga, a radical black studies professor in California. Celebrated from December 26 to January 1, Kwanza purports to acquaint black Americans with their African culture, but, as the renowned black scholar Thomas Sowell has noted, "little or no African culture [has survived] among American negroes."[16] Initially, Karenga's holiday was celebrated primarily by radical black-nationalists. Today, given the mass media's favorable publicity of Kwanza, it is observed by considerably more black Americans, especially by those who espouse the values of multiculturalism.

Ron Karenga had no intention of giving Kwanza any religious significance. (In fact, he initially created it as a replacement for Western religious holidays, arguing that Western religions diminished human potential, although he has since changed his justification for the holiday.) But this did not deter the black Lutheran advocates who produced *This Far by Faith* from giving Kwanza a religious aura by appending a biblical passage to each of Kwanza's Seven Principles. The hymnal devotes an entire page to these Seven Principles.[17] They are *Umoja* (unity), *Kujichagulia* (self-determination), *Ujima* (collective work and responsibility), *Ujamaa* (cooperative economics), *Nia* (purpose), *Kuumba* (creativity), and *Imani* (faith). The third and fourth principles are socialist in nature, and the seventh (faith) bears no similarity to the biblical concept of faith in the New Testament, as enunciated by Jesus Christ and the apostles. In short, Kwanza (Swahili for "first fruits") and its Seven Principles are derived largely from African agricultural festivals practiced by pagans.[18]

Martin Luther King Jr. once pleaded, "Let us not be judged by the color of our skin but by the content of our character." Apparently, this plea was far from the minds of those who produced this hymnal, for

15. *This Far by Faith: An African American Resource for Worship* (Minneapolis: Augsburg Fortress, 1999), p. 108.

16. Thomas Sowell, *Ethnic America* (New York: Basic, 1981), p. 184.

17. *This Far by Faith*, p. 108.

18. Janice C. Simpson, "Tidings of Black Pride and Joy," *Time* (December 23, 1991): 81.

had they remembered King's words, they might have paraphrased them and said, "Let us not judge our present Lutheran hymnals by the color of those who wrote them, but by the content of their theology." That approach would have served and honored black Lutherans more nobly than a hymnal which reflects more the values of multiculturalism than of confessional Lutheran theology.

The Feminist Influence

The feminist influence of recent years has made significant inroads into American Lutheranism. As was touched on above, it has even affected the conservative Wisconsin Synod's new hymnal, which changed the Nicene Creed to say that God in Jesus Christ "became fully human" rather than "was made man," as it appeared in the traditional version.

One of the more significant effects of feminism in Lutheran circles today occurred in the ELCA when it opted for proportional representation of sex (as well as of race and ethnicity), also known as political quotas. The quest for quotas, an important facet of multiculturalism, has since the 1970s become a major part of America's secular politics, especially in the Democratic Party. And it did not take long for this political goal to find its way into the nation's liberal denominations, including the ELCA.

In 1972, the Lutheran Church in America (LCA), fifteen years before it merged with the American Lutheran Church (ALC) and the Association of Evangelical Lutheran Churches (AELC) in 1987, formed a group known as the Consulting Committee on Women in Church and Society (CCWCS). This group was given several charges; one was to devise strategies to increase proportionate representation of women in all LCA decision-making entities. Gracia Grindal writes that "The language suggesting quotas for the representation of women was disputed at the LCA convention, although an amendment to remove it failed."[19]

The CCWCS did not falter. In fact, it did its work so well that the

19. Gracia Grindal, "Women in the Evangelical Lutheran Church in America," in *Religious Institutions and Women's Leadership: New Roles Inside the Mainstream,* ed. Catherine Wessinger (Columbia: University of South Carolina Press, 1996), p. 185.

fruits of its labors carried over into the merger in 1987 when the ELCA came into being. Thus, not only do ELCA delegates at national conventions have to be selected on the basis of quotas, but delegates to regional synods also must be selected in that manner. The ELCA's *Constitution, Bylaws, and Continuing Resolution* commands that all synod organizational entities be 50 percent female and 50 percent male, and that "at least 10 percent of the members of these assemblies, councils, committees, boards, or other organizational units shall be persons of color and/or persons whose primary language is other than English" (5.01.f). Moreover, regarding quotas, the constitution leaves no wiggle room for any misunderstanding of the ELCA's multiculturalist objectives, for it specifies that "persons of color . . . shall be understood to mean African American, Black, Arab, and Middle Eastern Asian, Hispanic, American Indian, and Alaskan Native people" (5.01.C96). It is interesting to note that two years before the merger, and thus before this constitutional stipulation became a permanent plank, Lowell Almen (later elected secretary of the new body) warned with little or no effect that the ELCA was "becoming little more than the ecclesiastical wing of the Democratic Party."[20]

Another directive to the CCWCS was for it to create guidelines for implementing inclusive language in all published materials of the LCA. As with the matter of quotas, the committee's vigilant and aggressive pursuit in favor of inclusive language later also became an integral part of the ELCA in 1987.

Five years before the ELCA was formed in 1987, the Commission for a New Lutheran Church (CNLC), comprised of seventy members from the LCA, ALC, and AELC, was established to define a number of issues for the forthcoming merger of these three bodies to create the ELCA. In designing the new merger, the feminist leaders of the CNLC almost pulled off a major theological coup. Not only were they able to bring to a vote the issue of whether to retain or alter the Trinitarian formula of "Father, Son, and Holy Spirit" as part of the official theological position of the ELCA, but their desired change to "Triune God" lost by only three votes in a count of thirty-three to thirty.

---

20. Lowell Almen, "The Back Page," *The Lutheran Standard* (May 5, 1985): 30.

Multiculturalism's Presence in Lutheran Colleges and Universities

During the last decade or so nearly every Lutheran college, in a socially contagious sort of manner, has been promoting multiculturalism. Thus, in recent years Augustana College in Rock Island, Illinois, has been featuring an annual Kwanza celebration. This college, once prominently populated by conservatively minded students of Swedish background, also boasts having a Black Student Union, something now seen as being multiculturally sensitive and politically correct. In the 1960s and 1970s, however, a one-color group would have been a violation of the *Brown v. Board of Education* Supreme Court decision of 1954, which declared the separate-but-equal principle as unconstitutional. This all-black student group meets in the Black Culture House on the college's campus.

The current proclivity toward multiculturalism with its accent on "diversity" is, of course, also present at other ELCA colleges. For instance, Muhlenberg College in Allentown, Pennsylvania, in its publication *Prospectus*, cites students praising the college's diversity posture. Muhlenberg's *Cultural Club Quarterly* in one of its articles refers to a past event that occurred in "2696 B.C.E." This symbol and its counterpart C.E. are politically correct designations and have the effect of taking Jesus Christ out of history.

Perhaps the most remarkable example of multiculturalism's spirit and mind-set within the arena of Lutheran higher education occurred at Capital University, Columbus, Ohio, a Lutheran university of the old Ohio Synod that was in fellowship with the LCMS back in the 1870s. In 1999 this Lutheran school chose a Roman Catholic as its president. This election prompted Paul Williams, a Lutheran pastor and a member of the university's Board of Trustees, to say, "The Lutheran tradition is slipping away from us."[21]

Capital University's enrollment in the year 2000 stood at about 3,900 students, but only 20 percent of them were Lutheran. A decade earlier 30 percent of its students were Lutheran. It is not known whether this rapid decline in the number of Lutheran students on this campus and other Lutheran colleges is a direct result of multicultural-

---

21. Quoted in Monica Wilch Perin, "Still Lutheran? ELCA Colleges Struggle to Expose Their Identity in a Pluralistic Society," *The Lutheran* (November 2000): 57.

ism's presence and influence in recent years. But, given the continued presence of multiculturalism on the ELCA's college campuses, it is quite likely that the number of Lutheran students in the future will decrease even further.

In many respects there is very little difference between the ELCA and the LCMS colleges and universities with regard to their genuflecting before the altar of multiculturalism. The Missouri Synod's Concordia University (known as Concordia College until recently) in St. Paul, Minnesota, boasts having a Diversity Affairs Office, headed by a dean of diversity. And, consistent with multiculturalism's politically correct lingo, this office has a published circular about the school which says it seeks to "orient new Students of Color to services. . . ." These students also have "mentors of color." The situation is similar at Concordia University, River Forest, Illinois, which, in its *Forester* magazine, published an article in 1999 titled, "Making Every Day a Multicultural Experience."[22]

Valparaiso University, Valparaiso, Indiana, a school affiliated but not owned or controlled by the LCMS, also tries hard to promote what it calls the "Diverse Voices of Valpo," in part through its Office of Multicultural Programs. Ironically, the six-page brochure just quoted, which makes much of the school's accent on "diversity," completely ignores its Lutheran affiliation, hence prompting one to ask: Is being Lutheran not part of the university's understanding of diversity? The university also employs politically correct language; for instance, its *General Catalog* states that the student union "is fully accessible to persons who are physically challenged," rather saying "physically handicapped."

Homosexuality and the Lutheran Churches

According to the multicultural and politically correct mind-set, one is supposed to be affirming not only of all cultural practices but of a variety of lifestyles as well. One prominent objective of multiculturalism is the promotion and integration of homosexual behavior, despite the fact that such behavior is still largely a contra-cultural phenomenon in America. Given the ELCA's proclivity toward multiculturalism's em-

22. "Making Every Day a Multicultural Experience," *Forester* (Summer 1999): 8.

phasis on accepting virtually all kinds of cultural diversity, it is not surprising that the denomination has in recent years been making serious efforts to accept and accommodate the homosexual lifestyle within its theological parameters. In the year 2000, the Greater Milwaukee Synod (a regional unit) of the ELCA passed two resolves at its convention. The first one stated "that a committed relationship be defined as one where there is love, quality, faithfulness and endurance and mutual uplifting of spirits." The second resolve declared: "and be it further resolved that the Greater Milwaukee Synod recognizes and affirms the blessing of such committed same gender relationships by pastors of this synod after counseling with the couple seeking such a blessing."[23]

Although the ELCA has not, as of yet, officially adopted this regional synod's stance of blessing same-sex unions, it is clear that the secular society's advocacy of same-sex relationships, a major step toward accepting the legalization of same-sex marriages, has made significant inroads into the ELCA, and it is worthy of note that while the ELCA has not officially condoned same-sex relationships, it has also not condemned them. Hence, it appears quite likely that in time there will be more resolutions passed by congregations and regional synods within the ELCA, making it quite likely that eventually same-sex relationships will be approved by the church body as a whole.

The request for approving and blessing same-sex relationships has thus far not surfaced in the LCMS, nor has any request been made to ordain practicing homosexuals in the synod's ministry. It should be noted that the LCMS in its national convention in 1998 authorized the creation of a Task Force on Ministry to Homosexuals and Their Families. This task force prepared a report that was adopted at the synod's national convention in July 2001. The report, however, did not say or imply that same-sex relationships were acceptable behavior. In fact, it stated that homosexual behavior is "contrary to the created order . . . and intrinsically sinful."[24]

Although the issue has not arisen in the Missouri Synod, the push for the ordination of practicing homosexuals has had an influ-

---

23. Cited from a fax document I received from the Greater Milwaukee Synod (September 15, 2000).

24. "Ministry to Homosexuals and Their Families," Convention Proceedings, 60th Regular Convention, The Lutheran Church–Missouri Synod (St. Louis, 2001), p. 130.

ence on the ELCA (as well as on some non-Lutheran denominations). Thus, several congregations in the ELCA have recently ordained homosexuals, although without official ELCA approval. The most noteworthy example occurred on April 28, 2001, at St. Paul Reformation Lutheran Church in St. Paul, Minnesota, where Anita Hill, a lesbian, was ordained, contrary to the present official policy of the ELCA. Participating in this ordination were one active ELCA bishop (who after the ordination was asked to resign), three retired bishops, and 150 clergy (some of them non-Lutheran). To date, this congregation in Minnesota has not been disciplined, much less removed from the roster of ELCA congregations. Abiding Peace Lutheran Church, Kansas City, Missouri, another ELCA congregation, which in 2000 ordained Donna Simon, a lesbian, also has received nothing more than a censure from its bishop.[25]

Given that many in the ELCA favor blessing same-sex relationships and ordaining practicing homosexuals, it is not surprising to read positive portrayals of homosexual behavior in *The Lutheran,* the official monthly periodical of the ELCA. One such article, written by a lesbian, said that homosexuality is an acceptable lifestyle for Christians. This article also noted that 149 ELCA congregations and 12 synods, as of February 1999, had voted to become part of the group known as Reconciling in Christ, which welcomes practicing homosexuals into the life of ELCA parishes.

In addition, at its national convention in Indianapolis in August 2001, the denomination resolved by a vote of 899 to 115 to engage in a formal study of whether homosexuals may be ordained and whether same-sex relationships may be ecclesiastically blessed. The study will be presented to the next convention in 2005. Since some congregations in the ELCA already have ordained homosexuals and some have also blessed same-sex unions, it will not be surprising if this body of 5,200,000 members gives formal approval to both of these practices at its next national convention. If this happens, it will be a sea-change departure from the biblical Scriptures and historic Lutheranism, as well as a reversal of the early church's condemnation of the homosexual practices of the pagan Greeks and Romans. In this context it is noteworthy to recall that even while the early church was still an illegal entity in the

25. Russell E. Saltzman, personal communication (2001).

Roman world, it resolved at the Synod of Elvira (Spain) in A.D. 306 to deny baptism and catechesis to all homosexuals unless they repented and vowed to no longer practice this sinful behavior. The Council of Ancyra (Turkey) in A.D. 314 reaffirmed the decision of Elvira.

Whether looking at the "gay-friendly" disposition of the ELCA or its openness to other dimensions of the multiculturalist agenda, it is quite evident that confessional Lutheranism within the ELCA has essentially evaporated. The words of Michael C. D. McDaniel, once a professor of religion at Lenoir-Rhyne College and also a former ELCA bishop of the North Carolina Synod, come to mind. Diversity and inclusivity, said he, are so highly valued now by the ELCA that these two ideological principles of multiculturalism have "rapidly [become] a greater force in decision-making than either law or the gospel."[26]

Multiculturalism and the Zeitgeist

Although multiculturalism has made inroads in varying degrees into all three major Lutheran bodies in the United States, it not only has invaded but has also conquered the ELCA, which obligingly surrendered to it. Even though the LCMS has naively toyed with some aspects of multiculturalism, it has so far not embraced multiculturalism to the extent that the ELCA has. It has not accepted the corollaries of multiculturalism such as feminist-oriented theology and quotas based on sex, race, or ethnicity; nor has it ever considered formal proposals to approve same-sex unions or the ordination of practicing homosexuals. It is therefore not surprising that the Missouri Synod, at its national convention in July 2001, resolved that it no longer considers the ELCA "to be an orthodox Lutheran church body."[27] This action indicates that confessional Lutheran theology in the LCMS is still alive, and that it still has the potential to fend off further invasions of multiculturalism. Nevertheless, multiculturalism's ever-present accompanying forces of political correctness, diversity, and feminism do

26. Michael C. D. McDaniel, "ELCA Journeys: Personal Reflections on the Last Forty Years," *Concordia Theological Quarterly* (April 2001): 106.
27. "To Address Cooperative Pastoral Working Arrangements with Evangelical Lutheran Church in America," Convention Proceedings, 60th Regular Convention, The Lutheran Church–Missouri Synod (St. Louis, 2001), p. 142.

prompt the question: How long will confessional Lutheran theology, as it was once bequeathed to them by C. F. W. Walther, remain in the LCMS and WELS?

If informed, critical examination of multiculturalism, a major threat to confessional Lutheran theology, does not occur in both the LCMS and WELS — and thus far there has been very little of such examination — it would be difficult to argue why both bodies may not eventually succumb to this anti-Christian and anti-Lutheran Zeitgeist, as has happened in the ELCA. Were this to happen, the name "Lutheran" would have a vacuous sound and content, reminiscent of St. Paul's description to Timothy of those who in the last days will hold to "the outwardly form of godliness, but den[y] its power" (2 Timothy 3:5).

BIBLIOGRAPHY

All God's People Sing. St. Louis: Concordia, 1992.

Almen, Lowell. "The Back Page." *The Lutheran Standard* (May 5, 1985): 30.

Barry, Alvin L. "From the President: A Convention Overview." *The Lutheran Witness* (August 1994).

Culver, James Jr. "With One Voice." *Lutheran Forum* (February 1996).

Farnham, Margaret. "What About Same-Sex Unions?" *The Lutheran* (September 2000): 36.

"Fire and Faith." *Time* (September 29, 1987).

Grindal, Gracia. "Women in the Evangelical Lutheran Church in America." In *Religious Institutions and Women's Leadership: New Roles Inside the Mainstream,* ed. Catherine Wessinger. Columbia: University of South Carolina Press, 1996.

Gustafson, David A. *Lutherans in Crisis: The Question of Identity in America.* Minneapolis: Fortress, 1993.

Helme, Gavin L. "Same-Sex Unions." *The Lutheran* (October 2000): 57.

"Making Every Day a Multicultural Experience." *Forester* (Summer 1999).

McDaniel, Michael C. D. "ELCA Journeys: Personal Reflections on the Last Forty Years." *Concordia Theological Quarterly* (April 2001).

Perin, Monica Wilch. "Still Lutheran? ELCA Colleges Struggle to Expose Their Identity in a Pluralistic Society." *The Lutheran* (November 2000).

Schmidt, Alvin J. *The Menace of Multiculturalism: Trojan Horse in America.* Westport, Conn.: Praeger, 1997.

Simpson, Janice C. "Tidings of Black Pride and Joy." *Time* (December 23, 1991).

Solomonson, Sonia C. "Celebrating Diversity." *The Lutheran* (January 1999).

Sowell, Thomas. *Ethnic America.* New York: Basic, 1981.

Tessmer, Julie K. "The Changeless Gospel in a Changing Congregation." *The Northwestern Lutheran* (December 1997).

This Far By Faith: An African American Resource for Worship. Minneapolis: Augsburg Fortress.

Wentz, Abdel Ross. *A Basic History of Lutheranism in America.* Philadelphia: Muhlenberg, 1955.

Integrity and Fragmentation: Can the Lutheran Center Hold?

ROBERT BENNE

There is much discussion today about whether a "Lutheran center" or identity can hold in many Lutheran colleges. In my view, the Lutheran center cannot hold in many, if not most, colleges because it was never there in an articulated form in the first place. To paraphrase the words of James Burtchaell, "How can those colleges miss what they never had?" How can they hold now what they never held in the first place? A few Lutheran colleges have been able to articulate and hold a distinct religious center that has shaped and organized their lives as colleges. Though that center may be under constant discussion, it still provides the identity and mission of the college as a whole. Whether it can remain the organizing paradigm for the college of the future is an open question. But the fact that it is under intense public discussion is a good sign.

Mere discussion is not enough though. Discussion can lead to chaos or paralysis. (The whole faculty of Calvin Seminary was once dismissed by its Board because they had argued themselves to an impasse. The good Calvinist pastors on the Board held the quaint thought that the seminary should have a clear position on important matters of faith.) Ongoing discussion can also lead to notions of a center that in fact will marginalize or subvert any persisting Lutheran identity. That nuance, too, will have to be unpacked.

It is important to define at least provisionally and formally what is meant by "center." I would argue that the center for Lutheran liberal arts colleges ought to be religiously defined. That is, a religious vision of Christian higher education should be at their center. This religious vision, which like the Christian faith is comprehensive, would have within it an interpretation of the role and nature of human learning. (This provision of course eliminates a lot of Lutheran colleges who would currently find it quite embarrassing to admit that their mission was religiously defined.)

The religious vision comes from a living religious tradition. Alasdair MacIntyre has famously argued that a living tradition is "an historically extended, socially embodied argument about the goods which constitute that tradition." Traditions extend through many generations. Lutheranism is such a tradition — or better, such a constellation of traditions — and it has sponsored many colleges and universities.

Differing Visions of Lutheran Colleges

In giving a rationale for its involvement in higher education, Lutheranism has never exhibited unanimity. But its religious commitments led it to establish colleges that had an educational purpose consonant with its perceived mission. Something in these Lutheran bodies impelled them to establish colleges. The problem for many Lutheran colleges is that they were not conceptually clear about what they were doing. The impulse was there but the sharp rationale — particularly a theological rationale — was not. These colleges were "Christ of culture" colleges.

H. Richard Niebuhr, in his renowned book *Christ and Culture,* identified five classic ways that Christian traditions have related Christ (the Christian vision) to culture. One of those, the Christ-of-culture tradition, identifies Christianity with the best of high culture. For example, during the Enlightenment many of the elite identified Christ as a sublime teacher of morality. He was a hero of culture along the lines of a Socrates. The way I am using the Christ-of-culture category is a bit different. I mean that for many Lutheran groups that established colleges, the Christian vision was deeply and unconsciously entwined with their particular ethno-religious culture. They were fairly homogenous groups that wanted their young to be educated within the ethno-religious culture that they prized. They wanted their laity-to-be to be immersed in the "atmosphere" of their culture. More-

over, they wanted that culture to encourage candidates for the ordained ministry who would then go on to seminaries of that tradition.

The Midland Lutheran College of my college days was such a
college. We were children of the German and Scandinavian Lutheran
immigrations to the Midwest. Most of us had parents who hadn't gone
to college, but we were encouraged by them and our local parishes to
go to "our" school. We were taught by faculty generally of that same
ethno-religious culture. Ninety-some percent of us were from those
backgrounds. How could such education not be Lutheran? Almost everyone at the college was Lutheran. Similar statements could be made
about Gettysburg and Muhlenberg colleges a generation or so earlier.
Many of the Lutheran colleges exhibited these characteristics.

But was there anything more specifically Lutheran about that
Midland of yore? Not a whole lot. Religion was a pretty inward, non-
intellectual matter. We had pietist behavioral standards that prohib-
ited premarital sex and alcohol. We had Bible courses offered at a low
level of sophistication. We had required chapel of a distinctly
nonliturgical sort. We had faculty who had committed their lives to the
college and who now and then would connect their Christian perspective with their teaching. By and large the faculty and administration
encouraged us as young Christians.

But there was no articulated center that sharply delineated the
mission of the college. The theological acuity to do that was simply absent, or was felt not to be needed. Lutheran theology and ethics were
not taught. Lutheran history was nowhere to be found. The Lutheran
idea of the calling was not explicitly taught to young people who had
had it bred into them in their parishes. There was no concerted intellectual effort to interrelate the Christian vision with other fields of
learning. We were simply Lutheran by ethos. We were immersed in a
Christ-of-culture educational enterprise.

When the colleges expanded their student bodies and faculties in
the late fifties and sixties, students and faculty members were re-
cruited who were no longer part of that ethos. Indeed, the ethos itself
was melting into the general American culture. Since the colleges had
no articulated center, they lost whatever integrity and unity they had.
Soon faculty appeared who were not only apathetic about the tradition
that originally sponsored them, but actually hostile. Raising any question about a religious center disturbed and offended them. The culture

that was friendly to Christ became one that either ignored or rejected him — and the college changed with that culture.

The loss of such a religious, Christ-of-culture orientation did not mean death for the colleges, some of which found new ways to define themselves. Gettysburg, among others, went for high quality and highly selective pre-professional education. This provides a certain kind of integrity and unity, but not one that is religiously defined. At most, religion is a grace note, a flavor in the mix, a social ornament — but certainly not the organizing center. It remains to be seen whether such an identity is satisfying enough to either college or church to maintain it.

Other Lutheran colleges, which Burtchaell calls the "confessional colleges," did have a more articulated center. That is, the religious vision that sprang from their religious tradition was more specific, often theologically stated. They didn't mind being viewed as "sectarian," an appellation from which the Christ-of-culture colleges fled. This theological distillation of the religious vision served as the paradigm around which was organized the whole life of the college — its academic, social, organizational, and extracurricular facets.

Two Lutheran colleges I recently studied are representative of these "confessional colleges."[1] St. Olaf College in Northfield, Minnesota, a college of the Evangelical Lutheran Church in America, and Valparaiso University in Valparaiso, Indiana, historically linked to the Lutheran Church–Missouri Synod, are both highly articulated colleges who have kept a robust connection with their sponsoring Lutheran religious traditions. They have organized their identities and missions around the Christian vision and ethos.

St. Olaf, stemming from a strong Norwegian Lutheran religious tradition, has had a long history of tending its Lutheran identity. In its early days, St. Olaf was so pervasively Norwegian Lutheran that it scarcely had to attend to its identity, but it did, mainly through the charismatic leadership of its clergy presidents. They were able to draw to St. Olaf some giants in the world of literature and music — for example, the author O. E. Rolvaag and the choral conductor F. Melius Christianson. From the beginning, the Lutheran idea of the calling of

---

1. See Robert Benne, *Quality with Soul: How Six Premier Colleges and Universities Keep Faith with Their Religious Traditions* (Grand Rapids: Eerdmans, 2001).

all Christians was a central organizing motif; it pervaded the consciousness of faculty, students, and staff.

After the Norwegian ethnic identity waned following World War II, St. Olaf began serious theological reflections about its identity and mission. These affirmed St. Olaf's commitment to an engagement between secular learning and Lutheran theology. They also insured a strong commitment to teaching required courses in Christian theology and ethics, and to encouraging exchanges between the Christian vision and secular fields of learning. This reflection and commitment continue at St. Olaf. It is a self-consciously Lutheran Christian college.

This articulation of the Lutheran identity of the college is bolstered by the ethos maintained at the college. Over 50 percent of the students are Lutheran, and the college would like to keep that percentage high. There is a highly developed daily chapel program presided over by a distinguished chaplain and his staff, and there are many active Christian groups on campus. Further, the famed St. Olaf choral and instrumental music programs draw the participation of almost half the student body. These programs, moreover, are not simply aesthetically oriented but are also religiously serious. Students are invited into a deeper exploration of their Christian commitments through them.

Much of a similar nature could be said about Valparaiso University. Its theater, choral, instrumental, and visual arts are flourishing. These programs in the arts are led by capable young Christians, and they become vehicles for the Christian formation of the students. While Valparaiso doesn't have the percentage of Lutherans that St. Olaf does, it appeals to large numbers of Roman Catholics. Together these two religious groups constitute roughly 60 percent of the student body. They worship together in daily chapel services in the stunning Chapel of the Resurrection, the largest and most architecturally interesting building on campus. The chapel was built to symbolize the Christian center of all learning. Emblazoned on its front is Valparaiso's motto: "In Thy Light We See Light."

Valparaiso is informally related but not legally tied to the theologically conservative Lutheran Church–Missouri Synod. Lutheran theology has provided its defining vision from its inception as a Lutheran school in 1920. That vision was given charismatic articulation by its longtime, larger-than-life president, O. P. Kretzmann. In his long tenure at the university he gathered a large group of impressive Lutheran intellectuals who taught and wrote at the university. He also founded literary journals, an honors college, and a liturgical institute, among other things. Throughout his tenure and beyond, the university has enjoyed a conspicuous flowering of Christian humanism, Lutheran style.

The university continues this heritage even though its relation to the Lutheran Church–Missouri Synod is ambiguous. It continues to be led by Lutheran leaders in its board, administration, faculty, and alumni. The Christian vision and ethos continue to be the organizing paradigm for its life and mission. Moreover, it has strengthened this commitment by garnering a number of externally funded centers, institutes, and programs that contribute directly to its religious identity and mission. It also fosters an ongoing public discussion about its Lutheran, Christian character, which witnesses to the fact that its church-relatedness is the crucial element in its self-understanding.

These two schools continue to exemplify a centered Lutheran version of Christian humanism. Throughout their histories, they have been led by people who have had a clear rationale for what they were doing. And this rationale has sprung from their religious tradition and has been theologically articulated. It has been supported by a board that has explicitly supported and prized that tradition. Above all, the schools have had the courage to select faculty who have supported such a notion of Lutheran humanism.

These two, and a number of other such Lutheran colleges, still exist, but they have an uphill battle to maintain their identity. Some schools that once had a clear rationale are, in fact, already losing it. A number of reasons for this are obvious. Some colleges fight for survival and are willing to adapt to market conditions even if it means giving up their religious center. Others are seduced into giving up their religious center by the lure of a glorious worldly success. Some have increasing numbers of administrators and faculty who simply do not see the point in trying to operate from a religious center. They do not believe that the Christian vision is any longer an adequate vision for organizing the life of a college. For many of those administrators and faculty, religion is a private, interior matter that should not be publicly relevant to the educational enterprise. Some colleges can no longer agree on the center and fall into a kind of chaotic pluralism.

Then they cannot summon either the clarity or courage needed to hire faculty who support Lutheran humanism in higher education.

A number of Lutheran colleges fall between these two depictions. They are a bit more intentional than the Christ-of-culture types but less defined than the Lutheran humanist types. I do not wish to set up exclusive categories; but it does us no good for Lutherans to continue with self-congratulation concerning fidelity to a Lutheran center when so many of their colleges have little or no semblance of one.

Defining a Lutheran Center

All this brings us to the question: What would a Lutheran "center" look like? First of all, a Lutheran center is a Christian center. Lutherans share with other major Christian traditions a common Christian narrative — the Bible and the long history of the church. From those narratives emerged early on what we could call the apostolic or Trinitarian faith, defined in the classic ecumenical creeds. In the long history of the church much theological reflection took place; a Christian intellectual tradition was shaped. This intellectual tradition conveyed a Christian view of the origin and destiny of the world, of nature and history, of human nature and its predicament, of human salvation, and of a Christian way of life. This larger Christian tradition also bore Christian practices such as worship, marriage, hospitality, charity, and so on.

The Lutheran Reformation and its ensuing history arose from and expressed a Lutheran construal of this general Christian tradition. Many of the facets of that construal are ensconced in the Lutheran Confessions. Some of the more particular elements of that Lutheran construal will be discussed a bit later as I further delineate the Lutheran center for Christian higher education. This Lutheran Christian vision of reality, particularly in its intellectual form, constitutes the center. But how will it work out in the life of a college? How will it provide the organizing paradigm for the identity and mission of a college? How will it make a difference? What difference will it make?

Mark Schwehn, in a recent address at the University of Chicago (later published in *First Things*), provides a wonderful starting point. In his address he attempts to define the characteristics of a Christian university, one that, as I put it, employs the Christian vision as the organizing paradigm for its life and mission. Schwehn talks generically about "Christian" institutions but I will transpose his language for specifically Lutheran colleges. I will also abbreviate the rich elaboration of each of his characteristics.

First, Schwehn lists what he calls "constitutional requirements." A Lutheran college must have a board of trustees composed of a substantial majority of Lutheran persons, clergy and lay, whose primary task is to ensure the continuity of the school's Lutheran Christian character. This will mean appointing a majority of Lutheran leaders who are committed to the idea of a Lutheran Christian college.

These leaders will in turn see to it that all of the following things are present within the life of the institution: first, a department of theology that offers courses required of all students in both biblical studies and the Christian intellectual tradition; second, an active chapel ministry that offers worship services in the tradition of the faith community that supports the school (Lutheran) but also makes provision for worship by those of other faiths; third, a critical mass of faculty members who, in addition to being excellent teacher-scholars, carry in and among themselves the DNA of the school, care for the perpetuation of its mission as a Christian community of inquiry, and understand their own callings as importantly bound up with the well-being of the immediate community; and fourth, a curriculum that includes a large number of courses, required of all students, that are compellingly construed as parts of a larger whole and that taken together constitute a liberal education.[2]

Second, Schwehn develops three qualities that ought to be present in a Lutheran Christian college and that flow directly from its theological commitments. The first is unity. By that he means the conviction that since God is One and Creator, all reality and all truth finally cohere in him. Thus, the Christian college quests for the unity that follows from this theological principle. The second quality is universality, that all humans are beloved of the God who has created and redeemed them. All humans must be treated with dignity and respect. The third is integrity, which involves the belief "that there is an integral connection among the intellectual, moral, and spiritual dimensions of human

2. Mark R. Schwehn, "A Christian University: Defining the Difference," *First Things* (May 1999): 26-27.

life, and that these therefore ought where possible to be addressed concurrently within a single institution rather than parceled out into separate and often conflicting realms."[3] While these qualities may be grounded in other views of life, they are thoroughly grounded for a Christian college in Trinitarian theological principles.

Schwehn's final point deserves more attention because, at least as I am applying it in this chapter, it gets at the particularly Lutheran qualities of a Christian college. Schwehn argues that a "Christian university privileges and seeks to transmit, through its theology department, its official rhetoric, the corporate worship it sponsors, and in myriad other ways, a particular tradition of thought, feeling, and practice."[4] While one could spend a good deal of time on a Lutheran college's "feeling" (its aesthetic tone) and "practices" (its worship, its arts, its sense of corporate and institutional calling), I would rather focus on its tradition of thought, its approach to higher learning. This is shaped by the particular way that Lutherans relate Christ and culture, gospel and Law, the right-hand Kingdom and the left. And since the Lutheran approach is complex and dialectical, it is highly vulnerable to distortion.

Lutheran colleges respect the independence, creativity, and contributions of the many "worldly" ways of knowing. The disciplines are prized in their full splendor. Luther roared, "How dare you not know what you can know!" He also argued that Christians have to be competent in their secular callings; a Christian cobbler makes good shoes, not poor shoes with little crosses on them. Lutheran teacher-scholars teach and write well; their piety will not excuse incompetence.

The disciplines are not, however, given idolatrous autonomy, for they, too, are under the dominion of finitude and sin, and they often claim too much for themselves. Rather, the disciplines are to be engaged from the point of view of the gospel, and here "gospel" is meant to refer to the whole Trinitarian perspective on the world, not just the doctrine of the forgiveness of sins. That is, a Lutheran college aims at an ongoing dialogue between the Christian intellectual tradition — as construed in Lutheranism — and the secular disciplines. This is what is meant by a lively tension and interaction between Christ and cul-

3. Schwehn, "A Christian University," p. 28.
4. Schwehn, "A Christian University," p. 29.

ture, the gospel and the Law, and the two ways that God reigns in the world.

A genuinely Lutheran college will aim at such an engagement, rejoicing in the areas of overlap and agreement that may take place, continuing a mutual critique where there are divergences and disagreements, anticipating that in the eschaton these differing views will come together in God's own truth, but in the meantime being willing to live with many questions unresolved. Thus, in some areas of inquiry, a Lutheran college will recognize paradox, ambiguity, and irresolvability. But this recognition takes place at the end of a creative process of engagement, not at the beginning, where some proponents of "paradox" would like to put it. Those proponents then simply avoid real engagement by declaring "paradox" at the very beginning, essentially allowing everyone to go their own way and do their own thing.

A caveat should be entered here. This sort of engagement does not go on all the time and by everyone in every classroom. A good deal of the time of a Lutheran college is given over to transmitting the "normal knowledge" of the field or the bulk of the liberal arts core. But in probing the depths of every discipline, in addressing perennial and contemporary issues, in shaping a curriculum, in the kind of teaching and scholarship it prizes, and, above all, in the kind of faculty it hires, the college nurtures this ongoing engagement between the Christian intellectual tradition and other ways of knowing.

Unlike the Reformed approach, that of Lutheranism does not give an automatic privilege to the Christian worldview which in the end can "trump" the other ways of knowing. Unlike the Catholic approach, which sees all knowledge rising to a synthesis organized by Catholic wisdom, it lives with more messiness. But it respects those models of Christian humanism and finds itself closer to them than to the modern secular tendency to marginalize and then sequester into irrelevancy the Christian view of life and reality.

This genuine Lutheran approach also guards against its own Lutheran distortions, the prime one being the separation of Christ and culture, gospel and Law, and of the two ways that God reigns. This separation takes place in this way: The gospel is narrowly defined as the doctrine of justification, and this gospel is preached in the chapel and taught by the theology department. But it is not the full-blown, comprehensive vision of life explicit in the Trinitarian faith. It does not have the intellectual content of the full Christian vision.

In this flawed view, the Law (culture or the left hand of God) embraces everything else. All disciplines are under the Law and reason is the instrument for understanding them. Indeed, those who advocate this view often appeal to Luther's understanding of reason, which sounds like an affirmation of autonomous reason set free from Christian assumptions. If that is the case, then a Lutheran college simply allows all inquiries shaped by reason to proceed freely. The results of these inquiries are respected and left pretty much unchallenged. The best available faculty can be hired for this exercise of autonomous reason without regard to their religious convictions or their interest in the theological dialogue I outlined above. A Lutheran college, in this view, is simply one that encourages the exercise of autonomous reason. Or, in postmodern terms, it respects the various perspectives that people bring to learning from their social locations.

There are enormous problems with this approach. For one thing, it assumes that Luther meant the same thing by reason that we do. On the contrary, the reason that Luther respected was thoroughly ensconced in a Christian worldview. It was a reason that could affirm the Good, the True, and the Beautiful in a way that was consistent with Christian presuppositions. But such a view of reason is long gone. Reason has been removed from the religious traditions within which it worked, and now operates from very different assumptions, usually characterized by a pervasive philosophical naturalism (the modern) or by an arbitrary epistemological tribalism (the postmodern).

Allowing such an exercise of reason to go unchallenged in a Lutheran school is irresponsible because it leads to the bifurcation of the minds of students and faculty alike. Christian faculty who worship God on Sunday teach a view of the world that shuts out God and human freedom on Monday. Students live their faith and intellectual lives in two separate compartments. To combat this unhappy situation, the disciplines must be engaged by the gospel, the Christian vision with its comprehensive claims to truth. This does not mean, however, that the Christian vision is itself immune to challenge; the disciplines also engage the Christian vision. In any genuine conversation there is the chance that both conversation partners' views may be changed. What's more, Christian claims are often of high generality;

the claims of the disciplines more detailed and concrete. One often needs the other. Engagement does not always create conflict; it often reveals the two parts of the dialogue to be complementary.

The distorted Lutheran approach I have depicted above splits Christ (the Christian vision) from culture (the academic enterprise), the gospel (in its full elaboration) from the Law (the exercise of reason). This separation of the Christian intellectual tradition from secular learning is as dangerous to Lutheran colleges as the separation of the gospel and politics was to the Germany of Nazi times. Certainly the stakes are quite different, but such a separation will lead to a realm of secular education unchallenged by the Christian vision, just as it led in Germany to a political movement unchecked by that same Christian vision.

Such an approach, which often is used as a rationalization to disguise the prior lapse into secularization, can then well appeal to paradox, ambiguity, and uncertainty, since it will have nothing but a cacophony of voices each claiming their little corner of the college. Such a condition, which is not too far from the one prevailing at many Lutheran colleges, led one graduate student who attended a Lutheran education conference a few years back to say, "Gee, from what I gathered there, a Lutheran college is a wonderful place because everyone can think and do whatever they wish. It's a free-for-all."

Desecularizing Lutheran Colleges — A Case Study

Those colleges that approximate such a view of Lutheran higher education — Lutheran humanism, if you will — will have a good idea of what to aim at. But what of the many colleges who have long lost a Lutheran center, a religious vision that shapes the life of the college? What of the many colleges that find my ideal Lutheran vision simply impossible? One might answer that we can't put Humpty-Dumpty together again. But a fraction of these schools — it would be difficult to see in their number a trend — are making efforts to reconnect more seriously with their heritage. Good evidence for this phenomenon is the number of schools that have joined the Lilly Network of Church-Related Colleges and Universities and the Rhodes Consultation on the Future of the Church-Related College. Both of these well-funded programs intend to help schools strengthen or restore a meaningful relation to their sponsoring heritage. While some of the stalwarts of both programs have never "left the faith," perhaps a greater number are trying to "regain the faith."

Such is the case of Roanoke College, the Lutheran-related liberal arts college of seventeen hundred students where I have taught for eighteen years. From a point in the early 1980s when the college almost lost any meaningful church connection, the college has moved to one in which the Christian perspective is strongly represented among the other voices that constitute the college's life. It appears that there is strong momentum to increase our movement toward a more systematic intentional pluralism. Roanoke is a member of both the Lilly Network and the Rhodes Consultation, but those memberships are more the result than the cause of its efforts to restore a meaningful relation to its Christian heritage. Several new board members of strong Lutheran conviction have been appointed. A young and vigorous new bishop of the Virginia Synod is now on the board and, more importantly, on the executive committee of the board. The college provided space for the Virginia Synod headquarters and the bishop and his staff have become a familiar presence on campus. A director of church relations was hired, and she has opened the college to many church functions — youth events, synod assembly, continuing education events, and synod council meetings — and has been very successful in recruiting Lutheran donors for the specifically religious activities of the college. For example, the chaplaincy and its staff have recently been completely endowed.

Two successive deans have been sympathetic to the notion of "institutional fit" in the hiring of faculty and have attempted, with mixed results, to screen faculty for their sympathy for the religious dimension of the college's mission. Reengagement with the Christian heritage was beginning to move from the periphery to the center of the school's life — its academic program. Yet the majority of faculty were not "on board" in that process of reengagement. Had a public conflict taken place at that point, the Christian partisans would certainly have been trounced.

A Faith and Learning organization was begun which has grown to a membership of near forty. It meets regularly to reflect on the college's religious character and to support efforts to strengthen it. The president of the college and most of his cabinet participate regularly. This grassroots organization has been crucially important. As it has grown it has given the administration increasing stimulation and support. It has broadened support in the faculty by making a persuasive case for the viability of the Christian intellectual tradition. When the most recent public showdown between proponents and opponents of reengagement occurred, this support was indispensable.

Even with strong efforts to recruit Lutheran students, the Lutheran composition of the student body remains low — about 8 or 9 percent — mainly because our region is sparsely populated with Lutherans. Our Lutheran students seem, however, to make an impact beyond their numbers. Moreover, there are many religiously serious evangelical students drawn from the region who provide the strongest religious presence in the student body. Our effort to endow a professorship in evangelical studies is intended both to nourish and recruit more evangelical students, as well as to study a major American religious movement.

In a very important move, the college has again put a required religion/philosophy course, called "Values and the Responsible Life," into the general education curriculum. Prior to this requirement, a course in religion/philosophy had not been required for twenty years. The new course challenges each student with central Christian moral and religious claims, along with those of other normative perspectives, but there is little doubt where the course "is coming from."

This change came around 1990 and occasioned the first public showdown between those supporting reengagement and those resisting it. The faculty narrowly allowed a "values course" to be developed by the religion and philosophy department. When the faculty realized that the required values course would include the Judeo-Christian tradition as a source of religious and moral values along with other perspectives, its suspicions grew. The course was monitored more closely than any other course in the general education curriculum. When evaluation of the whole general education curriculum took place in the mid nineties, a number of faculty protested anonymously that the course was "Sunday school proselytizing" with weak intellectual content. In response, the college held a summer workshop that served as preparation for faculty beyond the religion and philosophy department who might wish to teach the course. After members of the department "walked through" the course during the workshop, the word spread that indeed there was intellectual challenge in the course and that the department wasn't coercing faith among the students, if indeed that were possible. Since that workshop there has been little further carping, and the college touts the importance of the course far and wide.

The momentum toward reconnection led to recent important revisions in the college's statement of purpose. One of those revisions was the occasion for a second showdown. The new statement emphasizes spiritual growth and participation in religious and service activities more than the former, but the real step forward was the way that the new statement spells out what it means to "honor our Christian heritage," which was a phrase in the old statement. The new version states that the college "honors its Christian heritage and its partnership with the Lutheran church by nurturing a dialogue between faith and reason." This strong new addition came to the floor of the faculty via an amendment that members of the Faith and Learning Group had written. The group had prepared for a lively debate on the amendment by arranging for articulate spokespersons from the group to defend the amendment against objections that might arise. Curiously, no public arguments were made by the skeptics. The ensuing vote resulted in a tie, which the Faculty Moderator, a devout Catholic, broke by voting for the amendment. When a later attempt was made to reconsider the change, the faculty defeated it by a comfortable margin. The board accepted the change, and Roanoke College now has a mission statement far more religiously robust than before.

The story at Roanoke College is not, however, simply one of triumph. The college was invited to apply for a Lilly grant for "Theological Reflection on Vocation" in the spring of 2001. At the same time I wrote an article about Roanoke entitled "Reconnection — A College Recovers Its Christian Identity," which appeared in the *Christian Century* magazine. The combination of these two events was too much for the secularists among the faculty. They mounted a campaign to get the president to withdraw from the Lilly competition and to stop the "religionization" of the college. Fears were stirred up among even the more moderate but uncommitted members of the faculty that we were becoming a seminary or a fundamentalist college. The application to Lilly went on, however, and the initiatives set in motion to reconnect are still in motion. Nevertheless, the incident served notice that reconnection will not be easy and will take a long time. Only if the college has the courage to hire according to its new purpose statement will the future be won, one faculty member at a time, over a long period.

If Roanoke's story, warts and all, can be duplicated — and I certainly believe it can — then colleges that have come close to losing their connection can reverse that process and make important headway in the opposite direction. A determined but patient group of leaders who believe that the Christian account is publicly relevant to all facets of the college's life and mission can move such a college toward a new relation to its religious heritage. And, in many ways, that new relation may be more intentional, meaningful, and fruitful than its earlier one.

BIBLIOGRAPHY

Benne, Robert. *Quality with Soul: How Six Premier Colleges and Universities Keep Faith with Their Religious Traditions.* Grand Rapids: Eerdmans, 2001.

Burtchaell, James Tunstead. *The Dying of the Light: The Disengagement of Colleges and Universities from Their Christian Churches.* Grand Rapids: Eerdmans, 1998.

Schwehn, Mark R. "A Christian University: Defining the Difference." *First Things* (May 1999): 25-31.

Loose Bonds, Emerging Commitments:
The Lives and Faith of Lutheran Youth

EUGENE C. ROEHLKEPARTAIN

In congregations and communities across the United States, Lutheran youth are partnering with adults to plan and lead youth ministries. They are struggling to discern what it means to be a Christian growing up in a postmodern, post-Christian society. They are active leaders in their congregations, schools, and communities. They are worshiping, praying, and studying Scripture. They are putting their faith into practice through acts of leadership, compassion, and justice. In short, they are growing in faith and discipleship as full members of the Body of Christ.

Unfortunately, that isn't the story one generally hears when people talk about young people, including those in the church. More often, you hear consternation about young people becoming inactive in church after confirmation, not upholding orthodox Christian beliefs or values, and engaging in risky, health-compromising behaviors.

The reality is that both stories speak truth about the complexity of the religious experience of Lutheran youth. Lutheran youth are both growing in their faith commitments and, too often, loosening their connections to the faith community. The opportunity facing Lutherans is to create the environments and opportunities that tap the strengths and potential of young people more consistently so that they are more likely to become powerful, positive forces in the church for today and tomorrow.

In surveying the most current research available specifically on Lutheran youth and their faith practices, beliefs, and behaviors, a strong core of commitment — along with mixed, often loose, bonds to the church — emerges. And while Lutheran youth express many positive commitments, those commitments are not always followed through with faithful action. These findings highlight young people's experiences in and perceptions of congregations, suggesting areas of action that have the potential to strengthen young people's faith and commitment to the church.

Unfortunately, little current research is available specifically on Lutheran youth. Only two national studies, both conducted by Search Institute, were identified through an extensive literature search as including distinct samples of Lutheran youth. The first study, Effective Christian Education (ECE),[1] involved youth and adults in six major American Protestant denominations, including the Evangelical Lutheran Church in America (ELCA). A national sample of 656 ELCA youth was included in the overall sample of 2,365 Protestant youth. The second study, Congregations at Crossroads (CAC), was commissioned by The Lutheran Church–Missouri Synod and Lutheran Brotherhood.[2] This study included a sample of 486 youth, ages thirteen to nineteen. Though not fully comparable, they provide grist for exploring the faith and life experiences of a broad range of Lutheran youth.

These two national Search Institute studies are the heart of this chapter, and are supplemented primarily by two more recent but limited studies in the LCMS: a survey of 359 Texas youth who attend LCMS youth groups,[3] and a poll of about 1,600 youth at the 2001 LCMS Youth Gathering in New Orleans.[4]

1. P. L. Benson and C. H. Eklin, *Effective Christian Education: A National Study of Protestant Congregations — A Summary Report on Faith, Loyalty and Congregational Life* (Minneapolis: Search Institute, 1990); see also E. C. Roehlkepartain, *The Teaching Church: Moving Christian Education to Center Stage* (Nashville: Abingdon, 1993); E. C. Roehlkepartain and P. L. Benson, *Youth in Protestant Churches* (Minneapolis: Search Institute, 1993).

2. P. L. Benson, E. C. Roehlkepartain, and I. S. Andress, *Congregations at Crossroads: A National Study of Adults and Youth in the Lutheran Church–Missouri Synod* (Minneapolis: Search Institute, 1995).

3. Barna Research Group, *LCMS Texas Teens and Their Faith: A Study of LCMS Youth Group Attenders* (Austin: Texas District of the Lutheran Church–Missouri Synod, 2001).

4. T. K. Dittmer, *Summary Report of the 2001 Lutheran Youth Fellowship Youth Poll* (St. Louis: LCMS District and Congregational Services — Youth Ministry, 2001). Downloaded on December 27, 2001, from http://dcs.lcms.org/youth/lyf.htm.

The Faith Life of Lutheran Youth

Adolescence is a time of rapid change, and it is pivotal for young people's faith development. Not only do adolescents' cognitive abilities develop dramatically, moving from concrete to more abstract thinking, but they are in a pivotal time in identity formation — in which religious commitment and identity are integral. As scholars such as James W. Fowler have suggested,[5] adolescents typically move from a childhood faith that is essentially inherited from their parents to "owning" their faith, beliefs, and values — integrating them into their own identity and understanding of their selves.

This process is not just internal and individualistic; it is greatly shaped by the expectations and influences of those around them, including their families, peers, congregation, and community. And while some have viewed this stage as one defined by crisis and rebellion, more recent research suggests that it is better defined as a period of change and transition, because crisis and rebellion have been found to be neither universal nor inevitable.[6]

Surveys of youth and their self-reported views of their faith commitment suggest that faith is an important part of life for roughly half of all youth in America. For example, according to a Search Institute study of more than 200,000 public school students during the 1999-2000 school year, "being religious or spiritual" is quite or extremely important to 54 percent of middle and high school students.[7] This level of commitment changes relatively little between the sixth and twelfth grades.

Among ELCA youth in the ECE study, 95 percent said that their faith has at least some influence in their lives. Just 25 percent, however, said that faith is the most or a very important influence in their life, and just 17 percent agreed that it is mostly or absolutely true that faith is at the center of their life. No similar questions were asked in the national LCMS study, although the Barna study of Texas youth-group at-

---

5. J. W. Fowler, *Stages of Faith: The Psychology of Human Development and the Quest for Meaning* (San Francisco: Harper and Row, 1981).

6. R. M. Lerner, *Adolescence: Development, Diversity, Context, and Application* (Upper Saddle River, N.J.: Pearson Education, 2002).

7. Unpublished data of the Search Institute.

tenders found that 93 percent agreed that "the Christian faith is relevant to the way I live today."

Though it is helpful to gauge young people's perceptions about the role faith plays in their lives, a more thorough examination of their faith lives enriches our understanding considerably. Indeed, numerous studies have shown that people of all ages believe things to be important that they don't actually put into practice in their daily lives. To that end, both the ECE and CAC studies included a Faith Maturity Index, which seeks to capture "the degree to which a person embodies the priorities, commitments, and perspectives characteristic of a vibrant and life-transforming faith."[8] As such, it deals less with people's self-described faith or their orthodoxy and beliefs than with their faith practices or signs that their faith is shaping who they are and what they do.

The Faith Maturity Index is built around two dimensions of a life of faith: the vertical dimension, which emphasizes the relationship with God; and the horizontal dimension, which emphasizes relationship with and responsibility to others. Ideally, Christians have an integrated faith that is strong on both dimensions. It is also possible, however, to have a horizontal faith (high on relationships and commitment to others, but low on the vertical dimension), a vertical faith (high on the vertical dimension, but low on the horizontal dimension), or an undeveloped faith, which is low on both dimensions.

Table 1 shows the percentages of ELCA and LCMS youth who are categorized as having each faith type. Several patterns are worth noting. First, there is a compelling difference between the levels of integrated faith found in ELCA and LCMS youth, with LCMS youth being much more likely to have an integrated faith, and much less likely to have an undeveloped faith. It is interesting to note that ELCA youth are fairly consistent with other mainline denominations in the ECE study; LCMS youth are closer to the Southern Baptist youth in the ECE study, of whom 30 percent were found to have an integrated faith. While some of these differences may be due to sampling and the fact that different surveys were administered, they also may suggest that

8. P. L. Benson, M. J. Donahue, and J. A. Erickson, "The Faith Maturity Scale: Conceptualization, Measurement, and Empirical Validation," in *Research in the Social Scientific Study of Religion*, vol. 5, ed. M. L. Lynn and D. O. Moberg (Greenwich, Conn.: JAI, 1993), p. 3.

Table 1. Faith Types of Lutheran Youth (in percentages)

	ELCA*	LCMS†
Integrated Faith: High on both the horizontal and vertical dimensions of faith maturity	9	25
Horizontal Faith: High on the horizontal dimension; low on the vertical dimension	23	27
Vertical Faith: High on the vertical dimension; low on the horizontal dimension	3	10
Undeveloped Faith: Low on both the vertical and horizontal dimensions of faith	65	38

*Data from the ECE study (Benson, Williams, Eklin, and Schuller, 1990, p. 25)
†Data from the CAC study (Benson, Roehlkepartain, and Andress, 1995, p. 40)

differences in the way each church body approaches Christian education and youth ministry, in its expectations for youth, and in how it passes on faith to children merit further exploration and dialogue.

At the same time, the overall patterns are similar, and these general patterns that cross denominational differences are perhaps even more important. Only a minority of youth have developed an integrated faith, and the horizontal dimension tends to be stronger than the vertical dimension. Both patterns are partly explainable in developmental terms. A life-cycle perspective on faith development reminds us that faith continues to grow, develop, and transform throughout life; thus, it is unreasonable to expect that young people would typically have cultivated an integrated faith while still in the transitions of adolescence. In addition, the relative strength of the horizontal dimension of faith speaks to young people's developmental task of finding their place in society and being able to understand cognitively abstract concepts such as justice, equity, and other social issues.

These data also remind us that even those young people who see faith as an integral part of their life do not complete confirmation with a fully formed, fully integrated life of faith. Their faith life is still maturing, growing, becoming part of their personal identity. So while confirmation is an important early milestone on their faith journey, it is certainly not the culmination. Yet, as we will see in the next section, there are reasons to be concerned that too many youth, their families, and their congregations actually act as though confirmation is a point of completion, not a foundation for lifelong growth and discipleship.

Church Participation and Loyalty

Although most American youth say that faith or spirituality is important to them, this belief does not always translate into active participation in a congregation. So, in the face of ongoing concerns about declining — and graying — membership in Lutheran churches in the United States, it is important to gain perspective on participation patterns among young Lutherans.

In addition, active engagement in a faith community during childhood and adolescence remains a powerful predictor of faith and involvement in adulthood.[9] To illustrate: a poll of about one thousand American adults by Barna Research Group found that adults who participated in a faith community for some part of childhood or adolescence are almost three times as likely as those who did not to be involved as adults (61 percent versus 22 percent).[10]

Unfortunately, existing research does not clearly identify the proportion of children baptized Lutheran who are active in congregations into adolescence and beyond (since surveys of church members inevitably over-represent those who stay involved or at least connected). Thus, if anything, the findings from studies of churched youth may overestimate actual levels of church involvement.

Among the LCMS and ELCA youth surveyed by Search Institute, 68 percent and 60 percent, respectively, say that they attend worship "about once a week" or more. A third (33 percent LCMS; 31 percent ELCA) say they also volunteer in their church at least three hours a month by teaching, leading, serving on a committee, or helping with some program or event.

Among the Texas LCMS youth surveyed by Barna, 64 percent also said they attend youth group weekly, with 28 percent indicating

9. Benson and Eklin, *Effective Christian Education.*

10. Barna Research Group, "Adults Who Attended Church As Children Show Lifelong Effects" (November 5, 2001, press release). Downloaded on January 2, 2002, from www.barna.com.

that they attend once, twice, or several times a month. In addition, about half of these youth (47 percent) indicated that they attend almost every special event that is promoted through their youth group.

These global numbers may mask a troubling decline in church participation among young people. There is evidence — bolstered by widespread concerns among church leaders and other observers — that many young people drop out of church following confirmation and that, as a result, many congregations offer less and less programming for older youth. For example, in the ECE study, ELCA church leaders indicated that 67 percent of elementary-age children and 70 percent of seventh- to ninth-grade youth who are part of their church participate in Christian education. But that perceived involvement drops by more than half to 32 percent for grades ten to twelve. (Lest adults become too judgmental, the Christian education participation rate for ELCA adults was only 23 percent.)

Unfortunately, more recent data are not available to determine whether the perceived new interest in spirituality among the current generation of young people has reduced this "dropout rate." Broader trends of religious participation have not, however, changed significantly in the past decade, and clergy and youth workers continue to report this widespread and vexing challenge.

One might argue that it is okay for young people to "take a break from church" during high school when so much else is going on. There is growing evidence, however, that young people who leave the church during adolescence may not ever return. Indeed, Roland Martinson of Luther Seminary, St. Paul, Minnesota, estimates that 50 to 60 percent of baptized and confirmed youth who stop participating in worship and congregational ministries by age twenty-one will not return to participate in any faith community by age thirty-five.[11] When asked about the long-term prospects for their own church involvement, only 21 percent of ELCA youth said "there is an excellent chance I will be active in the church when I'm 40." (The average among the mainline churches studied was 34 percent.)[12]

---

11. R. M. Martinson, Untitled presentation to the consultation to the ELCA Bishops' Initiative on Children, "Treasured and Safe" (January 4, 2002, Chicago, Illinois).

12. P. L. Benson, D. Williams, C. H. Eklin, and D. Schuller, *Effective Christian Education: A National Study of Protestant Congregations — A Report for the Evangelical Lutheran Church in America* (Minneapolis: Search Institute, 1990), p. 30.

This prediction isn't necessarily a reflection of general dissatisfaction with their current church participation. Almost three-fourths of Lutheran youth (70 percent of ELCA youth; 73 percent of LCMS youth) say they feel at home in their church, and most (62 percent ELCA; 70 percent LCMS) say their church matters a great deal to them. Nevertheless, only half said they would feel a great sense of loss if they had to change churches (54 percent ELCA; 55 percent LCMS).

Beyond satisfaction with and loyalty to a local congregation, a broader question is the degree to which their specific faith tradition or church body is important to young people — particularly given that most young people will move many times as they enter and make their way through adulthood. When asked how satisfied they are with their denomination, 76 percent of ELCA youth and 73 percent of LCMS youth indicated that they were satisfied or very satisfied. They were less likely, however, to say it is important to be in a congregation of their denomination. Only 55 percent of ELCA youth and 58 percent of LCMS youth indicated that it is important or extremely important to attend a church affiliated with their denomination.

To some extent, these findings present a fairly mixed, even confusing picture. On one hand, young people continue to indicate that their faith is an important part of their lives, and many of them are regularly involved in and satisfied with their congregations. At the same time, many congregational leaders perceive declining congregational engagement, particularly after confirmation. An examination of the various dimensions of faith and congregational life may well point toward strategies for helping young people stay engaged and active in their churches.

Young People's Religious Knowledge, Beliefs, and Practices

When we examine Lutheran young people's knowledge, beliefs, and practices, it appears that, for the most part, their beliefs are consistent with traditional, orthodox Christian theology, as shown in Table 2. While there is certainly some variation between church bodies and among individual items, Lutheran youth fairly consistently see God as loving and powerful, they accept basic teachings about Jesus, and they see the Holy Spirit as active in the world.

Table 2. Lutheran Youth's Religious Beliefs (in percentages)

	ELCA*	LCMS†
Beliefs about God		
God is loving.	97	
God accepts me the way I am.	94	
God is active in the lives of individuals.	81	
God decides everything I do.	52	
God created the universe.	95	
Beliefs about Jesus		
I know that Jesus Christ is the Son of God who died on the cross and rose again.	88	98
Jesus is a friend who cares for me each day.	82	
Jesus is a teacher who shows me how to love and serve.	77	
Other Beliefs		
I believe the Holy Spirit is at work in my life.	73	93
I believe in life after death.	57	85
I believe that the devil is a real power in the world.	77	

*Data from the ECE study (Benson, Williams, Eklin, and Schuller, 1990, p. 25)
†Data from the CAC study (Benson, Roehlkepartain, and Andress, 1995, p. 40)

Lutheran youth are somewhat less knowledgeable about Scripture and theology. Among LCMS youth, only 50 percent of those surveyed correctly answered seven out of ten multiple-choice questions designed to indicate whether they were familiar with the basic content and structure of the Bible. Similarly, only 53 percent demonstrated an accurate knowledge of the Lutheran distinction between Law and gospel, a percentage based on their ability to answer at least seven of ten statements in accordance with the Lutheran confessions. (Among the statements were "God's law places obligations on us that no one can completely fulfill" and "Salvation is a gift that no one deserves.")

Thus, many (though certainly not all) Lutheran youth understand basic theological concepts, and about half have a working knowledge of Scripture and a core Lutheran belief (the distinction between Law and gospel). Yet when we ask how much that faith is shaping their lives and their choices, that knowledge may not be moving from their heads to their hearts.

As shown in Table 3, only one-quarter to one-half of Lutheran youth say that their faith is having a powerful impact in their lives. (LCMS youth break this pattern when 68 percent indicate that their faith makes an important difference in helping them know right from wrong.) Nor do a majority of Lutheran youth engage in personal practices of spiritual nurture, such as prayer, sharing one's faith with others, Bible study, and seeking opportunities for spiritual growth.

In addition, the surveys asked young people about their pro-social attitudes, such as being engaged in promoting social justice, speaking out for equality, giving time and money to help others, and accepting people with different religious beliefs. In most cases, fewer than one-third of the young people indicated that these issues were high priorities for them (that each statement was "always" or "almost always true"). In the wake of the terrorist attacks of September 11, 2001, however, it is significant that — even a decade earlier — seven out of ten Lutheran youth indicated that they accept people with different religious beliefs.

It is striking that LCMS youth are more likely than ELCA youth to indicate active involvement in speaking out for equality, working for equality, and doing things to protect the environment, when the emphases of the two church bodies would have suggested the opposite patterns. It is difficult to know how to interpret these differences. They could reflect the general contrast that the LCMS youth surveyed generally are more active in church and more likely to express a high level of faith maturity. We can only speculate as to whether such differences are due to differences in sampling or are true differences in the levels of engagement in the two church bodies.

Faith in Action: Service to Others

Through the 1990s, young people in the United States became increasingly engaged in serving others. A Gallup Youth Survey found that nine out of ten teenagers believe that doing charitable or volunteer

Table 3. How Faith Shapes the Lives of Lutheran Youth

Percentages of youth who indicate that each statement is always or almost always true (6 or 7 on a 7-point scale)

	ELCA*	LCMS†
Impact of Faith in Life		
My faith helps me know right from wrong.	38	68
My life is committed to Jesus Christ.	34	51
My life is filled with meaning and purpose.	37	50
I have a real sense that God is guiding me.	25	48
Faith shapes how I think and act each and every day.	26	42
Spiritual Nurture		
I take time for periods of prayer and meditation.	22	37
I talk with other people about my faith.	10	21
I seek out opportunities to grow spiritually.	9	20
I devote time to reading and studying the Bible.	6	9
Prosocial Attitudes and Actions		
I accept people whose religious beliefs are different from my own.	71	73
I speak out for equality for women and minorities.	14	34
I do things to help protect the environment.	18	34
I am active in efforts to promote social justice.	6	15
In my free time, I help people who have problems or needs.	14	13
I give significant amounts of time and money to help other people.	6	10

*Based on ECE data
†Based on CAC data

work is an important part of being a good citizen.[13] This common assumption reflects the intentional, systematic efforts to increase youth service involvement nationally. Analysis of school-based service learning by the National Service-Learning Clearinghouse (NSLC) found that, in 1984, only 27 percent of high schools offered some sort of community service. By 1997, 96 percent of high schools offered some sort of service opportunities. NSLC estimates that, in those thirteen years, the number of students involved in school-based service projects increased from approximately 900,000 in 1984 to 6.1 million — an increase of 686 percent.[14]

Lutheran youth are certainly part of this broader trend. Leaders in Lutheran churches (like those in other denominations) note the growth and expansion of service projects, mission trips, and engagement in a wide range of "service-learning activities," or service experiences in which intentional learning and reflection are integrated. These opportunities are becoming increasingly common as part of confirmation programs as well as becoming standard components of youth ministry. Youth are engaged in service within the congregations, in their communities, and through national and international work camps.[15]

This background offers important perspective and caution in interpreting data on youth service among Lutheran youth that is (in the case of the ELCA) more than a decade old. One would expect that, if asked today, more Lutheran youth would be actively engaged in serving others. Even with that caveat, roughly half (49 percent) of ELCA youth reported a decade ago that they spent at least an hour in the past month making their town or city a better place, and 50 percent said they donated at least an hour in the past month helping children, youth, or families in their town or city. They were less likely (33 percent) to have spent time promoting social justice or world peace.

For many Lutheran youth, then, serving others is an important

13. G. H. Gallup Jr. "The Spiritual Life of Young Americans: Approaching the Year 2000" (Princeton, N.J.: George H. Gallup International Institute, n.d.).

14. R. Shumer and C. C. Cook, *The Status of Service-Learning in the United States* (St. Paul, Minn.: National Service-Learning Clearinghouse, 1999).

15. See E. C. Roehlkepartain, E. D. Naftali, and L. Musegades, *Growing Up Generous: Engaging Youth in Giving and Serving* (Bethesda, Md.: Alban Institute, 2000).

opportunity to express their faith and values. Church bodies and other youth ministry organizations have been able to tap into and fuel this interest and commitment by developing service experiences (such as work camps, servant events, and mission trips) for young people. The challenge for churches is to build on and expand this interest and experience so that it becomes a lifelong commitment.

Involvement in Risky Behaviors

Unfortunately, too many Lutheran youth also engage in various risk-taking behaviors, though their levels of engagement are generally lower than young people who are not religiously active. (In some cases, their levels of engagement are comparable with surveys of youth in general, which include many young people who are also religiously active.)

If one looks at individual risky behaviors (Table 4 shows the seven risk behaviors that were examined in both Lutheran samples as well as in Search Institute studies of public school students), one might conclude that most Lutheran youth are not engaged in risky behaviors. But when ten different risk behaviors are examined together, one finds that 76 percent of ELCA youth are engaged in at least one of ten high-risk behaviors, and 32 percent are engaged in three or more of the ten high-risk behaviors measured in the ECE study. Among LCMS youth, 69 percent are engaged in two or more of the ten high-risk behaviors measured in that study (not the same ten as in the ECE study).

These findings remind us that churchgoing youth are not immune from the troubles and challenges that face young people in our society. Yet, too often, churches assume that these problems do not directly affect the young people who come to church — or that by simply being at church or in a youth group, young people are protected from these dangers. For example, only 26 percent of ELCA youth in the ECE study had spent at least six hours in their lifetime learning about or discussing alcohol and other drugs, and just 22 percent spent that much time learning about or discussing sexuality.

Only slightly higher percentages of ELCA youth gave their church credit for helping them with life issues. For example, 57 percent of ELCA youth said their church did a good or excellent job helping them make

Table 4. Risky Behaviors among Lutheran Youth and U.S. Youth (in percentages)

Note: Because these data are from different surveys taken in different time periods, caution should be exercised in drawing conclusions based on comparisons across groups.

	ELCA*	LCMS†	U.S.‡
Got in trouble at school, once or more in the past year	65	54	61
Hit or beat up someone, once or more in the past year	43	42	38
Had sexual intercourse, in lifetime	20	18	27
Stole from a store, once or more in the past year	17	23	25
Drank alcohol, six or more times in the past year	29	18	22
Used marijuana, once or more in the past year	11	10	20
Used cocaine, once or more in the past year	3	1	3

*Based on ECE data

†Based on CAC data

‡Based on unpublished Search Institute surveys of more than 200,000 public school students (1999-2000)

decisions about right and wrong. Only half (48 percent) gave the same rating regarding helping them apply their faith to daily life. And just 32 percent said their church did a good or excellent job helping them develop responsible values and behaviors in the area of sexuality.

Lutheran Youth's Involvement in Community Life

The vast majority of Lutheran youth spend most of their time in communities and schools, not in their congregations. They therefore experience both the benefits and challenges of being young people growing up in this society and in their communities.

Roughly two-thirds of ELCA youth report participation in co-curricular school activities at least one hour per week (63 percent), with 63 percent participating in sports and 62 percent participating in music. (These activity levels are similar to the percentages of youth who regularly attend worship services.) More than one-third (37 percent) participate in clubs or organizations outside of their church or school.

On the one hand, many church leaders view this kind of involvement as "competing" with church activities. And, in many cases, it can. It is important, however, to balance such concern by remembering the positive effects that can accrue from this community involvement. Rather than seeing such activities as competition, church leaders need to discover innovative ways to work together with those sponsoring these activities to ensure that young people have well-rounded opportunities for growth and development.

What Shapes Young People's Faith, Values, and Well-Being?

These studies underscore the reality that Lutheran youths' lives reflect the same range of complexities and contradictions that are part of being human and part of being an adolescent in this society. Lutheran youths see faith as an important part of life, yet most don't follow through with the practices to which that faith calls them to aspire. Many engage in risky behaviors, yet they are also likely to be actively involved in helping others.

One could look at this research and conclude, "That's just the way it is. It's just part of being an adolescent. They'll grow out of it." But while it is true that adolescence is an important transition period in the life cycle, there's growing evidence that many young people don't just "grow out of it." Furthermore, we are also learning a great deal about the kinds of experiences in young people's lives that increase the odds that they'll grow up faithful, caring, and responsible.

In recent years, many researchers have been studying factors that contribute to young people's healthy development and growth in faith.[16] For example, the ECE study identified a wide range of factors

16. See, for example, P. L. Benson, *All Kids Are Our Kids: What Communities Must Do to Raise Caring and Responsible Children and Adolescents* (San Francisco: Jossey-Bass,

that are related to growth in faith — and some that appear to have little or no impact. These findings are shown in Table 5.

Despite a widespread desire for simple, clear-cut answers and "magic potions," the reality is that development is a complex process that is influenced by many different things. The question is not, "Is it nature or nurture?" but, "How much nature, and how much nurture — and how do they interact with each other?" The question is not whether family, peers, community, school, or church are the key to young people's growth; rather, the question is how much each contributes to — or thwarts — healthy growth, while also reinforcing the other influences.

Developmental psychologists now describe human development in terms of an "ecological context" in which multiple factors and forces influence and shape young people's development.[17] The challenge for congregations, families, and others that seek to promote young people's growth and development is how to align and support multiple influences that can guide young people to make healthy, faithful life choices. Current research and theory[18] suggest that the following factors related to congregational life play an important role in nurturing faith and contributing to young people's overall well-being:

- experiences in family life, including a strong foundation of love, support, guidance, and boundary-setting, as well as the faith

---

1997); P. L. Benson and K. J. Pittman, eds., *Trends in Youth Development: Visions, Realities, and Challenges* (Norwell, Mass.: Kluwer Academic Publishers, 2001); E. C. Roehlkepartain, *The Teaching Church: Moving Christian Education to Center Stage* (Nashville: Abingdon, 1993); and P. C. Scales and N. Leffert, *Developmental Assets: A Synthesis of the Scientific Research on Adolescent Development* (Minneapolis: Search Institute, 1999).

17. See U. Bronfenbrenner, *The Ecology of Human Development* (Cambridge, Mass.: Harvard University Press, 1979).

18. See, for example, Benson and Eklin, *Effective Christian Education;* Martinson, Untitled presentation; E. C. Roehlkepartain, "Building Strengths, Deepening Faith: Understanding and Enhancing Youth Development in Protestant Congregations," in *Promoting Positive Child, Adolescent, and Family Development: A Handbook of Program and Policy Innovations,* vol.3, ed. R. M. Lerner, F. Jacobs, and D. Wertlieb (Thousand Oaks, Calif.: Sage, 2003); E. C. Roehlkepartain and P. C. Scales, *Youth Development in Congregations: An Exploration of the Potential and Barriers* (Minneapolis: Search Institute, 1995); M. P. Strommen and R. A. Hardel, *Passing On the Faith: A Radical New Model for Youth and Family Ministry* (Winona, Minn.: St. Mary's, 2000).

Table 5. Influences on Young People's Faith Maturity

This chart shows factors with the strongest and weakest relationships to growth in faith for youth, based on the ECE study of Protestant congregations. While these statistical correlations don't prove cause and effect, they do suggest areas of the greatest influence.

Strong relationship to growth in faith

- Lifetime family religiousness
- Lifetime involvement in effective Christian education

Modest relationship to growth in faith

- Lifetime church involvement
- Friends' religiousness
- Involvement in a caring church
- Involvement in non-church religious activity
- Serving others

Weak relationship to growth in faith

- Age
- Gender
- Geographic region

No clear relationship to growth in faith

- Income
- Denomination
- Congregation size

Source: Benson and Eklin, 1990.

practices and religious involvement of families, including conversations about faith between parents and children, family devotions or rituals, families serving together, and family participation in the faith community;

- engagement in quality, relevant religious education opportunities with caring, effective leaders, engaging educational processes, and content emphases that bridge theology, faith, and life;
- being actively engaged in serving others through the congregation and in the community;

- opportunities to be engaged in a range of positive developmental activities, including arts and/or sports;
- experiencing positive relationships with caring and faithful peers and adults in the congregation, including being supported and cared for during times of personal crisis;
- experiencing their congregation (and other places such as their schools and neighborhoods) as a place where they are valued, cared for, and challenged; and
- having opportunities to have leadership roles and be involved in decision-making.

Experiences in Congregations

If these types of experience play important roles in shaping young people's faith development and overall well-being, how likely are Lutheran youth to experience these positive influences in their lives? While a full examination of that question is beyond the scope of this chapter, suffice it to say that these kinds of positive, life-shaping resources in their lives and in their congregations tend to be lacking for too many of today's young people.

While the vast majority of Lutheran youth (like most youth in the United States) view family life as basically positive and caring, relatively few Lutheran families engage in the faith practices that play pivotal roles in nurturing young people's faith (see Table 6). Furthermore, most Lutheran parents do not perceive their congregations to be valuable resources to support them as parents. Over half of LCMS adults (52 percent) and nearly half of LCMS youth (44 percent) believe their congregation intentionally strengthens family life, yet only 20 percent of parents say their congregation helps them learn how to nurture the faith of their children.

Similar challenges are present within Lutheran congregations. While young people may feel that their church is a warm and caring place, they're much less likely to say that it challenges them to think, provides opportunities to lead and serve, connects them meaningfully with nonparent adults, or engages them in quality, meaningful Christian education experiences. In the CAC study, Search Institute identified 30 faith-enhancing qualities of congregations, including many of

Table 6. Faith Practices in Lutheran Homes

Percent of youth who say each occurs "often"

	ELCA*	LCMS†
Often talked with mother about faith	13	30
Often talked with father about faith	8	16
Often had family devotions or prayer at home	10	16
Often had family service projects	6	8

*Based on ECE data for youth ages 13-15
†Based on CAC data for youth ages 13-18

those mentioned above. Out of those 30, the average young person connected to an LCMS church experiences 12.2. Reflecting the broader concern about young people leaving church after confirmation, thirteen- to fourteen-year-olds reported experiencing 14.5 of the qualities, compared to 11.1 among fifteen- and sixteen-year-olds, and 11.4 among seventeen- to nineteen-year-olds surveyed. Among those qualities least likely to be experienced were the following:

- an emphasis on interactive learning in Christian education (18 percent);
- the congregation showing love and concern for people in the community (19 percent);
- the congregation involving youth in decision-making (20 percent);
- the congregation emphasizing evangelism and missions (23 percent);
- the congregation encouraging thinking, and expecting learning (23 percent);
- youth often experiencing care and support from an adult (27 percent).

Signs of Hope and Renewal

For the past fifty years (at least), there have been ongoing concerns about whether faith will be passed from one generation to the next in American Christianity. The title of John Westerhoff's now-classic book sums up the concern: *Will Our Children Have Faith?*[19] And, to be sure, there are some troubling trends that feed those concerns. Trend-watching is by no means an exact science, however (just listen to the prognosticators talk about the future of the stock market!), and cycles or waves are, perhaps, as likely or more likely than predictable trend lines. Several signs present in the Lutheran community and in society more broadly give reason for hope in the potential of renewal.

Numerous observers of today's young people point to a changing tide. In the midst of a hyper-culture of the Internet and the superficial culture of entertainment, advertising, and other media, there appears to be a growing yearning for and openness to religious community and meaningful purpose among young people. As evidence, look at the burgeoning of service projects and work camps among Lutheran (and other) youth in recent decades, so that service to others through servant events has become a primary emphasis for congregational and denominational youth ministries.[20] In addition, the growing peer ministry movement within Lutheranism (and other traditions), facilitated by the Youth and Family Institute, Bloomington, Minnesota, is helping a whole cadre of young people develop their skills and commitments as Christian leaders.

In another positive sign, market researchers now suggest that the emerging generation of young people is much more interested in finding meaningful, authentic experiences and relationships. Based on his research, evangelical pollster George Barna believes the following:

> Mosaics [his term for the current generation of young people] are looking for an authentic experience with God and other people. . . . Teenagers patronize churches and other event-oriented organizations because they are seeking a compelling experience that is made complete and safe by the presence of people they know and trust, and from whom they are willing to learn and take their cues. . . . Music and other ambient factors may attract them once or twice, but those elements will not keep them coming back for

19. John H. Westerhoff III, *Will Our Children Have Faith?* (New York: Seabury, 1976).

20. See Roehlkepartain, Naftali, and Musegades, *Growing Up Generous.*

more. There has to be sufficient substance, quality, hope, and genuine mutual concern and acceptance for them to return.[21]

These broader social and generational trends may be opening young people to meaningful engagement in faith, spirituality, discipleship, and mission. In addition, a wide array of innovative, diverse, and strength-building approaches to engaging young people in congregations has begun to emerge within and be adopted by Lutheran churches. Here are a few examples:

- Through its Child in Our Hands model, the Youth and Family Institute, Bloomington, Minnesota (www.youthfamilyinstitute.org), offers innovative tools and approaches for building a strong partnership for faith development between home and congregation.
- The Head to the Heart Senior High Ministries developed by Faith Inkubators (www.faithinkubators.com) integrates a small-group youth ministry model that includes active parent involvement, weekly peer small groups, monthly worship, and other activities.
- Search Institute's framework of developmental assets (www.search-institute.org) is being utilized by congregations to develop ministries that engage the whole congregation in ministry with youth within the congregation and in the broader community.
- The LOGOS System of Christian Nurture (www.logos-system.org), based in Pittsburgh, Pennsylvania, is a comprehensive model for intergenerational ministry with children and youth that centers around a midweek program of Bible study, worship, recreation, and family time.
- The Youth Ministry & Spirituality Project at San Francisco Theological Seminary (www.sfts.edu) is researching and developing a contemplative approach to youth ministry grounded in classical methods of spiritual formation.
- Using a framework of "faith practices," the Valparaiso Project on the Education and Formation of People in Faith at Valparaiso University, Valparaiso, Indiana (www.practicingourfaith.org),

---

21. Quoted in "Teens Change Their Tune Regarding Self and Church," a press release of the Barna Research Group, Ventura, California (April 23, 2002).

seeks to develop resources to help contemporary people live the Christian faith with vitality and integrity in changing times. One of its focuses is on helping youth.

Implications for the Future of Youth in Lutheran Churches

Each of these (and other) efforts to strengthen Lutheran congregations on behalf of children, youth, and families is planting seeds of hope for the future of Lutheran youth ministry. They are only beginning to take root, however, and the soil is not always fertile. Congregations resist change, and most youth workers do not have the power base, skills, or mind-set to introduce transforming innovations into congregational life and sustain them. Furthermore, like most national denominations, the major Lutheran church bodies have consistently found themselves having to reduce support for youth ministry as financial constraints tighten, and congregations increasingly look elsewhere for guidance, inspiration, and support for youth ministry.

On the one hand, such cutbacks can be viewed as nothing more than fiscal realities. On the other hand, they may be symbolic of a broader reality (also present in the broader society) that churches have "given up" on reaching youth, have simply assumed that a few professionals are responsible, or do not see an intentional focus on young people as a major priority worthy of significant investment. In that case, major efforts are needed to ignite the church's commitment to kids at all levels — efforts from individual members, local congregations, judicatories, colleges and seminaries, and national infrastructures.

It would be a mistake to argue for efforts to "rebuild" Lutheran youth ministry, as such an approach implies going back to the way it used to be. Rather, given the current realities and the decentralized society of "networks" and "webs" instead of "mainframes," the challenge is to find new, appropriate ways to support, sustain, and expand efforts that effectively engage today's young people in the kinds of authentic faith community and substantive commitment for which they appear to yearn.

REFERENCES

Barna Research Group. *LCMS Texas Teens and Their Faith: A Study of LCMS Youth Group Attenders*. Austin: Texas District of the Lutheran Church–Missouri Synod, 2001.

Benson, P. L. *All Kids Are Our Kids: What Communities Must Do to Raise Caring and Responsible Children and Adolescents*. San Francisco: Jossey-Bass, 1997.

Benson, P. L., M. J. Donahue, and J. A. Erickson. "The Faith Maturity Scale: Conceptualization, Measurement, and Empirical Validation." In *Research in the Social Scientific Study of Religion*, ed. M. L. Lynn and D. O. Moberg, vol. 5, pp. 1-26. Greenwich, Conn.: JAI, 1993.

Benson, P. L., and C. H. Eklin. *Effective Christian Education: A National Study of Protestant Congregations — A Summary Report on Faith, Loyalty and Congregational Life*. Minneapolis: Search Institute, 1990.

Benson, P. L., E. C. Roehlkepartain, and I. S. Andress. *Congregations at Crossroads: A National Study of Adults and Youth in the Lutheran Church–Missouri Synod*. Minneapolis: Search Institute, 1995.

Benson, P. L., D. Williams, C. H. Eklin, and D. Schuller. *Effective Christian Education: A National Study of Protestant Congregations — A Report for the Evangelical Lutheran Church in America*. Minneapolis: Search Institute, 1990.

Benson, P. L., and K. J. Pittman, eds. *Trends in Youth Development: Visions, Realities, and Challenges*. Norwell, Mass.: Kluwer Academic Publishers, 2001.

Bronfenbrenner, U. *The Ecology of Human Development*. Cambridge, Mass.: Harvard University Press, 1979.

Dittmer, T. K. *Summary Report of the 2001 Lutheran Youth Fellowship Youth Poll*. St. Louis: LCMS District and Congregational Services — Youth Ministry, 2001. Downloaded on December 27, 2001, from http://dcs.lcms.org/youth/lyf.htm.

Fowler, J. W. *Stages of Faith: The Psychology of Human Development and the Quest for Meaning*. San Francisco: Harper and Row, 1981.

Gallup, G. H., Jr. "The Spiritual Life of Young Americans: Approaching the Year 2000." Princeton, N.J.: George H. Gallup International Institute, n.d.

Lerner, R. M. *Adolescence: Development, Diversity, Context, and Application*. Upper Saddle River, N.J.: Pearson Education, 2002.

Martinson, R. M. "The Eight Keys of Faith Factors." A working document for the Faith Factors project of Luther Seminary, St. Paul, Minnesota, and Southwestern Baptist Theological Seminary, Ft. Worth, Texas (n.d.). Downloaded on May 13, 2002, from www.faithfactors.com.

———. Untitled presentation to the consultation to the ELCA Bishops' Initiative on Children, "Treasured and Safe" (January 4, 2002, Chicago, Illinois).

Roehlkepartain, E. C. "Building Strengths, Deepening Faith: Understanding and Enhancing Youth Development in Protestant Congregations." In *Promoting Positive Child, Adolescent, and Family Development: A Handbook of Program and Policy Innovations*, vol. 3, ed. R. M. Lerner, F. Jacobs, and D. Wertlieb. Thousand Oaks, Calif.: Sage, 2003.

———. *The Teaching Church: Moving Christian Education to Center Stage.* Nashville: Abingdon, 1993.

Roehlkepartain, E. C., and P. L. Benson. *Youth in Protestant Churches.* Minneapolis: Search Institute, 1993.

Roehlkepartain, E. C., E. D. Naftali, and L. Musegades. *Growing Up Generous: Engaging Youth in Giving and Serving.* Bethesda, Md.: Alban Institute, 2000.

Roehlkepartain, E. C., and P. C. Scales. *Youth Development in Congregations: An Exploration of the Potential and Barriers.* Minneapolis: Search Institute, 1995.

Scales, P. C., and N. Leffert. *Developmental Assets: A Synthesis of the Scientific Research on Adolescent Development.* Minneapolis: Search Institute, 1999.

Shumer, R., and C. C. Cook. *The Status of Service-Learning in the United States.* St. Paul, Minn.: National Service-Learning Clearinghouse, 1999.

Strommen, M. P., and R. A. Hardel. *Passing on the Faith: A Radical New Model for Youth and Family Ministry.* Winona, Minn.: St. Mary's, 2000.

Westerhoff, J. H., III. *Will Our Children Have Faith?* New York: Seabury, 1976.

Contributors

Robert Benne is the Jordan-Trexler Professor of Religion and director of the Center for Religion and Society at Roanoke College, Salem, Virginia. He is also the author of eight books, including *Quality with Soul: How Six Premier Colleges and Universities Keep Faith with Their Religious Traditions* and *The Paradoxical Vision: A Public Theology for the Twenty-First Century.*

Richard Cimino is editor and publisher of *Religion Watch,* a newsletter monitoring trends in contemporary religion. He is the author of *Against the Stream: The Adoption of Traditional Christian Faiths among Young Adults, Shopping for Faith: American Religion in the New Millennium* (with Don Lattin), and *Trusting the Spirit: Renewal and Reform in American Religion.* He is currently studying sociology at the New School for Social Research in New York.

Maria Erling is associate professor of the history of Christianity in North America and Global Mission at the Lutheran Theological Seminary in Gettysburg, Pennsylvania. She has written about mainline Protestantism in New England, Swedish immigration and religious life in America, and Lutheran history in America. She has recently coedited *The Role of the Bishop: Changing Models of a Global Church,* which explores aspects of the recent debate within American Lutheranism on the ecumenical agreement with the Episcopal Church.

Mark Granquist is assistant professor of religion at Gustavus Adolphus College, St. Peter, Minnesota. He has written a number of articles and chapters on the history of American Lutheranism, and has twice been honored by the Concordia Historical Institute for his contributions to this field.

Dan Hoffrening is associate professor and chair of the political science department at St. Olaf College. He is author of the book *In Washington but Not of It: The Prophetic Politics of Religious Lobbyists*. He teaches classes in American politics, particularly courses that focus on religion and politics, parties and elections, and the environment.

Robert Longman is an ELCA layman, freelance writer, and municipal planner for the Town of Babylon, New York. He is the author and manager of the Spirithome.com website that focuses on Christian spirituality and a veteran of college radio since 1984, at WUSB-FM in Stony Brook, New York.

Steve Montreal is the dean of the school of adult education and associate professor of political science at Concordia University, Wisconsin. He has previously written on issues of federalism and citizen participation in non-governmental organizations, and is currently working in the areas of religion and politics and crime analysis.

Mark Noll is McManis Professor of Christian Thought at Wheaton College. He is the author of *America's God, from Jonathan Edwards to Abraham Lincoln* (Oxford, 2002) and other works in the history of Christianity. His book *The Old Religion in a New World* (Eerdmans, 2002) contains substantial consideration of Lutheranism as it moved from Europe to North America.

James Petersen served on the national staff of the Evangelical Lutheran Church in America from 1988 until 2002, except for a two-year period during which he was Executive Director for Ministries at Community Lutheran Church in Las Vegas, Nevada. As a member of the ELCA's Chicago-based Evangelism Team, he spent extensive time between 1997 and 2002 traveling to and learning from flourishing ELCA congregations across the country, then developing workshops, seminars, and video-based learning tools in order to pass the learnings along to congregations. He is currently an assistant to the bishop of the Nebraska Synod, ELCA.

Eugene C. Roehlkepartain is the director of family and congregational initiatives for the Search Institute, a Minneapolis-based non-profit organization that provides leadership, knowledge, and resources to promote healthy children, youth, and communities. He is author or coauthor of more than twenty books and reports on youth, youth development, and congregations, including *Growing Up Generous: Engaging Youth in Giving and Serving, Strategic Youth Ministry,* and *The Teaching Church: Moving Christian Education to Center Stage.*

Alvin J. Schmidt is professor emeritus of sociology at Illinois College in Jacksonville, Illinois. He is the author of five books, including *The Menace of Multiculturalism: Trojan Horse in America, Under the Influence: How Christianity Transformed Civilization,* and *Fraternal Organizations.*

Scott Thumma is a faculty associate in religion and society at Hartford Institute for Religion Research, Hartford Seminary. In addition to teaching and research, he is the director of distance education and administrator of the seminary's Faith Communities Today web site. He is currently writing a book on megachurches in the United States.

Mary Todd is associate professor of history and assistant provost at Concordia University, River Forest, Illinois, where she directs the honors program. She is the author of *Authority Vested: A Story of Identity and Change in the Lutheran Church–Missouri Synod* and is president of the Lutheran Historical Conference.

Jeff Walz is an associate professor of political science at Concordia University, Wisconsin (CUW). His research has appeared in the *American Review of Politics, Political Research Quarterly, Publius: The Journal of Federalism,* and the *Southeastern Political Review.* Currently, he is examining the connection between religion and politics among Lutheran pastors.